Hacked Transmissions

Hacked Transmissions

Technology and Connective Activism in Italy

Alessandra Renzi

 University of Minnesota Press
Minneapolis
London

The University of Minnesota Press gratefully acknowledges support for the open-access version of this book from Concordia University.

The University of Minnesota Press gratefully acknowledges the work of Richard Grusin, editorial consultant, on this project.

Copyright 2020 by the Regents of the University of Minnesota

All rights reserved. No part of this publication may be reproduced, stored in a retrieval system, or transmitted, in any form or by any means, electronic, mechanical, photocopying, recording, or otherwise, without the prior written permission of the publisher.

Published by the University of Minnesota Press
111 Third Avenue South, Suite 290
Minneapolis, MN 55401-2520
http://www.upress.umn.edu

The University of Minnesota is an equal-opportunity educator and employer.

Library of Congress Cataloging-in-Publication Data
Names: Renzi, Alessandra, author.
Title: Hacked transmissions : technology and connective activism in Italy / Alessandra Renzi.
Description: Minneapolis : University of Minnesota Press, [2020]
Identifiers: LCCN 2019019309 (print) | ISBN 978-1-5179-0325-1 (hc) | ISBN 978-1-5179-0326-8 (pb)
Subjects: LCSH: Telestreet (Television network). | Pirate television broadcasting—Italy—History—21st century. | Television broadcasting—Italy—History—21st century.
Classification: LCC HE8700.7232.I8 R46 2020 (print) | LCC HE8700.7232.I8
LC record available at https://lccn.loc.gov/2019019309

UMP LSI

Con Nicol* Angrisano

Contents

Introduction: Co-researching Telestreet as a Form of Connective Activism	1
1. Making Sense of Telestreet: Three Compositions	19
2. Intimacy and Media Making: A Long History of Delirium, Care, and Social Reproduction	41
3. Delirium at Work in Berlusconi's Mediascape	65
4. Activist Energetics in the Information Milieu	85
5. Squatted Airwaves, Hacked Transmission	113
6. Subjectivity, Therapy, Compositionality in the Porous Spaces of Naples	133
7. Insu^tv, Media Connective	153
8. De/Re/Compositions, in Process	173
Epilogue: Repurposing Is How Connective Activism Happens	193
Acknowledgments	203
Appendix: List of Interviews	205
Notes	207
Bibliography	225
Index	245

Introduction

Co-researching Telestreet as a Form of Connective Activism

Movements that do not place on their agendas the reproduction of both their members and the broader community are movements that cannot survive, they are not "self-reproducing."

—Silvia Federici, quoted in Max Haiven, "Feminism, Finance and the Future of #Occupy"

From December 2007 to July 2008, national and international news circulated incredible images of mounds of garbage bags, several meters high, covering most of the streets of Naples in southern Italy. This garbage crisis was the worst to date, even though government corruption and collusion with the local mafia—the powerful Camorra—had regularly subjected Naples to such crises since the nineties. This time it would take the deployment of the national army and some draconian laws against protests to quell the growing unrest. During that period, together with the pirate microtelevision channel insu^tv—a node in a larger network of pirate television channels called Telestreet—I joined a media center set up near the barricades protecting the urban woods of Chiaiano, a small provincial park recently designated as a dumpsite. Like any other independent media center around the world, ours was one of the rare news sources that covered protests from the perspective of the communities involved, dispelling myths about their lack of civic interest and their complicity with the Camorra maintaining the status quo. Most importantly, the media center became a 24/7 point of connection for the population, linking local committees and grassroots projects promoting zero-waste and recycling policies, allies and members of small political parties joining in solidarity from other parts of Italy, social movements from the radical left, and Neapolitan media activists. The protest planning meetings, the media production teach-ins, the information sessions, the livestreaming events and socializing went on day and night for more than a month; we were not all that surprised when two goons on mopeds came to tell us that we had to dismantle our home

1

2 · INTRODUCTION

base and leave, immediately. We had clearly annoyed the local Camorra boss: whether it was because our rowdy assemblies bothered his sleep or because we were building a little too much awareness and solidarity, we could not be sure. Like many things surrounding the garbage crisis, it was unclear. What *was* clear, however, was the reaction of the inhabitants of Chiaiano, who did not want to let us go, and who, like many other groups involved in the nine-month-long mobilizations, came back to insu^tv with hundreds of hours of video footage asking insu^tv to help them tell their story.

Stories are rebellious creatures, especially when they are born of the hopes, friendships, and efforts of those struggling for a better world. Much to the chagrin of many a researcher, these kinds of stories resist all attempts to confine them to the neatness of printed pages. Here, as my accounts sneak away to meander through the trails of decades of Italian media activism and transnational social movements, they spin a web of practices and ideas that I use to define *connective activism*. Connective activism is a proposition for, as much as an analysis of, modes of struggle for justice that keep social connection and an ethics of care at the core of political organizing—in this case, organizing through collaborative media production and distribution. These pages adapt to the movement of rebellious stories while examining the relation of various media activist projects to the milieu that gave them life. To this end, the story of Chiaiano's media center does not announce the birth of connective activism, which has been around under different guises for a long time. Rather, this story opens a portal to Telestreet and its network of activists whose trajectories and work straddling media making and political organizing have much to tell us about resisting injustice and social isolation in today's hypermediated world. *Hacked Transmissions* digs for the roots of Telestreet; it probes its connective activist practices as they change with the environment and networks that engendered them. It grasps social struggle in its extended, ongoing mutation by looking at how activist formations recompose around new technologies, needs, and desires, across cycles of struggle. A long-term ethnography of a movement that spans more than fifteen years, the research for *Hacked Transmissions* also indissolubly ties its author to the stories told and the characters involved; in so doing, it lays out a collaborative research methodology that puts processes of subjectivation at the center and attends to an ethics of connection and care.

In my experience participating in movements for social justice, groups seldom have time to talk about the quality of their relations to other activists, unless they are seeking to build alliances, they are in a crisis, or they are involved in struggles over life lived, like those of racialized people. Also lacking are often conversations about the kinds of relations organizers establish between what they use to communicate and generate momentum and what they can achieve with those tools and infrastructures. This lack of shared reflection makes groups more vulnerable to fragmentation and isolation, surveillance, financial exploitation (data extraction), and to developing unhealthy communication habits (Renzi 2015; Klang and Madison 2016). Recently, it has fed many productive capacities to repressive policing entities and power-hungry media giants like Facebook and Google—whose sphere of influence has already entered politics and governance. My purpose here is neither to look nostalgically to the good old days of media activism nor to indict today's communication tools. It is much more about understanding these less visible and yet important relations, grasping the social transformation they foster as it is happening.

The recent cycle of struggles that followed the 2008 financial crisis drew the attention of social movement scholars and media theorists alike, partly because of the way they interpellated people simultaneously as scholars and affected citizens, and partly because of the extensive role media, especially social media, played in the mobilizations.[1] Networked communication platforms were sites and a means to feel united, to become collective subjects. "Social" media are often defined by their unprecedented capacity to link individuals for the purpose of communicating, sharing vast amounts of information as a form of participation in public life. In many cases, social media have indeed facilitated large mobilizations (Bennett and Segerberg 2012; Tufekci 2014). Still, the sociality of social media is not where one finds the modes of resistance I will describe as connective activism.[2] Those are to be found in the practices, ideas, and infrastructures that attempt to scale up political action by testing out indirect forms of resistance and social reproduction that prefigure different ways of being together. In search of a more subterranean recomposing field of struggle and care, this book redirects the focus away from livestreaming platforms, the People's Mic of Occupy Wall Street (OWS), or Twitter and Facebook in many recent mobilizations to where people and things *assemble* around pirate radio and TV, tech collectives, hacklabs, squats, and so on. *Hacked*

4 · INTRODUCTION

Transmissions follows Telestreet in this milieu to explore the transformations from Indymedia-style to social-media-based production and, more broadly, to interrogate how people come together, work together, and change *with* technology.[3]

The stories that I map in this book are largely about established and novel modes of social connection, forms of self-awareness, nonoppositional resistance, and politics that are made possible by the collective becoming of people, and media. Underpinning these stories is an understanding that humans hold less agency over technology than they would like to think. Correspondingly, I conceive of agency as emerging through the interactions among humans and technology, giving them both direction and purpose. *Agency is about the ability to come into composition.*

• • •

Starting in 2002 and lasting until Italy switched to digital broadcasting in 2010, Telestreet microtelevision stations transmitted at the neighborhood scale, using ultra high frequency (UHF) analog frequencies that commercial networks could not use because of physical, territorial obstacles. Italy had never had any community television channels. Telestreet programs offered Italians a variety of content produced collaboratively among neighbors: documentaries, cooking shows, replays of local sporting events, hijacked football matches from paid-access channels, comedy, city council meetings, footage of rallies and political events, experimental video, pirated films, soap operas, and more. Each of Telestreet's do-it-yourself (DIY) transmission systems was connected to an online peer-to-peer (P2P) network, sharing a web archive from which they could download autonomously produced broadcasting material, considerably reducing production and distribution costs. The video archive NGVision—one that anticipated platforms like YouTube and Vimeo but could circulate content even through dial-up internet connections—amplified coverage at a national level and allowed each node to maintain a considerable degree of autonomy in their programming choices.

"With 1000 Euro, I make my own TV" was the title of the text describing Telestreet's "standard kit" to build a microstation with an antenna, a transmitter (or a VHS player), a video camera, a video card, and some editing software at a cost of around 1,000–2,000 Euro (Telestreet n.d.).[4] The first task: find a shadow cone—an area that commercial frequencies cannot reach—and install the transmission apparatus; then set up a studio

Figure 1. The control room of Telestreet node insu^tv, assembled with refurbished and hacked technology in a DIY fashion. Naples, CSOA Officina 99. Courtesy of insu^tv.

space and go on air. Among the first Telestreet channels to appear on the mediascape in 2002 were OrfeoTv in Bologna, a central Italian town with a long history of free radio activism and autonomous cultural production, and TeleMonteOrlandoTV, a hobbyist experiment chronicling the daily life of Gaeta, a beach town south of Rome. In December 2002, striking workers of the Fiat auto manufacturing plant in Termini Imerese set up Telefabbrica to bear witness to their labor struggle. This undertaking only lasted three days before Italian police shut it down, but the project attracted considerable attention and was a huge source of inspiration. In the early twenty-first century, in a world of ongoing hypermediation and spectacle, DIY television lit the imagination of many and spread like wildfire.

But Telestreet was not born in a vacuum. A month earlier, at the European Social Forum in Florence, global justice organizers had brought the Indymedia open publishing ethics to grassroots television with Hub TV (Mediablitz 2004) and the following year, a similar kind of experiment—NoWarTV—went on air via satellite to protest the Iraq war. The mushrooming of grassroots television experiments was part of a surge in organizing for social justice that paid considerable attention to the role of media in

6 · INTRODUCTION

the production of consensus and the silencing of dissenting voices. The surge coincided, among other things, with the release of a variety of reports on media consolidation that highlighted how a few large corporations increasingly controlled what and how information circulates (McChesney 2015). Many media activist projects at this time were deeply intertwined with all sorts of campaigns against the rise of corporate capitalism and its neoliberal economic tenets. They challenged media monopoly, circulated alternative information, and worked as communication infrastructure for social movements. After all, this was the golden era of the global justice movement, with its large, theatrical protests shadowing every international governance summit. Media and activism reinforced each other at the grass-roots, one could say. They still do.

In Italy, where Prime Minister Silvio Berlusconi controlled more than 90 percent of the Italian mediascape, it was still possible to squat the airwaves without gaining access to cable broadcasting. Street TVs kept on appearing: insu^tv in Naples, opening with a transmission in a low-income housing complex; Rome's CandidaTV, producing experimental video art against the mainstream; Milanese Mosaico TV, founded by students and union organizers to cover labor issues; Padua's RagnaTele, bringing their cameras to the kitchens of Cameroonian and Moroccan migrants to learn about their culture; Telerobbinud in Squillace, livestreaming Sunday Mass for the elderly (Merani 2004); Disco Volante TV in Senigallia, run by a team of neuro-diverse individuals; SpegnilaTV [Turnoff the TV] in Rome; TelePonziana in Triest; Tele Ottolina in Pisa; and the list goes on. Like OrfeoTv, which had a transmission radius of only a few hundred square meters in the shadow cone beyond the reach of the music-channel giant MTV, the *televisioni di strada*, or street television channels, had a small audience and a larger network of collaborators on their teams, shaping the programming schedule from day to day in an open and horizontal manner. The more the merrier, what matters most is how many people make TV: this experiment was about media literacy, self-expression, and appropriation, not competition over eyeballs. Make no mistake, the language of street televisions could not be further away from traditional mainstream TV either: there were no moderators, little editing, and a lot of transparency about the production process (Mediablitz 2004). One could trip over the microphone cable used in the studio and have a laugh about it out in the piazza. By 2003, when Eterea, the first national meeting of Telestreet channels, was convened, dozens of microchannels had joined the roll call.

The meeting dealt with issues of legality, discussing freedom of speech and communication and the gray areas of regulation. For Telestreet media makers, the airwaves were a common good, a public space. People also discussed the future of grassroots communication and its links with struggles for global justice; they shared knowledge, skills, and content. After the meeting, the number and configuration of street television channels kept growing: it ballooned to more than two hundred around 2006 but would later shrink to only a handful.

I followed Telestreet's development for more than a decade, way past when the network exhaled its final breath in early 2008 in a couple of tired emails exhorting all the listserv members to pull the plug on the collective networked body, by then full of sadness, nearly comatose. Euthanasia seemed the best treatment to avoid the slow decomposition of Telestreet at the hands of internal friction, lack of resources, and the disappearance of node after node. The network was officially declared dead on the listserv in part because of frustration with the constant harassment and provocation by an incredibly persistent troll and especially due to its own online inertia. Telestreet could not retain cohesiveness after the initial euphoria also because it was a very heterogeneous network with different degrees of involvement of its nodes. This was as much due to the difficulty of sustaining individual street channels while tending to the life of the network as to the tensions between radical nodes and apolitical or religious ones. The fragmentation had already started at Eterea II in 2004 when members debated an official position on the legalization and possible financial support of Telestreet as a whole. Later on, in April 2005, an important split happened during the planning of the third edition of Eterea, spearheaded by a Telestreet node based in a parish. The presence of a priest overseeing the programming of the channel outraged some organizers who questioned the ability of the Catholic Church to run it without infringing on the anti-sexist and antihomophobic principles of the network. Further concerns about the transparency of the organizing process sparked more conflict and led many to boycott the convention.

Ultimately, Telestreet as a cohesive network never went out with a bang. A few months after Eterea III in 2005, activity dwindled on the listserv, the Telestreet website encountered technical problems and went in and out of maintenance breaks until it disappeared, and someone eventually declared it was over on the listserv. Despite petering out in this way—a perfectly normal end for activist projects such as this—Telestreet was an important milestone for media activism, and some of its microstations outlived the network (and the zombie listserv still mails a rare post, spam, and the odd obnoxious provocation). My interest persisted past this self-declaration of death through my involvement with the TV channel insu^tv in Naples, where the spirit of Telestreet is still alive today.

Street televisions were particularly active at an important time for radical media around the world, when people experimented with newly available technology and turned to communication itself as a way to fight back against the power of corporations. Activists worked together with hackers to build new communication infrastructure that was not-for-profit, free and open source, and could be adapted to their needs. Then, the interactive and participatory character of the web went in a flash from being the purview of hackers and media activists to being a commercial feature on proprietary interfaces.[5] During that brief moment of reorientation and potential, we called it the "social web"; then, all of a sudden there was social media, with its monopolistic character. Still, there is more to this story than killer apps. Telestreet embodied this time period in original ways: it combined tactical hacks through DIY media, horizontal media production, the subversion or jamming of televisual language, P2P technology, free and open-source software (FOSS), copyleft licenses like Creative Commons for noncommercial intellectual property rights, and more. There are multiple political and artistic traditions that influenced Telestreet—from Dada to theater, from political radio to militant research. So, while the importance of Telestreet for Italy was clear to many during its run, its contribution to media activism beyond national borders is more evident now when I retrace the trajectories that made the project possible and that, following the network's disappearance, led to a new chapter in media activism.

Movements are born of and driven by common dreams that cannot be forced into binaries like success and failure (Haiven and Khasnabish 2013, 488). They change and transform and, as they do, they leave traces and seeds that may grow somewhere else, if cultivated. Similarly, social and political transformations often traverse multiple cycles of struggles before they become visible and take hold. It is important to account for this continuity as a becoming of movements within a milieu where forces make and fold, unmake and unfold. These transformations are more than technological and straddle multiple cultural, political, and social worlds. Their study undoes the dichotomy between success and failure as much as between old and new media—and between the technical and the social.

Indeed, Telestreet has trained and inspired a new generation of media producers who see media as a tool for creative struggle and a tool to foster social reproduction outside the dominant system. Many of the innovations that Telestreet promoted seeped back into the global radical media scene (and were captured by mainstream media) through encounters and workshops with fellow activists in Italy and abroad, through contributions to media democracy debates and actions, and through a variety of collaborations from Bosnia to Palestine. Paying careful attention to this network's histories, recompositions, and recuperations allows us to dwell in the heterogeneous milieu of grassroots media and activism.

• • •

I had joined Telestreet after meeting some of its members in 2004 at the Berlin-based new media festival Transmediale, where they had been invited to rig up an impromptu TV studio. To an aspiring video maker and a media scholar who had left Italy shortly before Berlusconi's rise to political power in 1994, Telestreet's engagement with people through the medium of television was instantly compelling. Straightaway, I wanted to contribute to the project; but I also wanted to study it. Two months later, I was back in Italy, in Senigallia, for Eterea II, the second national meeting of the Telestreet channels. There, as electric debates about organization and the collective orientation of the network filled the days, I met more Telestreettari (members of Telestreet), reunited with organizers I already knew, and got a glimpse of the breadth and complexity of this movement. Not only could I not box Telestreet into the neat categories that the social scientists in my field had created for community media, but once my involvement in the project grew, it also became clear to me that I could not keep my political and scholarly engagements separate. But *activist* and *scholar* were predominantly seen as clashing and hard-to-reconcile subject positions in social and cultural studies of media, as well as among activists. Adding to this, as the research evolved, it drew me in, and in unexpected ways: being a subject-object of my own study required ongoing attention to my subjectivity or better, my ongoing subjectification.

Even when working within an established tradition of activist inquiry like participatory action research (Lewin 1946; Hale 2008), the balancing act between scholarship and activism is always tough. It invariably places the researcher in an arena where contrasting visions of valuable knowledge, ethics, and accountability constantly cast doubt on their research and the compromises it may demand (Peters 2016, x). In my case, the challenge was to develop an ethnographic study that did not simply memorialize Telestreet but produced knowledge that would be useful to activists and scholars alike while remaining aligned with the creative and political push coming from within the network. My study had to contribute to current discussions in the field of media studies, to exceed the practice of scholarly representation, *and* to function as an activist intervention itself, cutting across the scholar-activist binary. I found the tools for my inquiry in autonomist militant research, a tradition that is very much alive in Italian social movements.

Starting in the 1960s, activists of Autonomia Operaia (Workers' Autonomy) developed and performed *conricerca* (co-research) or simply *inchiesta* (inquiry) as a form of collaborative research with workers to understand the field in which labor struggle unfolded. Case studies like the ones with the Fiat factory workers (Alquati 1975) explored the new composition of the working class and bolstered emerging practices of resistance against labor exploitation. These studies were especially influential to identify the new tendencies in workers organizing and to provide a theoretical backdrop for the mass resistance that spread throughout the seventies. I reencountered *conricerca* in the early twenty-first century via the efforts of anti-precarity researchers seeking to understand the flexible and unstable labor conditions of the new, post-Fordist working class, the so-called *precariat* (Precarias a la deriva 2004). Not unlike participatory action research, *conricerca* places qualitative sociological research on its head: it uses traditional research methods like interviews, questionnaires, and focus groups but has different implications because it is also carried out by the subjects of research themselves, doing away with the separation between interviewer and interviewee (Whyte 1991; Greenwood, Whyte, and Harkavy 1993). During co-research, the groups taking part in the analysis actively participate in the construction of the tools for the study, so that the group itself defines the relevant issues and constructs the questions. At the same time, because of their co-involvement, for both activists and researchers the production of knowledge is immediately a mode of subjectivation—a shaping of conduct and personality—and development of political organization (e.g., Lazzarato 1993, 2001; Conti 2001a, 2001b). The prefix *con/co* in co-research refers to the two processes happening at the same time: the production of subjectivity and the production of organization. This is because the personal relations built among researchers and activists during the research and political activities help each to grasp these individual and collective expressions of subjectivity (Armano, Sacchetto, and Wright 2013).

All in all, the difference between co-research and more traditional forms of qualitative sociological and academic research (but also the workers' inquiry) is political rather than methodological because the research questions are already designed with political objectives in mind and the focus is to understand how people resist under changing conditions. *Conricerca* has much in common with participatory action research, especially in its radical roots of the barefoot researchers that framed it as a tool for problem solving, social justice organizing, and to initiate change (Lewin 1946; Fals-Borda and Rahman 1991; Freire 2007). While participatory action research has had a broader focus and a codified, multistep methodological process that leads toward specific goals shared with a community (MacDonald 2012), *conricerca* has mostly aimed its inquiry at labor and the reproduction of the labor force, that is, social reproduction (Del Re 2013). *Conricerca* foregrounds a process of unveiling emergent forms of conflict against exploitation that are often hidden but could scale up. This involves identifying the social needs, the traditions of struggle, as well as the practices of dissent that are already latent or present in hidden forms (Conti et al. 2007, 78). Co-researchers aim to provide concrete analytical maps of the *composition* of the new resistant formations and set the basis for future movements to come (Palano 2000). The process of co-research doubles as a form of organizing in that it also stimulates movement through participation and reflection (Conti et al. 2007, 80).[6]

In the context of researching media activism and mediated activism, the role of technology in the conceptualization of co-research is crucial. For pioneer co-researchers like Romano Alquati, the relationship between technology and human agents does not simply point to the creation of mechanisms of control through specific forms of labor (like the alienation of automated factory work) but also enables silent struggles that appropriate or sabotage these technologies (Conti et al. 2007, 80). This is no small insight today: with processes of capital accumulation rooted in communication technologies and so much labor centered on affective communication and on the commodification of sociality (Terranova 2000; Fumagalli 2007; Coté and Pybus 2011), the points of friction between media infrastructure, social control, and forms of counterpower are plenty and often hidden. This is where grounded, collaborative research can produce more analyses of the composition of contemporary collective subjectivities and

12 · INTRODUCTION

their relationship to the modes of production—that is, media as an extractive and subjectifying technology. These kinds of studies are necessary, not only to dismantle much of the hype around new technologies but also to better understand emergent modes of struggle around and through technology, centering new political subjects.

If, originally, *conricerca* focused on the working class and its labor struggles, my focus is broader—less focused on class and more on practices. In fact, I found that the focus on class distracted me from other kinds of struggles for social justice, for instance, those of women, migrants, colonized peoples, gender-nonconforming people, and the unemployed. I take my lead to rethink co-research from younger and feminist autonomist intellectuals who look at the *practices* recomposing a field of antagonism rather than at a collective antagonist subject defined solely according to its role in economic production (Palano 1999; Mellino and Curcio 2012). Thus, my research of recomposition in Telestreet investigates the assembling of social practices of resistance that fend off capitalist exploitation but also patriarchy, colonialism, racism, heteronormativity, ableism, and so on.

This approach framed particularly the case study of/with insu^tv, where I co-researched the transformations and practices of the collective, how insu^tv interacted with its broader networks to support local struggles, and how the project could grow.[7] In addition to running interviews and focus groups with current and past members, we sought out and experimented with different media, including livestreaming and facilitative co-production techniques. We also collaboratively developed and analyzed questionnaires to discuss the identity and orientation of the collective. We produced video, co-ran a media center with other activist groups, produced TV shows, and organized screenings and events. I participated as a member and as an observer. Individually, I also carried out further ethnographic research with OrfeoTv and Disco Volante TV and attended the national conventions and meetings. I did archival research and interviewed members of other Telestreet channels in Bologna and in Gaeta to set the historical and sociopolitical contexts and situate Telestreet's practices in space and time (Heller 2001, 118). Bologna played a key role in the prehistory of Telestreet through the autonomist Marxist movement's cultural and political activism with its free radios and zines in the seventies. These forms of political organizing are instrumental in understanding Telestreet's milieu, how it emerged from the history, culture, and society of Italy—and how it mutates across economically different Italian regions—while also being in conversation with the global trajectories of political movements. The political significance of many of the practices I discuss would be invisible without knowing these histories and ties. Beyond its use of television, the experience of street television provides a media model that cares for the connections among groups and that is part of the longue durée of Italian compositions in media and activism. At the same time, the long duration perspective of this study and the co-research deliver rare insights into the rhythms of movement and rest (Bratich 2014) of grassroots political formations.

Conricerca taught me that in order to deliver an account of how Telestreet and insu^tv emerged and recomposed over time, it is important to retain the liveliness of the stories that gave them life, as well as the heterogeneity of the experiences that shaped them. Historical documentation of both independent media activism and mainstream media trends in Italy were necessary sources of information, but so too were my friends' personal accounts.[8] My co-research process bears testimony to the potential for learning and collaboration through process-based research that produces knowledge *while* researching—simultaneously attending to processes of subjectivation. Once research becomes a catalyst for encounters that force us to think creatively while engaging the social field, the meaning attached to ethnographic work shifts from representation to localized collaborative creation. Thinking becomes a practice of learning through action, which relies on the willingness to challenge common assumptions and frameworks in order to experiment with newly acquired knowledge. The framing of connective activism and its attendant practice of *repurposing media* in this book are the product of my co-research exchanges. Connective activism and repurposing media are not part of a predefined political method adopted by Telestreet/insu^tv at any specific point in time. Rather, they are notions that I present to give some kind of consistency to the threads I untangle from the projects I encountered, for instance the use of collective aliases to build a common identity, tending to friendships and intimacy as a way of building cohesion during times of crisis, community research practices that foster porosity among groups, social therapeutic approaches to media making, to mention a few. Woven together, these threads of connective activism hold the intensity and potential of composing with others.

The writing that follows draws together theory, co-research, and political activism into a processual mapping of mutually elaborating registers of practice. The actual work of mapping begins by drawing contours and lines through the practices of a media scholar, an ethnographer, and a media maker. Practices are forces that continuously shape and reshape the individual and the social. Starting this inquiry *from* practice allows me to focus on the *relationships* and *resonances* among the elements that compose Telestreet and connect its people and transmitters. As a form of militant research, my practice exceeds naming a condition or relationship, or creating a concept that might provide a point of theoretical connection. It *embodies* the connection with others to create narratives about social change that embolden the political imagination. The emphasis here is on the potentials of embodied modes of connection that relay political practice rather than any specific political practice—this is part of performing connective activism. *The art of assembling in productive ways—the art of composition (of groups, networks, movements, and the like)—is one that is always refined in the throes of constant transformation and in fleeting becomings.*

• • •

As an offering of *conricerca*, *Hacked Transmissions* is a study of media activism, a theory of connective practices, and a storytelling medium that, in turn, aims at fostering new assemblages with its readers. The following chapters are tied together through a *social movement energetics*—an experiment in refocusing the reader's attention on the conditions and capacity for political *reorganization* across cycles of struggle. Why? Energy is key to these reorganizations because it is the product of (in)formation and collaboration: it pulses through the channels that bring together the groups I introduce and it courses through and connects the networks of humans and machines as I inquire into tenuous milieus of becoming.

In chapter 1, I take my cue from queer feminist philosophers of science Donna Haraway and Karen Barad: I think and write diffractively, or, in my own adaptation of this method, I think and write "compositionally" to gather momentum. My analysis begins with three propositions followed by compositions where I present a series of snapshots of Telestreet that situate the project in familiar contexts. The propositions discuss Telestreet as a social movement, tactical media, and community television while the compositions provide the theoretical foundation for a theory of emergence and change. The latter draws heavily on the work of Gilbert Simondon, Brian Massumi, and Gilles Deleuze and Félix Guattari, and will charge the energetics of movements I carry throughout the book. Additionally, chapter 1 outlines the parameters for one of the main practices of connective activism: the repurposing of media for social reproduction.

Chapter 2 looks back at the historical milieu that shaped Telestreet, especially its political and cultural relations to Italian autonomist movements from the seventies. The seventies were an important period for the development of political practices in Italy, often in conversation with movements abroad. In the fertile soil of the post-'68 countercultures and large, local mass movements, new and exciting forms of grassroots media carried with them an investment in aesthetic practices that stimulated Telestreet. The seventies also brought along new analyses of capitalist exploitation and patriarchal oppression. It is during this time that activists begin investing in processes of resubjectivation and social reproduction outside the logics of capital.

Chapter 3 carries on the archaeological media excavation (Parikka 2012), shining light on Silvio Berlusconi's own creative power to assemble media. This chapter chronicles the evolution of Italian neoliberalism by looking at the competitive privatization of its mediascape in the eighties and nineties, with the rise of strategies like differential accumulation (Nitzan and Bichler 2009). By the mid-1990s, Italian culture, spectacle, and politics blend into a powerful governmental assemblage (Foucault 2008; Grusin 2010), giving life to Berlusconi and Telestreet in surprisingly similar ways.

The energetics of the global justice movement and its media as explored in chapter 4 pay particular attention to the forgotten histories of the activist internet (bulletin board system [BBS], Okkupanet, guerrilla communication), their absorption into commercial platforms, and the spread of hacker and maker spaces. This chapter traces the movement of information and the energy it generates through new media activist tactics and projects that repurpose available technologies to produce powerful assemblages prefiguring Telestreet and social media alike. This is the period not only of well-known movements like the Zapatistas in Mexico but also of hidden gems like the fax-machine-VAX-computer networks that science students in China and Italy used to communicate secretly.

Then Telestreet returns to center stage in chapter 5, where I follow the movement of information through the bodies and other circuits of its DIY transmission assemblage, the individuation of the media activists and their audiences, and the technical objects that gained new functions in the process. Here, I unpack the functioning of the transmission system to understand how it works in interaction with its viewers. This chapter also tells the stories of nodes like TeleMonteOrlandoTV, Disco Volante TV, and OrfeoTv, drawing out the power of proxy-vision—the making of television in the community.

Chapters 6 and 7 examine insu^tv, the longest-lasting Telestreet channel, to flesh out a theory of connective activism and its attendant ethics of connection that repurpose media in order to break sociopolitical isolation. Insu^tv is deeply embedded in the Neapolitan activist field, supporting its struggles and fostering porosity among groups. My account of media activism in Naples tends to the relation *among* activist groups, one that is usually neglected in favor of studying the relation between specific groups and society, institutions, or the state. It is this attention to intergroup relations that reveals the value of connective activism as a set of practices that reconfigure the linkages between individuals, groups, and the broader activist field/society.

Chapter 8 then considers the eventual recomposition of the Telestreet/insu^tv media assemblage and the role of social reproduction within activism. It addresses the challenge of facing the decomposition of projects and movements. It provokes new questions about how to conceive of the relationship between communication infrastructure and practices of resistance.

I conclude with methodological considerations on studying movements informed by an ethics of connection. In the context of my own individuation as an activist researcher and as the author of this book, this form of ethics becomes a tool to challenge traditional models of knowing and envisioning social change and gestures toward the use of research methodologies that attend to the relation among political movements and the entanglement of the researcher and the assemblage being examined (Barad 2007). In this context, I apologize to those Telestreettari who may find themselves confined to marginal roles in an unavoidably incomplete and subjective narration of events, since this will not be the story of how they created Telestreet but of how Telestreet created them and others, including me.

Composition is a process that never simply vanishes when things come apart. It leaves traces: what I have learned with insu^tv marks all my work and thinking, and my being and ability to become elsewhere. Some of these traces are scattered among the pages of *Hacked Transmissions,* where I struggle to contain myself within the narrow confines of an authorial voice. The unstable transitions from the *I* to a *we* nest in the spaces that separate the words on the page and in the space of media practices that connect me to my *compagni* (comrades/friends), to the video camera and transmission kit, and to you, the reader of this book. More than as a transmission of data, I see the writing of this book as a means of producing and receiving resonances (Colectivo Situaciones 2005). *Hacked Transmissions* extends a call for research to be directly involved in the intensity of situated media creation and activism. The intensity—the *potential*—of an activist inquiry can never be fully communicated because so much of it is lived, and it deeply informs the processes of subjectivation of the researcher, as well as the collective individuation of the group. It is my hope that this book itself will engender a productive encounter with its readers, activists, and researchers to come.

1

Making Sense of Telestreet

Three Compositions

> How do gatherings sometimes become "happenings," that is, greater than the sum of their parts? If history without progress is indeterminate and multidirectional, might assemblages show us its possibilities?
>
> —Anna Tsing, *The Mushroom at the End of the World*

The battle to establish *what* Telestreet is and what media activism *does* unfolds in a clash of statements, of propositions and compositions, where the intangible power to define held by some has tangible effects on the existence and practices, the compositionality and movement, of others. Definition is fraught terrain.

Early on, the very definition of Telestreet was politically charged. In 2004 the Italian Ministry of the Interior's "Report to Parliament on Police Activity, Public Security and Organized Crime" included Telestreet in its special section on "Terrorism and Subversion," identifying it as "close to the squatters movement, broadcasting alternative programs that aim at creating a global network of independent channels for antagonistic movements" (Ministero dell'Interno 2004). This layered and loaded proposition defined Telestreet as a security threat while framing media activism in general as an oppositional force contra the state. In the Ministry of the Interior's report, state institutions, using their power to classify, compose a broad spectrum of media activists into a narrow (and hostile) ideological framework: "These diverse initiatives . . . are part of a larger project called 'Global Network' that involves the creation of a web for alternative communication using media channels (press, radio, television) . . . to promote 'bottom up communication practices that can crack the monopoly of local powers on the communication system'" (Ministero dell'Interno 2004, 16). In effect, the report recontextualizes the words of media activists with the aim of providing the state with a basis for dealing with groups like Telestreet using strategies reserved for terrorist or subversive threats.

This was all part of a broader, globalizing trend in securitization that is by now well known. The framing of security issues in the media and the new categorizations of threats by police and secret services have provided the language to define the activism of the extraparliamentary left as a form of extremism that threatens security (Monaghan and Walby 2011). These discourses function within a wider web of legal and juridical statements—both national and international (Braman 2011)—justifying the "security packages" that allowed the Silvio Berlusconi government to shut down, filter, or fine websites hosting antagonistic content.[1] While Telestreet was never directly censored, the security packages have allowed the police to surveil the communication and seize the data from the server they share with other groups and NGOs who rely on movements' tech collectives for their communication infrastructures (Autistici/Inventati 2017, 89). The policing of media activism is but one of the many threads tying Telestreet to activist projects that preceded and followed it.

Left-leaning parties and personalities placed Telestreet in the crossfire of institutional political battles between Berlusconi's ruling majority and those in the opposition. Green Party MP Mauro Bulgarelli was one of the politicians attempting to legalize Telestreet's status, recognizing its value for local communities and for the broader Italian mediascape: "These autonomous, nonprofit experiments should be supported and funded by the state, not depicted as dangerous breeding grounds for terrorism" (ANSA 2005). Unsurprisingly, Bulgarelli's denouncement of the government's attempt to criminalize social movements had no impact on state repression.

I say "unsurprisingly" because Telestreet does not simply exist in the fields of statements tended by activists and politicians. Discursive feuds in the form of proposition-counterproposition are part of a complex environment that engenders activist formations. All control, resistance, and subjectification processes unfold in unstable environments wherein activism becomes in the tension between being formed top-down (as "dangerous subjects," say, or cultural commodities) and the bottom-up process of proposing new visions and functions for society. At the same time, the discursivity of activist formations is but one element in a wider milieu of forces and relations that engender individuals and collectivities. One could say that this environment is *metastable*—it is in "a state that transcends the classical opposition between stability and instability, and that is charged with potentials for a becoming" (Barthélemy 2012, 217).

The metastable milieu holds activist formations forever open to their capacity to change. Social movements and other activist formations, including the ones that form around technologies, are therefore themselves metastable. Telestreet does not come after some discourses took hold but emerges and exists simultaneously with them, shaping and being shaped by the available technologies, the cultural and political practices, and the subjectivities the latter are tied to. Thinking about Telestreet in its ability to recompose (compositional thinking) versus thinking about it as an object to define (propositional thinking) refocuses the observer's attention on the capacity of activist formations to change. What follows in this opening chapter, and indeed in the rest of the book, is a way of defining, or better, making sense of, the movement and compositionality of Telestreet. The propositions I form describe some of what we know about Telestreet's features and history; the compositions then show what these propositions hide. The compositions are not negations but *extensions* that make an affirmative pass through the logical binary true/false typical of propositional thinking.[2] Each composition focuses on the emergence of differences or, if you like, singularities—on less obvious links between Telestreet and minor political and cultural histories like Tactical Media and the Situationists but also on events and technological affordances like media jacking.

I build on Gilbert Simondon's theories of emergence; his concepts of individuation, information, and transduction are useful in pursuing Telestreet *as a happening rather than a thing*. With Simondon, I contend that taking the reality of groups as a given misses what engenders the collective (and individuals, simultaneously) and distracts from an investigation of how societies and their groups change along certain conditions of quasistability. Thus, to understand change as emergence, or individuation, one might ask: "How do street televisions compose, pose together, in '*con*position'? How do they connect, disconnect, and reconnect?"

Proposition One: Telestreet Is a Social Movement

In publications ranging from the "culture jamming" magazine *Adbusters* (Bronson 2004) to the *International Herald Tribune* (Monico 2002), Telestreet has been celebrated as the forerunner of a new movement for communication democracy: "Street TVs have an extremely limited broadcasting range, covering just a block or two. But a blazing-fast growth rate combined with a very ambitious plan indicate they may soon start contending with bigger TV networks for local viewers," claims the *Hollywood Reporter* (Davidkhanian 2004). This is but one of countless enthusiastic responses to Telestreet from the national and international press. In many articles, "microtelevision" is posited as a neutralizer of mass media consolidation, not only in dystopian Italy where the government controls more than 90 percent of the media but everywhere it could be needed in the future. With this model, television is propelled out of the professional studio to crash the heavily guarded gates of cultural production.

Starting in 2002, public and private broadcasters and print media from the UK, France, Germany, and even Australia celebrated this David and Goliath media battle in Italy. The journalists marveled at the DIY street weapon Italians were using to sling shots at communication giants of the mainstream media. But a few months later, public attention toward the project faded, together with the international disdain for a prime minister who ran a European country despite having countless trials in criminal court, additional police investigations, and a blatant conflict of interest in his media ownership. If things do not change, they stay the same: Prime Minister Silvio Berlusconi with his media empire was active, but so was Telestreet. Yet, while Berlusconi was smiling for the cameras, standing next to those politicians who once felt good decrying the undemocratic turn of their neighbor, Telestreet was struggling and gasping for air in the gray underbellies of legalization disputes and resource allocation. In the mayhem of parliamentary politics, bills to legalize the network gathered dust while many of its nodes lacked the resources to scale up their transmission. Nodes sprang up; some foundered, and others were set up elsewhere, from garages to schools. Shutter speed and lens aperture swiftly altered the narrative depth of field of Italian politics, leaving only some parts of the photo in focus while the background was thrown into a beautiful blur.

The Telestreet group of activists and citizens has been described as defending freedom of expression and information with a bottom-up communication model that promises to take the broadcasting frequencies and media power distribution by storm. Many social movement scholars would say that Telestreet is a perfect example of how civil society works: if it is not the social capital of Telestreet that will lead the state to adjust its policies (Purdue 2007, 11), certainly the network's presence will at least function as a symbolic gesture by Italian citizens claiming their right to free communication (Tarrow 2004). Sure enough, parallel to the birth of Telestreet, a plurality of organizations from civil society coalesced around a series of actions and interventions against media monopoly. Telestreet became the poster child of this resistance.

Protests against Berlusconi's media monopoly ranged from the so-called Girotondi to events denouncing the purging of journalists and comedians from the mainstream media because they were critical of his administration. The Girotondi—the game of Ring-a-ring-o'-roses—started in 2002 to defend endangered media institutions: people gathered around the main studios of the Italian public service broadcaster RAI in nineteen Italian cities to protest Berlusconi's meddling in its administration (Societacivile .it n.d.). Many of the Italian interventions during the first and second terms of Berlusconi's government brought together different groups beyond traditional left-right political divisions. They did so partly with the help of creative organizing strategies and partly because their discourses focused on safeguarding basic civil rights rather than pushing a specific political agenda. These moments of contestation articulated political claims through contentious politics (McAdam, Tarrow, and Tilly 2001), often innovatively, like with the No Berlusconi Day, where thousands of people dressed in purple turned out in the streets on the same day (Mancini 2009).

In the context of Italy's climate of unrest against Berlusconi, Telestreet was a megaphone for the rights to media freedom that groups articulated in "an idiom that local audiences will recognize" (Tilly 2004, 4)—homemade television. This language spoke of a more democratic management of the Italian mass media and called for solutions to Berlusconi's conflicts of interest (Purdue 2007, 7). It also provided an alternative, where neighbors produced shows collectively for themselves and other neighbors. Telestreet became a badge that politicians and interest groups could wear as supporters of the freedom of communication and as critics of the Berlusconi government. Some Italian politicians and sidelined TV personalities praised the project and supported it very publicly (and pompously). This is because social movements often possess social capital that can be used as a bargain chip. With all this media hype and political attention, one could say that Telestreet *posed* as a social movement—it assumed a particular attitude or stance. Telestreet won awards at international art and activism festivals; its members were invited to teach media literacy workshops, they were at protests and in squares, magazines wrote about their hacks, and students flocked to the gatherings to write theses about them. This stance benefited the network and grew it considerably. And still, as is often the case with many social struggles, the Berlusconi government ignored all the actions and celebrations of Telestreet and the larger movement it represented. This comes as no surprise when scholars like Douglas McAdam, Sidney Tarrow, and Charles Tilly, for whom social movements are the carriers of social change (McAdam, Tarrow, and Tilly 2001), find it harder to conceive of a successful relationship between collective action and change in the present context of neoliberal governance, where strong alliances between a few very large corporations and a class of mostly wealthy politicians seem unbreakable (Harvey 2005; Klein 2008).

The Berlusconi government's tax cuts and privatization of services is strictly tied to neoliberal ideology and governance while the prime minister's backdoor connections between industry and politics have allowed him to become one of the richest men in Italy, with a staggering monopoly on media and a sprawling financial empire. In turn, politicians in the Berlusconi government have been able to design policies that undermine civil liberties and further widen the gap between the rich and the poor. With a stronghold on the media, they have attacked any opposition as personal persecution of the prime minister, jealousy, or "communist connivance" (e.g., Schrank 2009). The Berlusconi government has been a master at dismissing collective action and other accountability mechanisms. Calling Italian judges communists and dismantling the judiciary system to evade trials, Berlusconi is always smiling in his photographs. He also, still, smiles and promises happiness to all Italians through his suite of national channels, of which Rete Quattro long transmitted on frequencies legally assigned to a less powerful television channel (Kohl 2003). In this climate, it is not hard to imagine how the agency of social movements that function through oppositional politics is severely diminished. Telestreet's was no different.

If things do not change, they stay the same: Berlusconi smiled, but so did Telestreet, only not in photographs because people forgot about its presence. Once the momentum slowed down, the climate of political and social conflict fell into stupefied torpor, groups protesting refused to negotiate with those in power and were brutally repressed, and attention moved to the many scandals connected to Berlusconi's political life. But has Telestreet triggered no change? Telestreet's Cheshire cat smiles are not visible in pictures, but things do change, even when they seem to stay the same.

Composition One: Change as Individuation

Take two: Telestreet *poses* as a social movement but *to pose* does not mean *to pretend*; instead it is akin to *pausing*: "to assume or hold a physical attitude," *to stand in a position* for someone to observe. Press coverage, politicians' attacks and praises, art reviews, and award statements mediate the interaction between Telestreet and its observers. They all tell the same story of these humble citizens bravely fighting the embarrassing media giant and eventually, hopefully, succeeding. Posing, pausing, positioning: Telestreet is motionless in this picture, which still turns out to be out of focus because it was taken hurriedly on the way out to a new darling. This framing of Telestreet as an anti-Berlusconi movement positions it away from the daily experiences of producing media in the street where so much happens. Positionality is opposed to movement, and yet, is it not the latter that constitutes change—including the neighborhood's imperceptible, bracketed, qualitative change that precedes systemic shifts, ruptures, and visible transformations? How does positionality account for people meeting each other at a Telestreet event, people with disabilities making TV, children filming interviews that show on screen? The movement of subtle change triggered by OrfeoTv, Teleimmagini, TeleAut, and others is hard to see because the analysis of resistant collective actors takes place through the coding of a group's *positioning* on a social grid of signification, and all one can look at is their beginnings (we do not want Berlusconi) and ends (we still have Berlusconi). Here, one never sees movement itself (Massumi 2002, 2–3). So, while the exchanges that take place among the Telestreettari and their communities are fertile, lively, and hard to categorize, the social grid enables their representation via oppositional identities and discourses (as a framing of political messages). This is often the case with the actions and campaigns of social movements, like those advocating for environmental protection, gender and racial justice. Telestreet was a movement against Berlusconi's media control. Berlusconi's monopoly is intact; there was no change. I struggle to point at what changed with Telestreet because I am watching it *pose* (almost as a warrior stereotype) and I cannot see it *move*.

I could reconstruct what has happened in-between the day a manifesto for street television appeared online and the day an email announced the demise of the network: What were the terms and conditions of this change? Where is the change to detect? When I subordinate Telestreet's movement to the moments in time it connects, I still miss a notion of movement as qualitative transformation that attends to the changes in peoples' subjectivities, in their bonds with others and with places. This seeding of minute change among people, across the layers of affects, emotions, individuality, and collectivity, transduces behind or beyond what is visible every time a grandma shares her famed pasta recipe on TV while her grandchild is filming. In other words, I miss the individuation of Telestreet within its milieu. So, in order to look at the dynamism that constitutes change in Berlusconi's Italy, it is necessary to assign primacy to movement and consider position (or the finite product or object) as its derivative.

Relation is what happens before the coordinates appear; Telestreet emerges out of, and changes with, myriad relations among disparate components: the tools, the planning, the learning, the spaces, experiments, food, footage, family, and friends. Who asks the questions in an interview? Who holds the microphone and the camera? What if the interviewer and interviewee switch roles? These relations are at the basis of an ontogenesis of the social and of culture that leads to what is perceived as specific forms of culture and sociability (Massumi 2002, 9).[3] As I focus on the relations among the media objects and those who engage with them, I move away from a study of social morphology (of the dots on a grid) toward a conceptualization of emergence *in process.* My emphasis then shifts from describing how Telestreet and the Telestreettari retain their stability—their identity, configuration, and initial purpose—to how they cannot do so, passing thresholds after which they cease to be or take on different structures (Simondon 2006, 73).

The seeding of almost imperceptible transformation across the layers and components of the Telestreettari perception and individuality, their network and its milieu, is called *transduction.*[4] Transduction refers to the exchanges of energy and information between a system (a crystal, a cell, an individual, a group) and its milieu, causing change and becoming (often something different). In media too, transduction transforms different types of energy; for instance, a microphone transforms sound into an electrical signal. Transduction conceptualizes the level-specific process of emergence (the reorganization of a system) and its transmission of generative impulses to other levels or systems while allowing differentiation to the nature of these serial transformations. Transduction is the connecting thread of movement energetics, looking at the relation between Telestreet and its milieu. The energy traversing the network is what gives it the consistency that the coverage described cannot capture.

If one takes into consideration the networked aspect of much activism (Castells 2012), then it becomes useful to conceptualize *the transductive relations that shape and engender* Telestreet's nodes, other groups, and their environment rather than simply focus on their constituted parts. What engenders a network? What makes a node? If contemporary societies are increasingly built upon functional networks connecting different processes, resources, and parts (networks of activists, communication means, technologies, economies, institutions, and so on), then it is crucial to understand how to talk about the changing relations rather than just focus on Telestreet's repertoire of contention, how it makes video, and what the videos say. There is value in using and then discarding the category of social movement, as Telestreet did. Telestreet is a social movement; for a while, at least, it was positioned as one because it stood in for everyone who opposed Berlusconi. Most importantly, Telestreet *poses the question of movement in the social—that is, the question of individuation and becoming social in composition.*

Proposition Two: Telestreet Is Tactical Media

In the week leading up to September 21, 2003, the walls of Rome's historically working-class district of San Lorenzo were covered in posters declaring *"Totti libero!" "Montella libero!"* (Free Totti! Free Montella!). Puzzled by the enigmatic incitation directed at their football stars, the inhabitants of this Roma FC–mad area tore down some of the ads, until another campaign of flyers explained what was happening (Anonimo 2003). These new posters and flyers announced a free broadcast of the Juventus-Roma match on UHF channel 26 the following Sunday. A decryption card connected to a television transmitter made the game available without paying a subscription. This was a protest against the media monopoly and allowed thousands of underprivileged football fans to once again afford to be an audience. The groups behind the action included some street television channels—SpegnilaTV, TeleAut, AntTV, OrfeoTv—and the subversive communication agency Guerrilla Marketing. On the day of the match, polls conducted through the houses' intercoms made sure that the enthusiastic inhabitants of San Lorenzo were receiving a clear signal while they enjoyed a free performance of their favorite team. At the bottom of the TV screen, the logo of Disco Volante TV declared solidarity with the disabled-run Telestreet channel shut down by the authorities a few days earlier. The show also opened with a communiqué denouncing the planned eviction of more than one hundred Italian and migrant families from an occupied building in the area. The advertising intermission showcased Telestreet's own video spots and an interview with Roma FC fans denouncing the commercialization and enclosure of football through pay TV and unaffordable stadium tickets (Anonimo 2003). The independent broadcasting of the game, facilitated by Telestreet, was also interspersed with information on the background of Rupert Murdoch—who owned the Italian sport pay-TV channel Sky—and with homemade commentary on the game (Blisset 2004). Match score: Juventus 2, Roma 2.

Already in the press release that preceded the action, the coalition had drawn attention to the underlying connections between intellectual property and the consolidation of monopolies on information, as is the case with football. It is precisely at this intersection that the groups involved saw a perfected separation (Debord 1983) between the business and spectacle of marketed football and the sport as a moment of sociability and popular culture, constantly produced by fans around the world. For the groups involved, "no monopoly should be allowed to encrypt the richness of the streets and of the stadium terraces. . . . The public is not for sale" (AntTV et al. 2003). The hijacking of the encrypted signal of the match created an interference with "the *massmediocritised* communication flux" (AntTV et al. 2003) and made immediately visible the separation between football as business and spectacle and football as a catalyst for aggregation. The combination of television transmitter and a rigged decoding card materially inverted the power relations organizing the functions and qualities of the sport. Its operation decrypted and broke down the links among football, business, and spectacle in which the form of content (capital) and the form of expression (sport) are seen as necessarily coupled. Sociability and popular culture once again were expressed in football.

On Monday, February 2, 2004, I received an email from the Telestreet listserv passing on the news about a similar decryption action a day earlier in Scampia, one of the most degraded areas of the Neapolitan outskirts. Ma.gi.ca TV, named after three historical stars of the Napoli FC football team—Diego Maradona, Bruno Giordano, and Careca (Antônio de Oliveira Filho)—had delighted its audience with another free match, as well as with footage of local kids' games. Although Napoli FC lost, "Sky must've had its grief too," the email joked. Match score: Telestreet 2, Sky 0. At another level of this sociotechnical formation, one that ties broadcasting dynamics to dominant cultural production, Telestreet triggered a similar inversion of power, this time through the simple switching of two connectors in an antenna's box. The switched cables changed the device from a receiver of signals to a sender—from passive to active medium. This reverse engineering of media and its social functions, for Telestreet node CandidaTV, points at "the intention to radically remold the perception of media, which means eliminating the prejudices about its non-interchangeability. Instead of one-way communication, from one to many, . . . communication going from many to many" (CandidaTV, qtd. in Janković 2004).

These actions blow up the traditional communication model: the big bang of Telestreet forms a complex *assemblage*—a heterogeneous sociotechnical system that synchronizes behaviors, desires, languages, and ways of thinking. Assemblages describe specific interlocking and overlapping territories made of biological, social, and technological fragments that present unique properties that emerge from the interaction between their parts (practices, power, etc.). Within assemblages, technological elements are interwoven with elements of the social and with bodies, producing emergent unities (Deleuze and Guattari 1986). Defined in this relational manner, media are assemblages, institutions are assemblages, networks are assemblages, and so are nation-states and what we call "society." Simondon (perhaps ventriloquized by Gilles Deleuze and Félix Guattari) would say that *assemblages individuate.* Their components clinch together, turning into something more powerful than the sums of their parts. At this moment of media jacking, the Telestreet assemblage emerges from tech rigs, traditions of resistance, and discourses about consumption, among other things—it achieves the power to reverse power.

Temporary reversals of power are what characterize the practices of rebels who use tactical media "as a set of tactics by which the weak make use of the strong" (Garcia and Lovink 1997). "The ABC of Tactical Media," a manifesto for DIY media tacticians, is one of the many texts that call for creative resistance from those who are excluded from the wider culture (Garcia and Lovink 1997). Inspiration comes from the work of the Situationist International, with their subversive habit of *détournement,* which appropriates the existing means of consumer cultural expression to critique the "society of the spectacle" (Debord 1983). Tactical media engineer hit-and-run actions, ad hoc stunts, and pranks that can cause a shift in the perception about dominant forces (Raley 2009). The tactical media assemblage is a temporary grouping of people and technology who compose around an action, only to disperse again and maybe regroup under a different guise for future undertakings. What the Situationists wrote in the sixties found a captive audience in the nineties, when consumer electronics, digital media, and DIY technology enabled artists, hackers, and activists to rethink the role of communication and media as tools to confront dominant powers.

Telestreet comes into a world of tactical media; it suitably assembles in a milieu that Gilles Deleuze (1995b, 178) famously called societies of control, where individuals enjoy a high degree of freedom while being subjected to indirect yet equally powerful forms of control. Control societies center computers and other information technologies with their shift from production (of goods) to metaproduction, selling services and buying activities. Here, the transition of waged labor from factories to cognitive and affective labor—the service and creative economies—blurs the boundaries between work and leisure and sets the ground for the new arrangements of power and control, pervading society like a gas (179–81).

In a society of control, the commodification of information and lifestyles is inextricably connected with the development of cybernetics—"a theory of messages and their control" (Crary 1984, 292). The new social functions of television take root at this intersection between information technology and information as commodity, increasingly overlapping and networked with other forms of cross-platform consumer electronics, especially computers. Television's content no longer merely constitutes a simulacrum of life but reduces all signs to free-flowing elements that can be made compatible and sold with the rest of the available information flows (287–89). The increased connectedness among different information distribution media and the content transmitted have effects that range from the boom of the entertainment industry thriving on these flows to the creation of a mass-mediated social imagination based on consumer identities—a society of the spectacle on steroids, *pace* Debord. Production in the society of control is directly the production of social relations for capitalist accumulation, and the "raw material" of the new forms of labor is subjectivity itself, as well as the environment in which subjectivities are reproduced (Lazzarato 1996). Affect, before emotion, is the vector of information to the brain of individuals. Affect is the vector of psychosocial individuation of the subject—it carries *information.*

The transduction of affects across the circuits of interoperable television involves complex, multiscale dynamics that reach deep into human perception and desire (Lazzarato 2014) and deep into the material circuits of information distribution.[5] The sensory and cognitive stimuli that circulate between individuals and machines establish a relationship between interiority and the world that becomes a site of governance. As Richard Grusin demonstrates in his book on affect and mediality, we can think in terms of affect, beyond signification, to conceptualize how "media function on the one hand to discipline, control, contain, manage, and govern human affectivity and its affiliated things 'from above,' at the same time that they work to enable particular forms of human action, particular collective expressions and formations of human affect 'from below'" (2010, 79). Information is not just the commodity of contemporary capitalism; it is also what transduces across organic and inorganic elements of an assemblage. Information is data, content, and perceptive stimuli. It produces meaning across culture, the economy, computation, and subjectivity. Information makes different relations possible precisely because it entangles a variety of elements and processes.[6]

Tactical television tackles control societies' expanding grid of control by constantly intervening in these information flows and in the power relations they sustain. The capture and co-option of symbols and practices for market purposes become the main reasons to opt for ephemeral and nomadic structures. So, then, tactical media's *purpose,* if there is a clearly definable one, is nomadism, mobility, always opening up new cracks, platforms, and channels for rebellion and questioning: "Once the enemy has been named and vanquished it is the tactical practitioner whose turn it is to fall into crisis" (Garcia and Lovink 1997). Tactical media practitioners study "the techniques by which the weak become stronger than the oppressors by moving fast across the physical or media and virtual landscapes" (Garcia and Lovink 1997).

Tactical media thrived in Italy's vigorous society of the spectacle. Telestreet's second national meeting, Eterea II, was held in Senigallia in March 2004, in support of its node Disco Volante TV, based in that town and closed by the authorities a few months earlier. The founding members of the tactical media movement flocked to Eterea II to learn about Telestreet, now almost two years old. In the first interview I conducted on behalf of Telestreet, tactical media guru David Garcia foresaw the end of Telestreet once the Italian political crisis was over (Telestreet 2004). It was

32 · MAKING SENSE OF TELESTREET

not to take on the infamous prophetic role of Cassandra but in the spirit of tactical media that Garcia celebrated the reversals of power brought about by Telestreet, while emphasizing that it could only uncover the problematic arrangement of media in the country. Unless new effective strategies were developed, Telestreet's endurance and potential institutionalization would inevitably constitute its capture and demise. Two more years and the media tactician pronounced the death of tactical media as an effective activist practice because of the commercial cannibalization of creativity. For Garcia, neoliberal rhetoric of freedom and creativity have reopened an old fault line between artists and activists, depoliticizing tactical media. As mere epiphenomena of communicative capitalism, tactical media are not only tolerated but also consumed with glee (Garcia 2006). Garcia (2006) called for new connections between short-lived tactics and more sustainable strategies of dissent. The Situationists' strategies to undermine the spectacle in society have turned themselves into a spectacle—RIP, tactical media.

Composition Two: Assemblages and Transindividuation

If mere inversions of power and constant movement are no longer enough to effectively resist in a society of control, what is Telestreet's purpose? And how does it function? Garcia's call for sustainable strategies has not gone unheeded. Or better, long before Garcia's pronouncement, activists had already incorporated aesthetic tactics into their modes of protest, and Telestreet is not just an attempt to invert power. Telestreet doubles the bet, moving beyond temporary inversions of roles and power by embodying both social critique and a possible solution to the problem it addresses. Tactical media appropriate signs and symbols to deterritorialize the codes that fix the social imagination along the logic of the market. Telestreet *détourns* tactical media; it pushes this practice to its limit by *being the medium* that others can use: "We are television and we circulate messages that disturb and change the spectators' usual perspective. In this way we . . . create visions of multiplied reality," says Agnese Trocchi of CandidaTV (Janković 2004).

Media activism is often associated with the discursive, with attempts to portray events as unfiltered from the bias of corporate media and the codified language of media industries in general. Yet, since the language of television is never neutral and always manipulative, many street television channels openly, humorously, and *purposelessly* embrace this manipulation, offering visions of possible worlds that push manipulation into creation. We can think of Telestreet and other similar assemblages as milieus for the individuation of different collectivities, as I will argue in more detail in the next chapters.

Whenever I browsed the Telestreet video archive, I marveled at the quirky, deliriously creative character of many of the shows: EmisioNeokinok.tv's experimental television, OrfeoTv's performances live on screen, CandidaTV's programs made by children from the Roman periphery, and the adventures of pot-smoking Rotsuma by Teleimmagini are only a few examples that break the mold of what it means to make television— together, as friends. In these videos, criticism and creation go hand in hand, but criticism is only implicit in the process of creating something outside of what is allowed on TV. This means that to tell the story of Telestreet as an anti-Berlusconi movement, or as tactical media, is to tell only part of the story because Telestreet's productions do not aim to make evident and fill the gaps left by a media monopoly on information. Defying much of the media attention that hyped the project, the Telestreettari do not strictly see themselves as the paladins of the antimedia consolidation crusades. Granted, they developed as Berlusconi rose to power in the government and are critical of him, but Telestreet shows are very, very distant from the entertainment and news that are typical of Italian mainstream TV, be it Berlusconi's or public service broadcasting.

With the traditional television model morphing into a networked grid for the flow of heterogeneous data, symbols, and codes, it becomes harder to talk about a simple reversal between spectators and creators of content, consumers and producers of desires and lifestyles—what Axel Bruns (2008) has called produsage. Could one argue that a remolding of this medium takes place with a simple reversal? Through the antitelevision model of communication "from many to many" taking over the traditional broadcast system, Telestreet investigates the interoperability of television with other forms of accessible technology (P2P networks, Linux Operating Systems, social media platforms, etc.) but also with alternative modes of socialization that surpass communicating and distributing information: "If television killed the streets, we return it to the site of the crime. . . . Television is a weapon. The screen reality must be squatted. Weapons are in our hands, beware! If there is a big brother, Candida [TV] is his little sister" (Janković 2004). CandidaTV words set the record straight. Squatting sometimes requires weapons and, for Telestreet, the weapons are psychosocial as much as technical. I present these weapons as partaking in a *technical individuation,* where machine components come to assemble a technical system that is conducive to sociotechnical individuations (Simondon 1989).

Street television materially and figuratively becomes a way of (re)directing codes and flows of meaning and relaying multiple realities. Street television pushes past reversal, in order to *connect,* interface, and more efficiently relay these multiple realities. Telestreet *détourns* tactical media. It hacks the television system and its monopoly on shaping reality, moving from symbolic temporary inversions of forces between mainstream and independent media to a perversion of the television model into an interoperable assemblage always in motion because it is rooted in its collectivism. Way before dominant television took over multiple platforms, the interoperability of the pirate television assemblage displaced TV to a variety of contexts (community centers, the streets, the neighborhood, the art gallery, the protest, etc.). This kind of interoperability supports the strategic embodiment of plural experiences through "active participation in socialized knowledge" (Virno 2004, 13). The knowledge is partly created in the act of working together and partly in that it is connected to existing spaces and practices of resistance: for instance, using the production of a show to engage youth at risk. Thus, the Telestreettari find their fulfillment in the pleasures of being together and not in any specific content production. To paraphrase the Situationists one last time, Telestreet refuses traditional forms of communication but also turns this refusal into a constructive project (McDonough 2004, 134) of collective creation. Telestreet is not a tactical media practice but it draws on it and hacks it into a strategic, autonomous medium for the creation of multiplied reality, transforming those who come into contact with it—*transindividuation.* In a milieu of *trans*individuation, individuals and groups become in relation to each other and to media technologies.

Proposition Three: Telestreet Gives Voice to the Voiceless

Telestreet announced its irruption into the mediascape with the following manifesto (and a few more followed).

One, two, three, many . . .
STREET TELEVISIONS
Street TV, housing estate TV, neighborhood TV, condo TV,
micro TV, personal TV . . .
The televisual ocean we swim in seriously smells of monoculture
A single type of fish has taken over the waters of the info-sphere
Biodiversity has been wiped off
The banana fish is eating all the others
CALL FOR ACTION
To all free and strong fish which still love swimming
Empty your hearts of all sorrow
Let your imagination and creativity find their power again
Let friendship and risk lead us into the open again:
Where danger is, there grows the saving power
It is high time we came out of the fish tank
Let's go down the street, let's call our friends, our life compan-
ions, all those still alive, who have a mind and voice, let's buy an
aerial, a modulator and a TV transmitter, let's find a room, a garage,
a shed, let's gather our Sunday video cameras, a VHS from home, a
TV set, some lamps for a bit of light.
We can start now . . .

The first four lines of the text denounce the dire situation of media monopoly in Italy and justify the birth of the project as a rebellion against hegemonic and oppressive media powers. The remaining part of the manifesto
calls to those who feel alienated by the tyranny of Berlusconi to no longer
feel powerless and appropriate broadcasting technology for independent
transmission. For researchers of bottom-up communication models, the
narrative of Telestreet's empowerment and "giving voice to the voiceless"
(Ardizzoni 2008) is a compelling one (and often rightly so). Clemencia
Rodríguez (2001), Chris Atton (2002), Nick Couldry and James Curran
(2003), and John D. H. Downing et al. (2001) have all discussed the power
of citizen media to open up the space for minority groups challenging
social codes and legitimizing their identities.

In my own interviews with Telestreet's members, I have been exposed to
similar narratives. For instance, in one of the most exciting conversations
about the *becoming of a media activist,* my interviewee told me of a 2003
summer camp to protest the presence of detention centers in southern

36 · MAKING SENSE OF TELESTREET

Italy, where, more or less by chance, Nicola ended up with a video camera in hand while gate-crashing a detention center to document the infrastructure of the camp and the stories of its inmates. Still more or less by chance, Nicola managed to hide the tape with the footage before the police destroyed all visual evidence of the event. In the confusion caused by the invasion, some inmates escaped. Rumors have it that one of them is now a football player, and others found work. The video circulated widely, marking an important moment in Italian No Borders politics (Frassanito Network 2004). "Ale, since then I could not put the camera down" (interview with Nicola, 2008) is all Nicola needs to say. It is evident from the tone that there is a feeling of power in wielding a camera as a weapon against those who have a monopoly on the definition of violence.

I examine the video of the detention center action (Noborder 2003). I watch a fence, and pliers cutting it. I watch people sneak in with their cameras and a banner. I hear them chant, "No borders, no nations, stop deportation," and the detainees' answer, "Freedom! Freedom!" I am made into a witness to the bruises the migrants have from the police beatings, seeing them through the metal mesh of the dehumanizing cages they speak from. I startle at the sight of the soldiers and police appearing to arrest the protesters, and through that experience I am able to connect to those defending the rights of migrants and their autonomy to choose freedom of movement over artificially imposed borders. From the late nineties on, activists have been increasingly using cameras for documentation purposes but also to produce proof of police brutality during rallies and on other occasions. Simultaneously, the independent, grassroots documentaries available online and through activist networks have multiplied. Migrants to Italy have also moved behind the cameras with some Telestreet nodes. Whether it is explicitly for political purposes, to reveal the hidden or forgotten, or for community cultural production, there is power in autonomous media production. I have myself been there and felt it. This excitement goes to the core of the self, as Rodríguez (2001) emphasizes: it boosts a person's identity—whether it is a minoritarian identity or that of a Telestreettaro or Telestreettara. Telestreet empowers, (in some cases) gives voice to the voiceless, challenges in its own (small) way the monopoly of the banana fish swimming in the televisual ocean, and emboldens the little fish. Still, as I pop my head out of these metaphorical waters, my field of vision expands past the immediately visible social categories and identities of citizen media. I consider the information flows traversing Telestreet—the content, affects, and other perceptual stimuli—and how these do not only shape people into a coherent public.

Composition Three: Repurposing Media for Connective Activism

There is more to the No Borders camp story, more about the transformation from an activist camper to a member of insu^tv. In the same interview, Nicola tells me about joining the camp to cure activist burnout without completely disengaging from politics; Nicola had felt disillusionments with crystallized and stagnant local discourses on organizing and needed a break (interview with Nicola, 2008). Once the activist chanced upon the camera to document the treatment immigrants receive when they land on the shores of the so-called garden of Europe, the energy generated triggered some imperceptible change: the individuation of Nicola-as-media-activist-part-of-a-movement-of-media-activists (psychosocial individuation) and that of the camera-as-weapon (technical individuation). Assemblages are compositions that individuate and possess a kind of sociotechnical agency; they can become political.

The camera mediated a system of relations between the individual and the collective that are not pregiven but are exactly what shapes both terms through interaction: the media activist and media activism. This means that individuation, both personal and collective, takes place through practice—in this case, media practice. Simondon points at information and communication technology as important factors in processes of individuation, resonating with memory and social intelligence but especially with sensibilities and affects. Key here is the role of technical objects: a technical object expresses mediation between a person and the natural world (Simondon 1989). This kind of mediation implies that the technical object is endowed with a potentiality that can inspire a reconfiguration or creation of sociotechnical assemblages. The capacity for technical mediation, as is the case with the camera, is revealed when a certain kind of culture of technology grasps its effective reality and implications for human beings and for the social field in general. However, despite its potential to affect social dynamics, the technical object that is reproduced and marketed by industries often loses its singularity and potential. When the technical object is a mere tool, it does not have the same meaning for the individual: most technical objects take on a specific role when they establish themselves in society, becoming normalized (Simondon 2006, 251–53). Television in Italy is certainly an example of this habituation—until Telestreet. Nicola and Telestreet more broadly show that it is possible to rediscover an object's "essence" by drawing on a specific sensibility and creativity that enables one to move beyond its function as a tool (Simondon 2006, 263). This is where I start seeing the deeper effects of the encounter between Nicola and the camera: the creation of new relations and eventually the emergence of a Telestreet node. Importantly, mediation here refers to the ability to bring about, to foster new assemblages, not to the memetic ability to reproduce reality. The rediscovery of a creative attitude toward technology is a repurposing of sorts. It requires people to come together around a technological fix, often moved by specific events like the No Borders camp, or a Telestreet convention, or a hack of a pay-TV card. Other campers and activists joined Nicola to create Ma.gi.ca TV in Scampia and then insu^tv. I describe the practices of Telestreet nodes like insu^tv as *repurposing media*. Repurposing functions on multiple levels and at multiple scales to describe the hacking of media, sociality, and knowledge production.

First and foremost, of course, Telestreet repurposes available technologies (antennas, computers, etc.) and spaces (airwaves, the streets, etc.) and yet the repurposing is less about the reuse of discarded technical objects or neglected spaces and more about the harnessing of encounters and events within an expanding field of social relations. From this perspective, repurposing describes a set of alternative media practices that bend and hack what is available to foster social cohesion rather than communication—the stress here is on the *purposing* more than the *re*. Repurposing becomes a way of folding technology into new sociotechnical assemblages that, in turn, enter into composition with their environment, forging connections with other groups and individuals. For example, the documentary on the illegal dumping of toxic waste in Naples that insu^tv produced does not simply remedy a lack of information about this issue, nor does it just give voice to the communities protesting the garbage crisis (insu^tv 2009d). *Wasting Naples* is the culmination of years of outreach activities and technical and political support to bring people together around issues that affect them directly; this outreach is then reabsorbed into community organizing through screenings and a variety of thematic collaborations. This is part of the set of practices that I have come to understand as *connective activism*.

The following chapters will get into the details of how the repurposing of media fosters porosity among activist groups, how it draws on a variety of histories, traditions, and technological resources to build community and foster dissenting subjectivities. It is no coincidence that insu^tv views itself as a media *connective* instead of a collective: for this group, the engagement with DIY media production acknowledges the need to create and tend to the spaces and infrastructures where collectivity emerges through a set of shared creative practices. Repurposing also speaks to the movement of individuation that connects the individual and the collective at different scales, the *I* and the *we* that co-individuate. When seen as a way of connecting activist groups and communities, the repurposing of media brings to the fore the value of media activism for the creation of social assemblages in which the "media" literally *mediates* between individuals and among individuals and their environment, instituting and developing new relations (Simondon 1989). In this sense, I mobilize repurposing as a way of conceptualizing the unique, creative character of some struggles over social reproduction that autonomist feminism calls for (Serra 2015; Thorburn 2016). I offer up the concept of *repurposing* as one of the core practices of connective activism. This concept is a means for thinking *with* Telestreet, especially its node insu^tv.

I started this chapter with an analysis of the discourses and categorizations that support criminalization and surveillance; their force often drives the decomposition of social movements but it also triggers recompositions into new assemblages—this is what resistance looks like when one considers it from the perspective of ongoing change. Each transformation leaves a residue and plants new seeds. In a sense, the seeds that generated some of the practices of connective activism came from repression. Insu^tv was born from the burnout and fragmentation that followed the crackdown on the global justice movement after the protests at the 2001 summits in Naples and Genoa (interview with Asterix, 2008; interview with Sara, 2008). Steering away from any form of movement organizing and identitarian stances, the insulini (people from insu^tv)—video camera in hand—chose to coexist, conjugate, and connect with the most disparate assemblages, ranging from parishes and fair-trade associations to No Borders organizations. As it rejects identitarian positioning, insu^tv coexists, conjugates, and connects on a plane on which there are no dots that indicate their position—their closeness to or distance from others. To coexist, conjugate, and connect are the modes of an antidialectic, strategic logic that promises no resolution in a unity. This is not only a theoretical shift from *position* to *relation* but, especially, a practical move from position as a form of organizing alliances in movements to *composition* as a mode of sociopolitical relation (and consolidation) among heterogeneous groups—a movement building of sorts. It is particularly pertinent at times of fragmentation and crisis. In some cases, Telestreet may give voice to the voiceless and be a megaphone for identity. Still, before form, there is process and that process is part of political engagement in the form of *repurposing media for connective activism*. To fully understand Telestreet as a happening, it is necessary to investigate its historical and political origins first. Similarly, it will take some forays into the past to find the taproots and seeds of the intimacy, care, and friendship that instill energy into connective activism. By the end of this book, connective activism will have transduced from this initial composition to a fully fledged phenomenon that connects media practices and projects across time and space, entering through Telestreet and the example of its node insu^tv.

2

Intimacy and Media Making

A Long History of Delirium, Care, and Social Reproduction

Let a hundred flowers
bloom,
let a hundred radios transmit,
let a hundred pages
prepare
another
'68, with different
weapons

—Collettivo A/traverso, *Alice è il diavolo*

The young soldier Franco "Bifo" Berardi was taken to the psychiatric ward after refusing to leave his sentry post once his shift ended: he wanted to remain on guard for as long as he had strength. During ten days under medical observation, Bifo was generally compliant and claimed to be fine. Still, there was one troubling symptom: his uncontrollable impulse to remember and add up numbers on car license plates whenever he saw them. The doctor, upon releasing him from military duties, complimented him on "his excellent performance if he was faking." And yes, the soldier's performance had been top-notch, the fruit of intense study; he was diagnosed with a classic case of obsessive delirium (interview with Bifo, 2008).

Back in 1974, one of Bifo's friends had given him a book by a French psychoanalyst who had looked at the world from the perspective of a patient. Félix Guattari's *Una tomba per Edipo* (A grave for Oedipus, 1974) proved to be a great book for learning how to "play mad" and get out of compulsory military service: "During my experience, I understood something about schizoanalytic thought," he told me. "Folly—madness—entails a strong element of choice, of desire, of intention, and construction. . . . I started seeing Guattari as my savior."

Three years went by and Bifo, this time on the run to avoid prison, invoked "Saint Guattari" once again. Like many of his comrades, he was hiding in Paris, and he went searching for Félix.

When I tell the story like this, you see, it says nothing, but if we follow the thread of madness, things take on a different meaning. . . . My encounter with Guattari was like a kind of cry for help. I was like a patient searching for help but not to get out of madness, like Breton says: "It is not the fear of madness which will oblige us to leave the flag of imagination furled."[1] In a sense, it was a reversal of the fear of madness. Madness should not be scary, madness seen as delirium, from *de-lire*, to exit, to get out from the reading, from the structure, from the text.[2] . . . Madness can be a way of finding your way. (Interview with Bifo, 2008)

This use of madness to capture a certain attitude toward experimentation is not meant to irresponsibly romanticize a condition of suffering; the trope has less to do with mental illness and more with a reference to creative *delirium* and to some of the practices of the antipsychiatry movement of the time, where Guattari was involved.[3] Many departures from dominant structures of sense making and from the canonical readings of the time shaped the political and aesthetic practices that developed in the seventies in Italy.

Bifo's life-changing encounter with Guattari was not unique during that period, when Gilles Deleuze and Félix Guattari's *Anti-Oedipus* ([1972] 1983), the first volume of *Capitalism and Schizophrenia,* had arrived immediately after publication. One among many seminal works of unorthodox philosophy to reach the country, the book had made its way to Bifo's prison cell after he was accused of placing a bomb in the headquarters of the Christian Democrats. Bifo was subsequently acquitted (Berardi 2008, 3), but reading *Anti-Oedipus* left a mark on him, as it did on many other political activists who were inspired to experiment with alternative practices of cultural production. Their experiments, several of which revolutionized media making, draw out the micropolitical potential of practices that build on the friendship and intimacy of creating together. Some of the roots of Telestreet's connective activism can be found in these alternative practices of cultural production. They reveal a side of resistance that can only be sustained in experiments with different ways of being (together).

When I spoke with Bifo, he explained that *Anti-Oedipus* offered a radical departure from the dogma of traditional psychoanalysis and Marxism, introducing a new conceptualization of subjectivity into political militancy (interview with Bifo, 2008). In Deleuze and Guattari's schizoanalytic thought, processes of subjectivation unfold alongside and through practices that invest a-signifying elements with meaning and functions. Deleuze and Guattari's notion of a proliferating "unconscious as a factory" rejects the psychoanalytic tendency to discover links with the unconscious in favor of a focus on the constituent elements of social reality that shift the collective flows of signification and communication.[4] Deleuze and Guattari were not alone in questioning what had become the pillars of political thought—both France and Italy had strong antipsychiatry movements and new currents of thought questioning Marxist orthodoxy. Starting with the movement of 1968, the political ferment of the time triggered an exodus from spaces engaging with traditional psychoanalysis and party politics toward autonomous sites for political, social, and aesthetic experiments that in many ways still characterize the present. These experiments tackled capitalism as a system of value creation and accumulation, and as an assemblage of libidinal drives and desires expressed in individual and collective subjectivities.

In Italy the momentum of 1968 lasted for nearly a decade and carried with it a critique of the older generation's values, such as traditional family structures, authoritarianism, individualism, and uncritical consumption. There are various terms that describe the mass movement that grew in that decade. I have chosen to use the more common term *autonomia* to avoid confusion and because it foregrounds an important aspect of the relationship between politics and subjectivity that cuts across its heterogeneous groups and projects—and can be found in Telestreet as well. In its most generic sense, the word *autonomy* refers to a disenfranchisement from party politics and orthodox Marxism, and to the prioritization of the agency of the worker over processes of capital accumulation. *Autonomia* was a large, heterogeneous movement traversed by several currents, from feminism to vanguardism, from spontaneism to armed struggle. As such, no account or label can do it justice. However, what I rather grossly simplify as *autonomia* (or autonomist activism), in its many incarnations, indissolubly links the constitution of a polymorphous anticapitalist social configuration to a recomposition of the subjectivities of its intellectuals and activists through a process of self-valorization. In other words, *autonomia* was a movement that brought a variety of people together inside and outside the factory gates to rethink how capitalism oppresses, how one lives, and how one struggles in novel ways.

I follow the thread of delirium to chart some of the lines of flight of *autonomia*. Autonomism produced a rich body of theory and culture; it inserted the struggle over processes of subjectivation into organizing practices and forged influential concepts like "the social factory," the "refusal of work," "self-valorization," "class composition," and "antagonistic social reproduction." Media production, proto-media activism, *conricerca*, and experimental socialization feature heavily in my account as I too get off the furrow, reading the history of *autonomia* outside its own prevailing narratives—state narratives that brand the movement as violent and terrorist and those shaped by the few theorists who have become internationally renowned.

As I interviewed people in Bologna to take a snapshot of the original scene, I sensed the depth and breadth of the social upheaval of the time and the diffused desire to flee a coercive postwar society with its state-sponsored industrial consumerist machine. The cultural production of the period echoes these feelings as it departs from the hegemonic narrative and social script and ventures into a radical politics of exodus. I place the somewhat delirious autonomist media—books, magazines, journals, and radio—at the center of my reading because they take me to places that a historical or political-economic approach to the movement cannot: the sites of friendship, intimacy, and collectivity. Here, signs are not just used for signification but are also affective devices that relay processes of socialization and politicization building on the materiality of this cultural production: the circulating literature, the prints, the fonts of the offset press, telephones connected to radio transmitters, and many others. I recognize many of the ideas and approaches to creating social infrastructure and some of the spirit of this period in Telestreet.

Cutting Up the Norm

Between 1975 and 1976, Bifo cofounded Collettivo A/traverso (Transversal Crossing) with a group of intellectuals from Bologna. The A/traverso collective published a cultural and political agitation pamphlet that advocated for a critical use of media and cultural production to "transform/collectivize the everyday" (*A/traverso*, no. 1, qtd. in Fiori 2011, 50).[5] Their publication elaborated new languages and forms of expression that sabotage traditional communication flows to foster social recomposition outside the structures of capitalist production (Collettivo A/traverso 2007, 10); their tendency to transversality and to undoing norms was already materialized in the forward slash that cuts the title.

A/traverso, and many other transversal sheets, called for "the appropriation and liberation of the body, the collective transformation of interpersonal relationships as the fulcrum from which to reconstruct a project of rejection of factory work and of any order based on performance and exploitation" (*A/Traverso,* no. 1, qtd. in Fiori 2011, 50). This was a response to a backlash against the movement of '68. Deleuze and Guattari's concepts of the transversal and desiring-machines from *Anti-Oedipus* echo throughout *A/traverso*'s pages together with a denunciation of the sadness, oppression, and irrefutability of traditional (Oedipal) family structures, and a rejection of the laws of the economy and of the sign. As an alternative, *A/traverso* celebrates the interjection of desire as a productive force that can abolish "the split between sign and life, let loose the signifying subject . . . in the outrageous space of practice" (Collettivo A/traverso 2007, 11–12). Its contributors call for new arrangements based on love, friendship, and the pleasure of being together, since practicing collective happiness is itself a subversive act (53).

Desire, for *A/traverso,* has very little to do with repression or pleasure and this is in keeping with the critique of psychoanalysis. If pleasure is only a temporary interruption of desire, the latter pertains to the drives that constitute what is commonly perceived as *an individual* (Deleuze and Guattari [1972] 1983, 35). Desire produces subjectivities but it is not simply personal; it has to be understood also as socialized within libidinal and political economies—it *produces production* (Deleuze 2004, 232).[6] Subversion becomes possible if one can redirect desire away from the social reproduction of the producers of surplus value for capital. In these cases, desire produces movements; it becomes part of that *energy* that often drives cycles of struggles. Desire connects.

A/traverso, as a "desiring-machine"—what I have been calling an assemblage—combines different elements and reinserts them into the social in a new configuration: the newly imported, more sophisticated technology of the offset press is combined with text and fonts rearranged from the mainstream press and, of course, with many words, ideas, and readings from books pushed to their limit of signification. DIY cut-up punk

46 · INTIMACY AND MEDIA MAKING

aesthetics meets *autonomia,* or the other way around. The resulting colorful and chaotic layout is an open invitation to join in a play of language and thought compositions. And join they did. The ideas circulated, as much as the sensory encounter with the magazine affected *A/traverso*'s readership. They catalyzed new possibilities for social connections through experimentation and collaborative cultural production.

Exodus, Autonomy, and Composition

The movement of 1968 had left more than just a seed of dissent in the fabric of society, and by the mid-1970s struggles peaked again. In 1976 organized groups of young proletarians in Milan protested the opening of the La Scala theater, blocking the entire city, and in 1977 a wave of antiauthoritarian student protests spread across Italian universities (Fiori 2011). More than just works like *Anti-Oedipus* and the transversal sheets, a wealth of autonomist publications also supported the new anticapitalist and antiauthoritarian discourses. The journals *Quaderni Rossi* (Red Notebooks, 1961–65), *Classe Operaia* (Working Class, 1964–67), *Potere Operaio* (Workers' Power, 1969–73) and *Rosso* (Red, 1973–77), to name a few, brought forward new interpretations of Marx that deviated from the orthodoxy, spurred by sociopolitical transformations that already started after World War II.

At that time, the Marshall Plan for reconstruction, currency protection, austerity measures, and hard working conditions had allowed Italy to complete huge public works projects, gear up for resource extraction, develop the car manufacturing and other heavy industries, and increase the internal demand for goods (Ginsborg 1989, 283–93). In the sixties, large numbers of young people who did not cross the ocean in search of better lives flocked from the poor south to the north of Italy, where the construction boom and the factories now required unskilled labor. During this so-called economic miracle, Fordist-automated production of goods and mass consumerism became the two pivotal mechanisms of growth and Italy became an important player in the economic field. Because the reconstruction effort had involved the exploitation of the workforce with the complicity of the Partito Comunista Italiano (PCI, Italian Communist Party), this new workforce was deeply mistrustful of the parliamentary left (Moroni and Balestrini 1988; Borio, Pozzi, and Roggero 2002). In the factories, schools, and universities, a new generation of youth demonstrated a marked antagonism toward the rigid social structures they inherited from the Communist Party and the Catholic Church alike.

The introduction into Italy of foreign literature and philosophy, the attention to social movement struggles outside the country (pacifism, feminism, anticolonialism, Black Power, and the LGBTQ movements), and the contact with countercultures like the beatniks, hippies, and later punk and dropout cultures fueled these feelings like gasoline. Not unlike their counterparts in other parts of Europe and North America, Italian students and workers celebrated new forms of music and art, free movement and travel, and countercultural fashion styles.[7] The seventies were the time of the first "centers of the young proletarians," what will later become Italy's social centers. The Centri Sociali Occupati e Autogestiti (Occupied and Self-Run Social Centers, CSOAs) are squatted houses run as communes, laboratories for countercultures and counterinformation, and spaces of aggregation against the isolation of young people and the valorization of free time. The seventies were also a time when intellectuals and artists otherwise relegated to the margins by a conservative cultural system could reach for available media production tools and started experimenting with radio transmission, video (Betamax and VHS), and audio recording. In particular, video was used for the first time to document the protests and political events of the day and to experiment with the fusion of art and politics as in the early works of Pier Paolo Pasolini and Alberto Grifi (Berardi, Jaquemet, and Vitali 2009, 77). This experimentation led to the emergence of Italian experimental film and to the free radio movement (Goddard 2018).

Many activist groups, like Lotta Continua (Ongoing Struggle), Potere Operaio (Workers' Power), and Autonomia Operaia (Workers' Autonomy), were founded during this period. The cultural work of their journals revolved around researching and understanding the composition of the new class of workers and their relationship to the local capitalist system, often through the activity of *conricerca* (co-research) (Alquati 2002, 6). Co-researchers were seen as "barefoot researchers" who fused theory and practice and were close to the groups they researched (Virno and Hardt 1996). As such, *conricerca* was a truly radical method. In the past, the labor movement, parties, and trade unions had relied on politically neutral knowledge that could be subsequently used for politics (Conti et al. 2007). Because in co-research, the studies were already designed with political objectives in mind, attention was immediately directed at the microconflictual, daily dimension within and outside the work environment. Co-researchers questioned the dominant sociological categories and tested them through different hypotheses that looked at day-to-day struggles constantly recomposing and stratifying the social tissue (Palano 2007). The barefoot researchers aimed to set the material (rather than just theoretical) basis for future movements in the path of "silent and subterranean" struggles, which were tied to each other in myriad bundled threads (Alquati, qtd. in Palano 2007). Inquiries in the factories brought to light elements of struggles in which workers already partook (e.g., sabotage, committees, and assemblies outside the unions, etc.). Since the seventies, *conricerca* has functioned as a mode of organizing (Conti et al. 2007, 80). This is because, while attending to the complexity of social struggles, research stimulates movement within fields of struggle through participation and interaction among all actors involved. The new notions of subjectivity (and desire) influenced this research method with co-researchers investigating the shifts in the subjective structure of the needs, behaviors, and practices of resistance of the working class but also the sedimentation of apparently spontaneous and unorganized antagonist cooperation (Armano, Sacchetto, and Wright 2013). The latter was thought to leave a sort of "political residue" in the subject positions of the groups and could become the basis for subsequent struggles.

A deviant reading of Karl Marx's work accompanied this research: autonomists thought anew the figure of the worker as well as the relationship between resistance, labor, and production.[8] The readings of *Das Kapital,* and especially the *Grundrisse*—the fragments on the machine—sought to represent the point of view of the worker, who ought to reflect on the historical stages of capitalism and understand their intrinsic forms of bourgeois antagonism to devise suitable strategies of emancipation (Moroni and Balestrini 1988, 38). Marx's analysis of the introduction of technology in the production process had rendered manifest a separation of labor into mental and menial that spoke to the economic context of the period. The economic development of postwar Italy had deeply affected the social fabric, giving birth, among other things, to (equally exploited) specialized workers and the so-called unskilled *operaio massa* (mass worker). Marx's concept of the *Gesamtarbeiter* (total worker)—that is, the combination of the workforce for production—paved the way to rethink exploitation as inherent to the production process instead of specific modes of labor

(1961, 531–32). As this rebellion against Marxist orthodoxy unfolded, attention moved *from labor to the worker* and radically changed how people understood struggle. Against the traditional Communist Party line, Mario Tronti was one of the first thinkers to invert the idea that class struggle can only take place once a certain level of economic development has been reached. Tronti ([1966] 2006) advocated for ongoing class struggle that reoriented the production process and forced capital to adapt to the workers' needs. He recognized that there is reciprocal presupposition of workforce and capital and that the working class has agency to enable or prevent production—to *become* capital or to divert its cumulative force toward the production of other forms of value.

More importantly, since at this stage of capitalist development social relations are entirely subsumed by capital, society itself is seen as an extension of the factory and an articulation of production. This theoretical breakthrough led to the conceptualization of the "social factory," a concept that still plays a fundamental role in the discussion of struggle against capitalist exploitation—and that has been popularized in books like *Empire* (Hardt and Negri 2000). Within this framework, antagonism is displaced from the factory to the social through a refusal to participate in the process of capitalist social production. The cooperative articulation of time spent outside the capitalist production process becomes an explicit practice of resistance. In the words of Antonio Negri, resistance against capital becomes a "movement of productive co-operation that . . . presents itself as the refusal of capitalist command over production and as the attempt, always frustrated but not less real, of constituting an autonomous time" ([1997] 2003, 73). This refusal to partake (as much as possible) in capitalist social production surfaces often not only in Telestreet but, increasingly, in the post–financial crisis movements, for instance at the encampments of the Occupy movement and in the economic platform of the Movement for Black Lives.

Unprefigured, ongoing, autonomous struggle immanent to capital's dynamic: this is where the meaning of autonomy goes beyond a disengagement from institutional politics to refer to the autonomy of the worker from capitalist development (through the self-valorization of needs and desire). Autonomy refers to the main characteristic of the subject in a communist society wherein she has control over her own multilateral productive potential (Negri [1979] 1999, xxx). Autonomy stays open to directions that can only form *during* the struggle rather than before it. Autonomist journals

50 · INTIMACY AND MEDIA MAKING

were the vectors that transmitted these ideas and proposed the *refusal of work* as a strategy of flight out of capital and to subordinate labor to the needs of the working class. This idea of the refusal of work dovetails with a belief in the possibility of more equal distribution of work to increase the development of a general social knowledge, or *general intellect*, often in connection with technological innovation (Marx [1857–58] 1973, 706).[9] Ultimately, for autonomists, the social liberation of the subject can only take place once an awareness of her own agency "within the contradictory structure of the relations of production" is reached and time can be devoted to alternative practices of self-valorization, and hence of subjectivation (Negri [1979] 1999, 160–63).

For nearly two decades, Italy became a laboratory for new social experiments and individuals entered a process of resubjectivation (Borio, Pozzi, and Roggero 2002, 72–73) through a long period of production sabotage, factory and university occupations, permanent assemblies, wildcat strikes, and autoreduction of prices of transportation. Self-valorization involved the theoretical analysis and collective development of alternative forms of socialization. *A/traverso* and Radio Alice are attempts at this kind of autonomous social production and resubjectivation in radical and irreconcilable opposition to the majority.

Radio Alice's Technosocial Wonderland

The deviations and contradictions of the seventies in Italy lead me into the cultural and political climate of an important moment for the emergence of social movements, when the writings, media, and delirious creations were indispensable elements. Like the viruses described in William Burroughs's stories that inspired activists like Bifo, the deviant readings traveled. They were translated and read collectively and in connection with other ones, with the realities in which they appeared. They were cut and pasted into zines and pamphlets. They produced new political and aesthetic options. Like a virus, the first issue of *A/traverso* was presented as a project in multiplication, not only making words proliferate on paper but also announcing events that would "reinstate life in place of the economy" (Collettivo A/traverso 2007, 10). *A/traverso* made the words spill out of the pages and shaped other kinds of situations for encounters and proliferation. Radio Alice, one of the first free radios in Italy, was born when one of these situations brought together Lewis Carroll's heroine, a cheap military transmitter, a telephone, some texts and records, and a desire to experiment, shared with many.

Radio and television in Italy had been under state control until 1974, when the Supreme Court declared this monopoly unconstitutional, enabling the birth of the "free" radios. Within a year of this ruling, the Italian airwaves were already teeming with more than 150 radio stations, and by the end of 1976 there were 1,500 (Orrico 2006, 5), run mostly by youth eager to infiltrate a mediascape that left very little if no space for their needs and tastes. There were many who seized the opportunity to finally air the newest international trends in music and countercultures, but others reached for the airwaves to support autonomist political organizing. Here, again, the prehistory of Telestreet finds its anchor. The institutional Italian left, especially the Italian Communist Party, traditionally had opposed the privatization of the mass media for fear of a capitalist takeover of the communicational superstructure. Quite the reverse, many in the free radio movement recognized the potential of the medium to bypass the control of a clerical and conformist Italian culture and create a space where political groups could come together on the airwaves—a place for delirious creation and collective becoming. Many free radios became the voice of the students' and of the young workers' movement: Radio OndaRossa in Rome, Radio Sherwood in Padoa, and Controradio in Florence were born then. These free radios, and a few more, will play a crucial role all the way to the present, importing new musical genres like hip-hop to Italy, hosting a bulletin board system (BBS), and training media activists. Radio Alice came on the scene in Bologna as an extension of *A/Traverso* and suitably retained a heterogeneous character that refused any internal political positioning and organization, even though it still reflected many autonomist ideas.

If there is a buzzword that characterizes its approach to mediatized aesthetics and politics, it is Radio Alice's subversive Mao-Dadaism. The old Dada utopia to abolish art and life is enacted through new forms of communication that subvert the medium of radio and blur the distinction between art and daily life. The following is from Radio Alice's first broadcast, on February 8, 1976:

An invitation to not get up this morning, to stay in bed with someone, to fabricate musical instruments or war machines. This is Radio Alice. Finally, Radio Alice. You are hearing us on 100.6

megahertz and you will hear us for a long time, unless the krauts kill us. Alice built herself a radio but in order to speak she continues her daily struggle against zombies and jabberwockies. Radio Alice transmits music, news, flower gardens, rants, inventions, discoveries, recipes, horoscopes, magic filters, loves, or war bulletins, photographs, messages, massages, lies. Radio Alice gives a voice to those who love mimosas and believe in paradise, those who hate violence and beat up the bad guys, those who think they are Napoleon but know full well that they could be an aftershave, those who laugh like flowers and cannot be bought up with love gifts, *those who want to fly and not sail, the smokers, the drinkers, the jugglers and musketeers, the jesters and the absentees, the mad ones and the tarot magicians.* (Collettivo A/traverso 2007, emphasis added)

Mao-Dadaists proliferate pervasive and polycentric communication technologies that recompose the relation between sociality and production outside the capitalist system (Moroni and Balestrini 1988, 604–5). Mao-Dadaism starts from the lesson of Dadaism with an understanding that the avant-gardes of the early twentieth century failed to abolish the separation between art and life, trapped as they were in the "illusory kingdom of art" (Chiurchiù 2017, 101). Mao-Dadaism has its starting point in Dada but the separation between art and life is abolished with *transversalism*: "on the practical terrain of existence, of the refusal of work, of [capitalist] appropriation," Mao-Dadaism calls for "the transformation of time, of the body, of language" ("Countermanifesto mao-dada," qtd. in Chiurchiù 2017, 101). The open-door studios of Radio Alice became a space for Mao-Dadaism, autonomist self-valorization, and the subversion of dominant circuits of libidinal and economic production—that is, for deviant, delirious media production.

Radio Alice's assemblage emerges outside the conventional logic of individualized identity (Collettivo A/traverso 2007, 14), folding in a variety of disparate groups (not always in agreement with each other) and fostering a process of collective subjectification that is inclusive while retaining all elements of heterogeneity.[10] Radio Alice had minimal editorial input that was made possible by an open mic; it broadcast without a program schedule. As Ambrogio, one of the founders, explains, the project brought together different ideas and people, turning the channel randomly into a performance stage, a soapbox, a confession booth, a roundtable, and so on.

Radio Alice represented "the movement of differences" at a time when identity politics was otherwise strong (interview with Ambrogio, 2008). Not unlike *A/traverso*'s chaotic layouts and playful texts, the experimentation with alternative uses of language and communication structures was one of the main tools of Alice's Mao-Dadaism. At the same time, the ability to hack the functions of the available technology added some important elements to this emerging assemblage. Humor, satire, fake news, music, rants, readings from the avant-garde, live telephone pranks, literature, and whatever else that was brought to the programming were interspersed with direct phone-in interventions from the audience. From a technical perspective, the simple telephone-radio hack turned Alice in a pliable and multidirectional medium with a potential unseen before. For Ambrogio, this groundbreaking feature, one that will soon be adopted by the mainstream, opened up the microphone to multiple subjects—from policemen to sex workers, from nurses on night shifts to street cleaners. It made the radio station into a reference point for many Bolognesi (interview with Ambrogio, 2008). This recomposition of collective subjectivity from homogenous to a multiplicity in constant flux is an important aspect of Telestreet and is key to my understanding of connective activism.

The Delirium of Domestic Labor

Heterogeneity notwithstanding, there was no space in the autonomist organizations to discuss gender. Even when they were on the front lines in groups like Lotta Continua and Potere Operaio, women who contributed a gendered perspective to the conversation were accused of distracting the groups from class struggle. And yet so much organizing work that changed Italian society in the seventies is tied to a feminist reconceptualization of the function of women in capitalist systems.[11] Above all, autonomist feminism has to be credited for locating social reproductive labor (elderly and infirm care, child bearing and rearing, education, affective labor) and domestic labor, as well as physical and sexual violence against women within a Marxist analysis of capitalism—an important derailing of the conversation, a going off topic that led to new radical directions in feminism internationally.

The feminist analysis of the "capitalist function of the uterus" (Dalla Costa and James 1975, 13) revealed the "arcane of reproduction" (Fortunati [1981] 1995) as the unseen basis of capitalist accumulation. Here the family functions as the site of production of the labor force whereas up to that point the family had been considered a place for consumption, for the production of use value or to provide reserve labor force (Dalla Costa 2002). Instead, women writing for the magazine *Le operaie della casa* (The house workers) were very clear about how to view this onerous yet unpaid labor that is so fundamental in the process of social reproduction: "life as work, always. Affection as work, sexuality as work, smiles as work, caresses as work, voice intonation as work, even dreams are hard work" (Comitato per il Salario al Lavoro Domestico di Padova 1976). Only the recognition of this invisible exploitation could propel class struggle forward, they claimed.

The research and rereadings of Marx by thinkers like Mariarosa and Giovanna Franca Dalla Costa, Silvia Federici, and Leopoldina Fortunati led many autonomist women, though not all, to demand remuneration for the work of social reproduction in the home and that the state cover its costs outside the home.[12] This economic recognition could level the playing field with their male comrades in the struggle against exploitation. The investigations into the work of social reproduction expanded and harnessed the theorization of the social factory but they also politicized the struggle against patriarchy as anticapitalist. Feminist readings of Marx revealed domestic labor exploitation and male physical and sexual violence as tools to discipline the subjectivity of the house worker. In other words, they mediated the violent relationship between women and capital (Cuninghame 2008). Patriarchy became no longer a matter of oppression but one of exploitation (Dalla Costa and James 1975, 10) and "if you don't know how women are exploited, you can never really know how men are" (18).

Nationwide groups like Lotta Femminsta (Feminist Struggle) led the movement Wages for Housework and were connected to similar campaigns in the United States and Canada as well as in European countries like Great Britain and Germany.[13] Salaries for housework were strategic to acknowledge the importance of housework for the reproduction and care of the workforce in the capitalist economy, which happened for free: "All this work that the woman does, an average of 99.6 hours weekly, without the possibility of strikes, nor absenteeism, nor to make any demands, is done for free" (Lotta Femminista, qtd. in Cuninghame 2008). The recognition that class exploitation was "built upon the specific mediation of women's exploitation" (Dalla Costa and James 1975, 23) led to a series of considerations that have framed political and social struggles in the so-called social factory all the way to the present.

The unacknowledged exploitation and isolation of women entwined with discussions of alternative processes of subjectivation outside domestic labor—what was called a process of self-identification (Dalla Costa 2002). Finding "a place as protagonist in the struggle" was crucial because "in the sociality of struggle women discover and exercise a power that effectively gives them a new identity. The new identity is and can only be a new degree of social power" (Dalla Costa and James 1975, 20). This engagement in struggles outside the home offered a place outside the circuit of capitalist social reproduction, refusing domestic work, its attendant subjectivity subservient to male expectations, and confronting men on different terrains that *presuppose* the home. Women were reframed as the central figure of social subversion: "Woman . . . had in her hands a fundamental lever of social power: she could refuse to produce . . . a struggle that could lead to a radical transformation of society" (Dalla Costa 2002).

This analysis of social reproduction also intersected with a discussion of a new relationship to sexuality that not only escaped an intrinsically violent reproductive function but allowed for a different connection to the body and its subjectivity: "most of housework and discipline which is required to perform the same work over every day, every week, every year, double on holidays, destroys the possibilities of uninhibited sexuality," declared Mariarosa Dalla Costa and Selma James in *The Power of Women and the Subversion of the Community* (1975, 26).[14] It is in this context that the first self-managed centers for the health of women were created to focus on general women's health and in particular on gynecology and family planning (Dalla Costa 2002).

Feminist groups close to the autonomist "area," like the Lotta Continua's Women's Collective, developed around the refusal of work, around the auto-reduction of bills and other essential domestic resources, but also against discrimination in the workplace, deregulated labor, and prisons (Cuninghame 2008). In general, women mobilized en masse to advocate for better social services, the creation of nurseries, and a less masculinist health care system where they had more control over their own bodies. This mass movement earned a series of hard-fought victories, including the diffusion of information about birth control, legislation supporting abortion, divorce, and the criminalization of domestic violence. Women also mobilized to improve public education, picketing and occupying schools and blockading roads. Although some parties, unions, and autonomist groups joined on the streets, the feminist movement emphasized its autonomy from institutional and male-dominated group politics (Cuninghame 2008).

Mao-Dadaism had its transversal sheets, zines, and radio; *operaismo*'s theories spread through its journals. It is no surprise that the archives and footprint of autonomist feminism are considerably smaller than those of autonomist work focusing on class struggle. This is partly due to the fact that much of the struggle consisted of direct action and partly because, with care and domestic work still a reality to abolish, there were simply less time and resources that could be devoted to cultural production: "What was striking was the level of extreme poverty of the means with which all this activity was carried out. The means of communication were mainly the leaflet and the paper, called *Le operaie della casa*" (Dalla Costa, qtd. in Cuninghame 2008). Nevertheless, even though journals like *Malafemmina, Noi Testarde,* and *Le operaie della casa* had a much smaller circulation, autonomist feminism left an important, albeit buried, legacy in Italy and abroad. This legacy led to new understandings of work in contemporary neoliberal capitalism with its precarious labor conditions; it has provided the scaffolding to study unpaid and affective labor in information economies; it has bolstered the conceptualization of the universal basic income; and it has fostered discussions of the issue of social reproduction and the need for commons in social movements. Theories of social reproduction have also broadened critical intersectional theories of race as well as analyses of access to basic resources and services (Thorburn 2016).

The feminist movement decomposed at the end of the seventies, during the large wave of repression of *autonomia*. In part, the decomposition was the result of exhaustion and burnout; in many cases, women still had to make life choices that distanced them from feminist militancy. What followed was "an adverse political will and a profusion of studies on the feminine condition from a different perspective.... On the study of the feminine condition, institutions used all their power, funding was redirected, networks and research were carefully channeled. The problem of reproductive work was not addressed. The discourse about the retribution of domestic work was also indicted" (Dalla Costa 2002). Many of the figureheads of the movement redirected their attention to the global condition of women, often in the context of colonization.

Desiring Friendship

The openness and euphoria characterizing *A/traverso* and Radio Alice's brief existence arose from a series of positive political events that included an electoral victory of the Italian left against the Christian Democrats (with their oppressive religious ties to the Vatican), the end of the Vietnam War, and a series of successful openings of autonomous "young proletarian centers" throughout the country (Berardi 2007, 158). However, behind the radio's carefree façade, there lay the drama of a generation of youth torn by internal political friction and external government repression that already followed the political turmoil of 1968.

By 1968/69, the Christian Democratic government was attempting to put an end to a decade of successful workers' and student struggles. The so-called *strategia della tensione* (strategy of tension) set out the secret services and collaborating fascist groups to undermine the movement's credibility through a series of violent terror attacks.[15] By the early seventies, police repression, the weight of the oil crisis, unaddressed inflation and unemployment, and an attempted fascist coup d'état moved discourses about the relationship between subjects and the state from one of exploitation to one of domination.[16] For some in the autonomist movement, this condition could only be overcome by force. As the Communist Party came even closer to moderate politics through the "Historical Compromise" with the Christian Democrats, armed cells like the Red Brigades mushroomed across the country. During this period, some political groups dissolved, and many of the people involved in political organizing went through a phase of disillusionment, inactivity, depression, and solitude. Alice's founders belonged to the dissolved political organization Potere Operaio and spilled from the latter into new politico-aesthetic experiments that influenced Italian media activism.

Sitting in a house in Bologna's old historical center that saw so much of the political upheaval of the time, Ambrogio told me about the birth of Radio Alice and political militancy at the time: "There were a few years of silence, years made of many discussions, many doubts, many deaths." He paused. "Many deaths, mainly by heroin, by police bullets. My very first girlfriend was shot dead in a Turin bar, basically executed by the Carabinieri [Italian military police] because she had become a Prima Linea militant [Front Line, an armed militant cell, similar to the Red Brigades], well, she had gone underground." Ambrogio is referring to the armed struggle

58 · INTIMACY AND MEDIA MAKING

against the Italian state that brands the history of that time as the *anni di piombo* (years of lead).

> The movement became fragmented: we went from spending most of our time together to clashing in a hard way, some decided to take up arms, some of us decided that that could not be the way. . . . What happens is that a twenty-five-year-old, like me, loses his friends. Some disappear; they go underground, some overdose. At the age of twenty-five you experience what usually happens to someone who is seventy or eighty, because friends die of old age or illness. They were tough years. Now, the discussion divided those who decided to face life with weapons and those who decided to do it with words, because this is what the dilemma was really about. . . . This created a difficult situation where, for instance, some of my friends called me traitor because of my decision to take up words. The same applies to the group that was behind Alice. So that, to start Alice at that time was not only an idea that turned out to be beautiful, and reasonable, but it also represented a choice that did not only have to do with politics but with our daily life in general. . . . You have to imagine groups of people, men and women, who had lived together, had all woken up at six in the morning to distribute fliers outside the factories, boyfriends and girlfriends . . . and then this sudden, violent separation. Our decision to start Alice was a choice that brought together once more long friendships and loves; it was a deeply important choice. Some others, those who had made a different choice, even tried to stop us. . . . I am telling you these things because I am sure that Franco and the others haven't. These are things that are rarely told. When Guido Chiesa started his interviews to make the movie about Alice [Chiesa 2004], I realized that these things are never told, but they are very important. This is one of the things that are not told, that that situation had created a sort of war: friendship had turned into betrayal, love into hate. (Interview with Ambrogio, 2008)

Telling me about the time when the Communist Party took his membership away from him because it considered Radio Alice a hideout for terrorists, Ambrogio helped me realize the importance of this radio project. Four roommates—Ambrogio, Luciano, Stefano, and Paolo—and some friends and lovers, faced with a choice between weapons and inaction, chose words: a life choice that short-circuits available subject positions. The desire to be on the part of life and creation: this was an opportunity to resist state repression with words for many of those trapped in the dregs of heroin, passivity, or violence.

At the same time, Alice's unwillingness to align with any specific identity takes on an additional dimension. This was an attempt at survival and refuge as much as one to cut transversally across the fragmented activist field, materializing its alternative in the structure and functioning of the channel. The context of emergence of Telestreet pales in comparison, and yet projects like insu^tv were born out of a somewhat similar existential crisis that started with the fragmentation of the global justice movement in the early twenty-first century. It is important to note the therapeutic value of this kind of creative and joyful media project as reference territories for individual and collective resubjectivation and as spaces for social reproduction. Friendship is a crucial element for social reproduction away from isolation and social conflict.

In a climate of harsh repression that spared no one, Alice's subversive power for technosocial connection was folded back into the struggle in an unexpected way. Unrest had been building up for years and 1977 started under the aegis of violent clashes between demonstrators and police. In 1975 the government had passed a law that enabled the police to shoot and kill any time they felt a threat to public order. Other laws had already increased preventative jail sentences to eight years and targeted individuals in possession of weapon-like items and garments that may be used for disguise.[17] These tactics did little to reduce opposition to the state and kindled more protest fires. In March 1977, the police killing of the student Francesco Lorusso during a protest triggered three days of riots, which only ended when the then minister of interior Francesco Cossiga sent tanks into Bologna.

Because of the combination of radio and telephone, Radio Alice quickly became an important communication medium during the clashes. After an initial call denouncing the shooting—only a few minutes after it took place—the radio was spontaneously turned into a coordination mechanism for the riots. At nighttime, the police raided the studio, confiscated the transmitter, and arrested those who could not flee.[18] Thirty years after these events, even then police chief Ciro Lomastro testified to the power of this assemblage: "They were better organized than us. We had our walkie-talkies but it was one-to-one communication. . . . They sent instructions to

60 · INTIMACY AND MEDIA MAKING

everyone who had a transistor radio, collected information through the phone calls and broadcast them. Incredibly efficient" (Smargiassi 2007).

Not so much a matter of voluntary organization but one of emergent properties of the assemblage, Alice had expanded the potential of distributed transmission. What had been created as a laboratory for resubjectification that was open enough to connect a variety of ideas and groups also provided a platform that was adaptable to new uses just by interjecting an additional element (in this case students and workers carried radios with them during the riots). Long before group SMS, Twitter, and livestreaming, Alice had brought together psychological, social, and technical components into a DIY assemblage for guerrilla communication. Most importantly, it had produced two defining features of the media activist technical culture this book deals with, its DIY adaptability and generativity, as well as its ability to *connect* disparate elements. I discuss this further in chapter 5.

Repression, Decomposition, and Refusal

Eventually, the steady escalation of conflict among *autonomia*, state, and fascist movements culminated in 1979 with the kidnapping and killing of Christian Democrat president Aldo Moro by the Red Brigades. The event triggered a witch hunt that put entire groups of intellectuals and activists behind bars. As is often the case, the violent actions permanently etched a homology in the collective imaginary of Italians between terrorism and autonomist political practices. The condemnation of the entire movement took place despite the fact that the makeup of groups like the Red Brigades was shaped by a rigid adherence to Marxist-Leninist dogmatism, distinctly Stalinist in theoretical-political grounding. Similarly, their actions were cut off and independent from collective class struggle, increasingly setting them apart from the development of *autonomia* (Berardi 2007, 160).[19]

The use of the label "years of lead" to describe the life of a large and heterogeneous movement denotes more than a simple value judgment on armed conflict. In fact, while the police and the legal system fulfilled their function of "establishing order," it was the sensational coverage by the media that steered public opinion about the events. The rampantly pro-government media disseminated contradictory, unfounded accusations against thousands before the judiciary legitimated them. It hid proof of secret services' infiltrations, stool pigeons, and unjustified life sentences in prison, swaying public debate and distorting the memory of a dynamic and powerful social phenomenon. These discourses against *autonomia* and its brutal and almost total repression played a key role in a process of counterrevolution (Virno 1996) that ushered in an individualistic mentality in the eighties, breaking up the fabric of society and supporting social isolation. The defeat of the autonomist movements came with the liquidation of their socialized values and their reference points for subjectivation, marking an epochal shift (Torti 2002).

Inside the movements, the call for radical change had cultivated processes of militant subjectivation that could be totalizing and left little space for the care and support that are needed during intense periods of political, social, and personal upheaval. With hindsight, feminists like Mariarosa Dalla Costa have talked about the exhaustion that came from that kind of militancy. In an interview shortly before her premature death in 2001, Maria Teresa Torti reflected on the shortcomings of the movement. She mentioned a lack of attention to the trajectory of growth of young people whose radical and sudden rejection of the dominant reference points for social subjectivation came with a fragility that easily led them to crisis, to destructive or self-destructive behavior. For many who escaped the pitfalls of terrorism and drug abuse, the choice was often a categorical closure with that experience: "I am simply disappointed with a political practice which made the prophecy of political autonomy too real in its totality, with no respect for the subjectivity of people . . . who could have grown, who had a path and was tearing through the codified social fabric. . . . This has been a serious shortcoming that may have accelerated untimely exits, closures, if not traumatic situations" (Torti 2002). Even though many other political, social, and economic factors (discussed in the next chapter) ushered in the counterrevolution that purged autonomist currents from society, it was not rare in the seventies and early eighties to see delirious creativity turn into mental affliction. Torti's pertinent remarks bring up the value of contemporary feminist thinking that has risen from the ashes of the seventies. This work stresses the importance of care for the processes of subjectivation that unfold as part of the work of social reproduction during struggle. Such work is still at the fringe of movements because it is often marginalized minorities who propose it. In the United States and Canada, the Movement for Black Lives and a variety of racial justice groups have created programs for education, support, and regenerative and emotional care (Books and Breakfast in Ferguson, Social Emergency Resource Centers in Boston, etc.).

In *The Delirium of Praise*, Eleanor Kaufman elegantly explains that madness has often been equated with the absence of work *(l'absence d'oeuvre)*, insofar as it is a language that merely folds onto itself while producing either nothing or too much (2001, 63, 82). For *autonomia*, madness, as delirious cultural production, was a choice to undermine the authority of sense as established by capital's axiomatics, and thus a refusal of the communicative aspects of capitalist social production altogether. This was the case, for instance, with Radio Alice, and it sowed the seed for some of Telestreet's nodes. Madness was also imputed to the countless women who were burned as witches at the dawn of capitalism and whose power is historicized in Silvia Federici's analysis of primitive accumulation. Feminists have often self-identified as witches (Federici 2014). In both lines, the *de-lire*, the exiting from the structure, takes place in the conversations ensuing in the contested sphere of social reproduction and subjectivation, where thought and creation meet in deviant readings, in folding others' works onto themselves. The encounter can take place *in* the thought of the "mad person," fairy-tale characters, the avant-garde, or the proletarian seen through the work of a political economist long gone, the thought of the housewife, the workingwoman, or the witch.[20]

Wrestling the functioning of knowledge from control and exchange value, and turning it into a productive force that consciously looks at the modes, the procedures, and the instruments of its development, has the effect of modifying the epistemological and operative structure of knowledge itself (Berardi 2007, 168). The rejection of work for capitalist social reproduction includes a refusal of thought and sense making according to prescribed logics even when it is still caught in a field of capitalist forces. Social reproduction can be *for* or *against* capital but not outside it. In the autonomist feminist rereadings of Marx, in the tales of Ambrogio and in the words of Maria Teresa Torti, I find an important thread to understand contemporary struggle and conceptualize connective activism as a practice for antagonistic social reproduction that harnesses communication and its structures. The latter is now a fully formed category of social reproduction.

Unpaid, feminized, and often racialized (Thorburn 2016) labor sustains movement struggles in many contexts; this unequal and unacknowledged labor distribution reproduces itself across generations in organizations as much as in the broader system of capitalism. Who, if, and when one performs the labor of care and social reproduction in social movements was a question for autonomia as much as it should be one for contemporary movements. Recognizing the work of people who attend to emotional safety in encampments, tech collectives, those who address violence within groups, and the artists, healers, and certain kinds of media producers is crucial to grasping what is required in the economies of resistance and in making movements more sustainable and scalable in the face of oppression. What kinds of encounters, materialities, practices, and languages are conducive of new forms of social reproduction? How does one unfold and proliferate processes of subjectivation in practice and thought, in the singular and the collective, transforming oneself while caring for each other?

From the eighties onward, subjectivities have been built around what Bifo calls "the dogmas of growth, competition and rent," and the only possibility of escaping exploitation and isolation is tied to an ability to reactivate the social body and resuture the social fabric of society to rebuild social solidarity (Berardi, qtd. in Hugill and Thorburn 2012, 213). The year 2011 was important for new cycles of struggle, with the rise of the European student movements, the Arab Spring, and the movements of the square, among others. In these movements, social reproduction has been a theme and a practice that developed with the creation of spaces for care, food provision, shelter, safety, and other daily needs (Feigenbaum, Frenzel, and McCurdy 2013; Thorburn 2016). These protests point to the potential of sharing spaces, of bodies coming together into collectivities, and yet the question of more sustainable strategies to retain the energy and encounters generated in these situations is still open, especially in the context of phenomena that are still marginal to a largely indifferent population. What I discussed in this chapter provides some concepts and histories of care and friendship to develop new experiments. The tales of Bifo and Ambrogio reestablish the dynamism to an account of emergence of media within a movement and clarify the role of a movement in the emergence of a medium. If it is true that participatory communication technologies are sites for the reproduction of the social (Thorburn 2016), then the history of certain strains of feminism opens up the space for more movement. In particular, the intimacy of media making for social reproduction provides a starting point to expand on forms of connective activism that I take up in the following chapters.

My own encounter with the delirium of *Anti-Oedipus* took place in 2004 at Eterea II, the network's national convention, during a conversation with a Telestreettaro. Carlo, a Roman media activist, excitedly dove into a long account of the power of desiring-machines, whipping the book out of his large corduroy pocket before I could even ask him why he had joined the Telestreet network. It was not until I too read *Anti-Oedipus* that I could take that bizarre conversation as a clear answer to my unasked question. Like Radio Alice's members thirty years earlier, Carlo saw in Telestreet a powerful laboratory for resubjectivation—one that had much to do with countering the effects of the rise of Berlusconi's entertainment industry.

3

Delirium at Work in Berlusconi's Mediascape

I was indeed a little mad. . . . True wisdom does not come from reason but from a far-seeing, visionary folly, which I believe guided me throughout this political adventure.

—Silvio Berlusconi, foreword to Erasmus, *In Praise of Folly*

On September 24, 1974, an attractive young secretary from Edilnord Constructions announced the birth of the cable television channel Telemilano2 (Gambino 2001, 105). Four years after broadcasting to the "satellite city" that Berlusconi had built on the outskirts of Milan, this channel settled into the citywide airwaves under the name Telemilano58. By 1979 Silvio Berlusconi had accumulated enough capital to invest more money into the mass media than any other entrepreneur, exploring the still uncharted territory of post-state-monopoly television. Two-and-a-half-billion Italian lire was an incredibly high sum of money for an investment with unpredictable capitalization in the newly liberalized broadcasting market. However, the rights to three hundred TV-premiere movies bought from bankrupt Titanus Productions could be easily sold to the many local broadcasters blooming throughout the country (Gambino 2001, 105).[1] What is more, it was possible to bypass legal restrictions on the local broadcasting radius by intervening in the perception of space itself.

Berlusconi's approach consisted of simply recording his newly acquired movies on VHS tapes and mailing them to the local channels that had signed up to his network. In exchange for competitive prices to transmit the movies, all these local channels kept identical schedules, offering synchronized programming across the nation and showing advertising from Berlusconi's other communication venture, Publitalia, already edited into the VHS recordings. It must have been his oft-flaunted passion for philosophy more than his law degree that led Berlusconi to understand space and its geometry differently from his business competitors. In fact, although many still see space as an absolute construct, holding its content while not being altered by it, in a Leibnizian turn, Berlusconi redefined space as emerging from the relations among the entities that constitute it. From now on, his television career would no longer be marked by the Euclidian-style measurements of his construction business. Berlusconi's new topological inspiration built on the structure of space *as* space and on the essential structure of figures despite their continuous variation. This means that the soon-to-be richest man in Italy could give up measuring metric space in absolute terms to creatively compose spaces that connect like patchwork— the spaces were amorphous, smooth, and not homogenous (Plotnitsky 2003, 99–102). They were plotted through the movements of the parcels with his films and ads.

Within a few years, Berlusconi's incipient broadcasting project had smoothed out the striated space of local television into a manifold of national broadcasting—a veritable assemblage.[2] Berlusconi's nationwide television was a collection of heterogeneous channels not formally attached to each other; its manifold character could only be defined *differentially,* in terms of conditions of frequency and accumulation of its parts (Plotnitsky 2003, 102). So, until Berlusconi had enough power to influence communication legislation, every local channel was only a fragment of the national space that was brought together through the tape delivery distribution method, competitive advertising, synchronization, and standardization— this process is called syndication. Syndication was the hack that placed Berlusconi in the position to beat his competitors and build his national media empire.[3] The Italian chaotic and corrupt socioeconomic context made the hack effective. In surprising ways, some of Berlusconi's assemblage-producing strategies are also the strategies Telestreet develops. Indeed, a syndication of sorts, perhaps a peer-to-peer syndication through the internet, is Teletreet's trick to nationwide proliferation and increased power.

The consolidation of power into the media tycoon's Midas hands (and into those of his cronies) is ultimately the story of the concretization of a new power diagram that gave life to Telestreet and whose shorthand label is Italian neoliberalism. When power becomes diffused (Deleuze 1995), counterpower becomes constituent (Negri 1998), and vice versa: the media- and information-scapes that feed Telestreet, and those that Telestreet rejects, are directly connected to productive communication networks that multiplied in the eighties. The eighties and nineties in Italy were a time of deep-seated transformations and of the fluidification of all forms of social and political control. More than an introduction to and critique of Berlusconi, this chapter outlines the shifty topology of the milieu of individuation of Telestreet and its connective activism from the perspective of the mediascape. Berlusconi has been deemed a key historical agent of change in Italian society. For me, the meaning and value of the story of Berlusconi's rise to power lie in using his parable to inquire into the relations between power and counterpower: the networking of connective activist nodes within what I call here, for lack of better words, the neoliberal-Berlusconian milieu. The neoliberal-Berlusconian milieu is a powerful and flashy kind of environment of individuation with properties amplified by the communication machine that gained consistency in the eighties and that gave origin to Berlusconi's entertainment and political assemblages alike. This particular configuration of neoliberalism arises from the swirl of global geopolitical and economic shifts, changes in Italian party politics, the institutional and social reactions to the political climate of dissent in the seventies, the rise of criminal actors as economic stakeholders, as well as developments in technology, the expansion of the entertainment and financial sectors, to mention only a few. Berlusconi gives this milieu its peculiar sheen but it is the intensification of the forces I discuss that constitute it. Berlusconi's assemblages are more product and less cause of Italian neoliberalism, even though they significantly shaped it in return.

The neoliberal-Berlusconian milieu illustrates perfectly how power can not be isolated from an environ that includes both economic actors and governments as one and the same (Nitzan and Bichler 2009, 8). As a matter of fact, in Berlusconi, as its façade, it is not even possible to separate the entrepreneur who accumulates capital—the media tycoon who influences public opinion—and the politician who develops policy (Lazzarato 2007, 88). But here I am not talking about *personal* roles because Berlusconi is a metonymy for the larger milieu where specific subjective, libidinal, social, cultural, and economic flows intersect and are channeled to exercise power. Paolo Virno has described the socioeconomic and subjective turn of the eighties and nineties as *counterrevolution* (Virno and Hardt 1996, 240): a subtle and pervasive process that radically transformed all forms of life, mentalities, cultural habits, tastes, customs, and social relations that had developed in the Italian social laboratory of *autonomia*. These changes unfolded while industrial production shrunk significantly, structural unemployment rose, and the economy transitioned into a booming service sector.

Like in other Western countries, electronic technologies became dominant modes of production that exploited the knowledge and communication skills of an increasingly precarious and flexible labor force. Ironically, the autonomist ideals of self-valorization through creativity and the refusal of work were recuperated into the backbone of circuits of cognitive capitalist production (Virno and Hardt 1996; Vercellone 2006). With the triumph of neoliberalism in Italy, it is no longer possible to distinguish political flows from productive and social flows, and this considerably impacts the processes of subjectification of Italians (Lazzarato 2007, 93–94). In all these transformations, communication and information are fundamental driving forces whose signifying and a-signifying processes are reorganized along market logics, be it business, the entertainment world of mainstream media, or institutional politics. Telestreet's individuation and that of a larger field of social movements and media activists unfolds in this milieu, with its structural, infrastructural, and discursive components. Telestreet is not just an antidote to Berlusconi's control of the media because Berlusconi is only a symptom of the problem that connective media activism aims to confront: the radical subjective turn and growing social isolation fostered in neoliberal power configurations, where communication is a tool to feed individualistic subjectivities and to accumulate capital at the expense of the vulnerable.

A Milieu behind the Sheen

Berlusconi's empire grew during dark and depressing times: at the peak of the brutal repression of autonomist activism and while the spread of organized crime seemed uncontrollable. To make things worse, inflation was on the rise and the country's economy had entered into recession. Contrary to what is commonly thought, dominant capital thrives during periods of inflation because there is a redistribution of capital from small to large firms (Nitzan and Bichler 2009, 370–75).[4] This is how Italy's economy once again found wind in its sails. In the eighties in Europe and North America, industrial production declined or was outsourced while corporations and oligopolies were able to profit from the elimination of antitrust legislation to grow and consolidate. The year 1980 opened with a defeat of the unions by Fiat, which would permanently gain the upper hand over its workers. By then Italian entrepreneurs had started investing in service-based and immaterial economies, contributing to the expansion of the tertiary sector.

During this period, capitalization—which I consider an encompassing *mode of power* instead of an economic category—reveals the real power of accumulation insofar as one sees how creativity and knowledge can be put to work to accumulate power by creating new forms and sites of productivity (Nitzan and Bichler 2009, 217–18).

Berlusconi harnessed the real power to accumulate already as he started building entire suburban neighborhoods and shopping malls in the late sixties, pooling together considerable amounts of investments from mysterious sources and obtaining building permits where no one else could (Gambino 2001; Barbacetto 2004). Clearly, his ability to rearrange the conditions for accumulation through less-than-transparent connections was fundamental to the process. Fininvest, his main investment company, was created in 1979 to coordinate and organize this growing empire, and from this point on, his career was marked by the continuous creation and relocation of sister companies registered under relatives' or friends' names (Barbacetto 2004). With a seemingly endless flow of cash, Berlusconi's activities branched out into finance and insurance, the entertainment business, advertising, publishing, and television. In all these sectors he beat the average accumulation rate by bringing his competitors to their knees through rock-bottom prices and takeovers, becoming more powerful than the rest. Tight relationships of nepotism, patronage, and debt that run along political party lines boosted the complex web of regulations, contracts, and shared worldviews in the background of Berlusconi's rise to power. In particular, direct and underground links between the heads of many financial institutions and state industry with private entrepreneurs facilitated secure investments, the allocation of tenders and contracts, and the privatization of important sources of profit. Working hand in hand, the new class of politicians and entrepreneurs was responsible for Italy's entry into the world of global business, the privatization of much of its infrastructure, and the slow demise of an allegedly unaffordable welfare state (Berardi, Jaquemet, and Vitali 2009, 47). These changes enabled more circulation of capital and new investments that consolidated the power of some economic (and political) actors while eliminating many others.[5]

It is not surprising, then, that even before Berlusconi's entry into politics, his empire fused politics and business. There is often a strong link between governments and corporations in neoliberalism, despite the common ideological opposition to state influence in the market. The Italian transformation took place by limiting access to resources through laws and norms, by excluding others from the game, and by taking away the power from certain actors—all thanks to deep-reaching ties between entrepreneurs and governing parties. This had *qualitative* repercussions on the distribution of power, especially in the media and communication industries. Modes of governmentality in both disciplinary and control societies bear on profitability in different ways, depending on the dominant material or immaterial economic structures that characterize them (Foucault 1979; Deleuze 1995). In either diagram, however, any kind of earning will be the outcome of a struggle among dominant capital groups to shape and restructure the direction of social production in order to create the conditions for capitalization. Since the accumulation of power is never absolute and always done in relation to other powers, the concept of the differential becomes useful to explore the development of the Italian mediascape.

Resubjectivation, Made in Italy

By the early 1980s, Berlusconi was able to wage war against the Italian public service broadcaster Radio Italia (RAI)—the only real contender and nationwide broadcaster. The first battleground was the field of advertising, where Publitalia—Fininvest's advertising wing—offered such low advertising rates for Berlusconi's TV network that it enabled even small companies to access this market. Previously, television advertising had only been open to businesses with enough capital to meet the high investment costs RAI demanded. With the arrival of Berlusconi, advertising became such a bargain that one would think Publitalia was heading for a financial crash. Instead, because the frequency and accumulation of ads during each show on its channels was unprecedented and the introduction of American movies and series through the VHS tape system stimulated nationwide distribution, Fininvest stole RAI's audience and revenues. It also changed the relation between audiences and ads, which became ubiquitous.

Paradoxically, it was not until a concern with media democracy was raised at the end of the decade that Berlusconi became officially free to dominate the airwaves with the help of the Mammì Law. This piece of legislation passed by his personal friend Prime Minister Bettino Craxi normalized the consolidation of his media empire, and Fininvest was allowed to keep three national channels. The Mammì Law did not include any antitrust regulations or limitations on advertising. Five months later, Berlusconi was also allowed to launch three pay-per-view TV channels

(Barbacetto 2004).[6] As a result, the Italian mediascape ended up divided into two poles: RAI, controlled by the government; and the channels owned by Berlusconi's Fininvest. With Berlusconi's election to prime minister, both poles fell under his influence.

The coalition between media, business, and politics became instrumental in pacifying discontent and stimulating consumption. Much of Berlusconi's ability to dominate the market derived from his companies' capillary expansion in many emergent sectors of the economy, from large supermarkets and shopping malls to financial and marketing services. Berlusconi's topological approach helped connect different commercial spaces and was boosted by his marketing and communication infrastructure. Most importantly, Berlusconi's control of the market helped saturate the increasingly mediatized environment with a flow of advertising images and symbols of new lifestyles that spoke to the desires of Italians to unprecedented degrees (Berardi, Jaquemet, and Vitali 2009, 28). These images worked well together with the television programs that mixed spectacular consumption-oriented and sexualized content with depictions of a new class of wealthy Italians.

During the period of passage from industry to business, one of the first systems to go had been the so-called point of contingency *(scala mobile)*, a mechanism that automatically raised wages in relation to inflation. Now, Italians had less money and more time to spend at home. TV became the most popular mass media in Italy. Police repression of activism and drug-related crimes made the streets unsafe for many, who came to prefer sitting comfortably in front of a TV. Fininvest's Canale 5's jingle aptly sums up the climate of the times: "Corri a casa in tutta fretta, c'é Canale 5 che ti aspetta" (Hurry, hurry home, channel 5 is waiting for you) (Berardi, Jaquemet, and Vitali 2009, 28). Here, Berlusconi's cutthroat competitive strategies met the needs of both investors and of audiences looking for entertainment and quickly took over RAI's role of family sitter. As an alternative to austere and conservative television programs, the new channels offered the excitement of the latest movies and TV series, the sappy romance of soap operas, the cheap thrills of soft porn, the best TV hosts and dancers that had jumped ship, and the promises of winning the countless variety and quiz shows. In a country with the highest TV viewership in Europe (Seisselberg 1996), the superficial and carefree nature of this programming contributed greatly to a climate of cynicism, opportunism, and crass hedonism, exemplified in one of the biggest successes of the time in Italy, the American television series *Dallas* (Berardi, Jaquement, and Vitali 2009, 28).

The ads and shows provided a template for a collective resubjectification of many who needed to compensate for a rather drab reality. The Italian mediascape, in which even RAI had to rethink its approach to entertainment to compete with Fininvest, established a relationship with its audiences that targeted their desires more than ever. For Maurizio Lazzarato, these developments sustained the production of the consumer as well as the individual of the neoliberal-Berlusconian assemblage because what was interpellated was a "political" rationality—an inclination to make choices and think about life in specific ways rather than simply as passions and emotions (2007, 91). This resubjectification is tied to a transition (never total) between diagrams of power—from discipline to control— from industrial to postindustrial (Foucault 1979; Deleuze 1995). Societies of control are marked by diffuse forms of hyperconnection, soft control, and surveillance in which life answers to the logic of capital.

As processes of subjectivation spill out of disciplinary sites of confinement (the factory, the church, the party, etc.), a subjective turn is shaped by the new environment, discourses, and infrastructure of value creation. This turn revolves around the creation of new desires, sensibilities, and aspirations at the intersection of social and economic production—what autonomist feminists would consider part of capitalist social reproduction (Serra 2015; Thorburn 2016). The professional and social requisites of the new power diagram are creativity, sociability, and communication skills, as well as the ability to adjust to change. As the movement of '77 is put to work in the creative industries, the new dominant processes of subjectivation become tied to advertising and consumption, which are supported by the introduction into the market of financial loans, installment purchases, and credit cards (Lazzarato, Manning, and Massumi 2009).[7] The new symbols of the time are no longer the Mao-Dadaist and the barefoot intellectual but the yuppie and the *paninaro*, the cynical consumer and logo-oriented youth who hang out in the new restaurant sensation: McDonald's fast food restaurants.

Technical Populism

These processes accompanied the "secularization" of culture from the church and from the religion-like doctrine of the Communist Party on the one hand and, on the other, the rise to power of a new generation of socialist politicians, led by Bettino Craxi (Virno 1996, 241). The politicians' rhetoric exhibited a *Dallas*/Reagan-style superficial optimism, hedonism, and individualism as well as an unprecedented openness to lobbying and corruption. Many of their illegal practices—Swiss bank accounts and off-shore warehousing of shares, money-laundering, association with the mafia, tax evasion, price inflations, complicity in murder, bribery of politicians and judges, shady mergers, takeovers, and so on—surfaced in 1992–93 during the Tangentopoli (bribeopolis) scandal. When the Mani pulite (clean hands) investigative team brought most politicians, many lawyers, judges, and entrepreneurs like Berlusconi's brother behind bars, Berlusconi found himself under investigation. With his business on the verge of financial collapse, no one in the parliament who had his back, and the new government pursuing its own punitive measures, urgent action was needed.

In 1994 the Silvio Berlusconi Publishing House launched a new series dedicated to great thinkers (Raboni 1994), starting with the ones who had most inspired its owner's "apprenticeship and audacity" (Letta 2008). Hot off the press came Thomas Moore's *Utopia,* Niccolò Machiavelli's *The Prince,* and Desiderius Erasmus's *The Praise of Folly.* In his personal foreword to Erasmus, Berlusconi shared how *The Praise of Folly* had influenced his visionary philosophy of life and work, for which folly is a creative, vital force.

An innovator is at his most original when his inspiration comes from the depth of irrationality. The revolutionary intuition is always perceived . . . as absurd, when it first comes. It is only later that this is recognized and accepted. . . . True wisdom does not lie in rational behavior, necessarily conforming to premises and therefore sterile, but in a farsighted, visionary "madness." . . . It was those very projects that people were opposed to and I was passionate about, my dear friends, those that came from the heart, not from cold reasoning, that were my biggest successes. (1990, ii)

A few weeks later, it was Erasmus's visionary folly that helped Berlusconi enter the political stage with a new party: Forza Italia (Go Italy!)—a football cheer. What Berlusconi did not invent but had come to perfect is a space (of manifolds, or assemblages) in which politics and business are sustained and mutually strengthened through strategic communication and marketing. The Italian "communication machine" was running now, well oiled, and Berlusconi may be seen as its mad pilot. Still, as mentioned, this communication machine grew from a combination of alliances, economic shifts, policies, and repression contemporaneous to Berlusconi's empire, such as the shift to post-Fordism with its technologies, the spread of flexible modes of labor, the financialization of information and expansion of the communication industry, an overall reorganization of labor market and socially necessary labor time, and the crisis of representative democracy (Virno 1996, 241). Ultimately, counterrevolution, Virno claims pithily, involved a transformation of the collective tendencies of the seventies into professional requisites (242). This means that on many levels, the sociocultural transformations resulted from the capture of the flows of desire and creative delirium that had been valorized a decade earlier by *autonomia*. Counterrevolution *put* creative delirium *to work*. Berlusconi's empire and the communication machine are not the same thing, but the communication machine as a vector of resubjectivation played an important role in making counterrevolution possible.

This is why it is not enough to look at Berlusconi's twenty-plus years in office as the result of his mediascape monopoly to understand how Italians—whose interests are not represented but actually damaged by this situation—have so enthusiastically bought into Berlusconi's "visionary folly." An analysis strictly focused on media consolidation misses the importance of the eighties' collective resubjectivation that embraced the values of neoliberalism, leaving them (mostly) unchallenged. This limited perspective also leads one to look for alternatives to Berlusconi's power mostly in practices of counterinformation that are doomed to fail because of the differential power he holds on the mediascape. If I reiterate that the communication machine is a major engine of the neoliberal-Berlusconian milieu, it is not simply because of his control of information flows but because it rechannels the flows of desire and captures affects and sociality into economic flows. Connective activism emerges as a strategy to liberate these flows of desire and reorient processes of subjectivation.

The Italian communication machine boasting 24/7 a new economic miracle while constructing a dreamlike world of consumption for television audiences was certainly an important means for the collective resubjectivation of Italians. The marketing and strategic communication methods from new creative enterprises like Benetton were developed and tested in the eighties and nineties; they also created Berlusconi and his party as an infallible and adaptable composite that brought Italy into twenty-first-century politics, where communication and the political are in reciprocal presupposition (Lazzarato 2007, 94). Using models tested in business, and reading the Italian sociopolitical transformations with a visionary eye, Forza Italia emerged as a new type of party—what Jörg Seisselberg dubs a "media-mediated personality-party" (1996). The irruption of communication into party politics is certainly not unique to Italy (it is especially common in the United States) because it is the result of widespread changes in the conditions of economic production, media penetration, and changing attitudes of citizens toward party politics in general. Still, Forza Italia is a compelling case for its intensity and the ease with which it took off in a country where television was the primary means of information, and where discontent with the political system was particularly acute.

Publications like *An Italian Story*—the high-budget picture books on the life of Berlusconi—convey the extent to which strategic communication had become the backbone connecting the heterogeneous elements of business and politics in Italy. These two volumes tell the glossy tale of the Berlusconi family and reveal the secrets of his success to readers. Forza Italia mailed the books free of charge to *every single* household in the country between 2001 and 2006. *An Italian Story* celebrates Berlusconi as a self-made family man, accessibly transposing onto his own image the aspirations of an entire epochal shift. Thanks to these discourses and to a common tendency to identify the agents of history in strong male figures, Berlusconi rises larger than life from a messy web of events and elements that characterize the political-economic context I described. Rather than a simple advertising strategy, the showcasing of Berlusconi as a winner, who is a self-made businessman and the president of the storied football club AC Milan, is an effective *marketing* maneuver. That is, if ads in politics are supposed to promote specific agendas and candidates to secure votes, the marketing of politics attends to the needs and desires of the "voters' market" as it translates their values into images and symbols. Marketing is not about selling a product but about shaping social relations and values in the market; this is why it deeply structures politics (Lazzarato 2007, 92).

At the same time, whereas the promotion of Berlusconi's leadership of the party harnesses the desires of Italians, his persona also effectively embodies and symbolizes the neoliberal ideals that Forza Italia promotes: competition, opposition to state regulation and taxation, private ownership, and so on. Seisselberg stresses how this combination secures the "best possible mediability of the party's political offer through the media" (1996, 721), no matter who owns the media. He also emphasizes how the pluralization of lifestyles and the loss of collective consciousness that marked the transition from the seventies to the eighties came with a decrease in party loyalties. In Italy as in other Western countries, this decrease was more the result of changes in the factors that produce social identities, in the rising emphasis on individuality, and in new consumption habits, and less the result of historical events like the Tangentopoli scandal. The satisfaction of needs that drives voter behavior today leads to "offer-oriented decisions" that are similar to consumer patterns (exemplified by the key role of polls), and parties in many countries recognize the importance of media penetration and personalized politics to retain voters' attention. For these reasons, marketing and strategic communication in Forza Italia were taken to an unprecedented level from the beginning, incorporating Diakron, a market research institute staffed with Fininvest's employees, directly into the structure of the party. Diakron steered a supple machine that was perpetually tuned into voter markets and public opinion (Ruzza and Fella 2009, 106). Because of Forza Italia's hierarchical party structure, marketing allowed for changes in the political offer, and in the mediatization of the party's leader—at the same time as it facilitated a transition from Realpolitik to symbolic politics (Seisselberg 1996, 721). Symbolic politics is characterized by a homogenization and simplification of information, by the power of naming in the political communication process and by affectivity (722). In the nineties, Berlusconi's visionary folly already tapped into information and data flows before this method could be perfected with big data analytics and social media dataveillance.

Forza Italia's party structure is the other site where Berlusconi's visionary folly delivers a product of its time. Since the mediation of politics is a high priority, Forza Italia has a highly hierarchical communication and organizational structure to help its president gain power. This organization resembles that of a business enterprise with a top-down approach, and with political candidates undergoing interviews and being screened for such attributes as persuasiveness and telegenics. At the bottom ranks of the hierarchy are the promoters—the grassroots activists who interact with citizens—and the clubs, whose members help with PR at the local level, organizing cultural events, party celebrations, banquets, balls, excursions, charity concerts, or sporting events (Seisselberg 1996, 718–29).[8] It is also worth noting the uniquely corporate terminology used in Forza Italia, where voters are referred to as the public or the audience *(il pubblico)*, which is not a common epithet for voters in Italian.

The lower party ranks in particular can be seen as an upgrading of Berlusconi's scheme of syndication (the nationwide network of broadcasters that used the VHS tape system to transmit simultaneously). Club members and promoters are not professional politicians and have no decision-making power within Forza Italia but have a similar relationship to the party as small companies to a franchising brand or mother company. They are able to gain symbolic and political power (and favors) at the local level in exchange for conforming with and promoting the values and images of the party: "In order to market their own political product, they have to rely on a recognized brand, but in exchange they have to follow precise rules of style and conduct, bringing a good name to the company whose label they work" (Virno 1996, 257). Overall, the character of the neoliberal-Berlusconian milieu speaks more to the features of neoliberal information-based capitalism than to a simple media monopoly.

Powerful capitalists tend to shape the market for their own interest and disadvantage smaller actors, and yet discourses about the free-market economy commonly establish that big businesses will automatically boost production and help industry thrive, thereby also supporting small businesses (the so-called trickle-down effect). These beliefs recruit smaller entrepreneurs into supporting the party's economic, political, and social agenda even though they do not have lobbying power like the bigwigs of Forza Italia. Forza Italia's agenda is not much different from the mantra of many other parties embracing neoliberal policies: less state control on the economy; less investment in government bonds and more trust in privately owned saving and investment plans; less taxes; privatization of state services like health, education, and insurance; more consumption to promote the economy; and more surveillance (Berlusconi 1994a, 1994b; Redazione 2009). They promote a free market (though in reality only free for a few) and private initiative, profit, and individual leadership.

Above all, Forza Italia makes more sense in the context of the Italian neoliberal milieu if we link Berlusconi's topological approach to accumulation. For Forza Italia, change is the differential outcome of "the free input of many people, each different from the others" (Berlusconi 1994b). As an assemblage, Forza Italia is a "free organization of voters of a completely new kind" (1994b). It is not the homogeneous, ideology-based space of the party but a new force that unites and smooths the space of politics, eliminating any distinctions between government and economy, entrepreneur and politician, citizen and consumer. It is only fitting that the party's

78 · DELIRIUM AT WORK IN BERLUSCONI'S MEDIASCAPE

vision is one that promotes a kind of competitive democracy whereby "democracy is achieved, not primarily through conflict *with*, but through competition *between* parties" (Seisselberg 1996, 727). Since the political struggles no longer rely on a clash of ideologies but on the relative hold on voters, power is accumulated differentially. This vision translates into a rejection of inner-party democratic decision-making processes typical of Western democracies because the focus is on the party's external and media-compatible success.[9] The role of marketing and strategic communication in shaping the "voters' market" by adapting to opinion trends in the electorate and maximizing success in relation to other parties takes the Berlusconi assemblage beyond simple populism into the realm of what had been described as "technical populism" (Seisselberg 1996, 730). Technical populism is the name of the business-oriented, marketing-based, personality-focused populism that thrives in the Italian mediascape. This term brings to light important forces that shape the relationship between politics and the economy in many other countries, and it draws attention to the import of communication and information in contemporary power arrangements, debunking the simplistic equation between mainstream media control and unrivalled power. If there is a way in which media penetration has an impact on the rise of technical populism and overall social control, it is through governmentality and its attendant subjectivation.

Television as a Governmental Machine

In Berlusconi's Italy, as in other neoliberal milieus, affective manipulation is a pillar of governmental control strategies (Grusin 2010, 80). Governmentality is concerned not only with people but also with the *organization of things*: governmentality involves the distribution of the mediascape, the regulation of access to frequencies and methods of transmission, the allocation of advertising, and the standardization of television's aesthetic language and narrative strategies. In other words, governmentality entails the configuring of the context for the emergence of everyday practices that interweave media like television into people's lives, creating continuity and familiarity between content and media use. The diffused and subtle background relation between everyday uses of media and the cognitive and sensory functions involved in engaging with media is called *mediality* (Grusin 2010). In Italy, the mediality of television—a mediality that involves the consistent conflation of entertainment and information—modulates collective affective orientations and mobilizes populations in politics and everyday life alike.

As I watched the 2001 electoral battle on television, it was hard not to notice the beginning of a new grammar for Italian politics: the campaign no longer rested on a clash between opposing ideologies, as was common in Italy. Instead, the race relied on the images and appeal of two opposing leaders—Francesco Rutelli and Silvio Berlusconi—and their ability to capture the imagination of their voters. Forza Italia established the mediatization of symbolic politics as an indispensable political strategy (Seisselberg 1996), and Berlusconi's 2001 election campaign marks this important transition from the consistent mobilization of affect in television entertainment to electoral media coverage. Thanks to the professional management of the persona of Forza Italia's president, Berlusconi's televised speeches and promotional videos were delivered amid screaming crowds of fans who sang his campaign song ("Meno male che Silvio c'è" [Thank God Silvio's here]). The images of him smiling triumphantly over the crowds as if he had already won the elections were ubiquitous. Primetime broadcasts of his fatherly discourses on protecting the interests of common people touted his success in business and with women and positioned him as a benefactor and role model for Italians. These dazzling electoral shows seemed to replace, convincingly, a widespread fear of precarity with the excitement about a future in which Berlusconi will reward the common person—like he does in the countless reality and quiz shows of his TV networks. Even if I did not buy his story, it was hard not to be swept away by the spectacle and the grandiose promises.

Crucially, the affective responses to Forza Italia's campaign were not just my reaction to the content of the images; they were also *premediated* (Grusin 2010); that is, they mobilized an already existing connection to the medium of television through a reaction to stimuli that are usually experienced outside electoral politics, when watching TV for entertainment. The aesthetic register of the delivery—the colors and lights of the shows, the cries of the crowd in the background, the music—were enthralling because they blurred the line between politics and entertainment. As an agent in the governmental assemblage of neoliberal Italy, Berlusconi's constellation of media outlets helped shape that mediality as well as the larger sociotechnical milieu in which his voters subjectivate, or individuate. In this sense, Berlusconi premediated his victory and thereby made it possible.[10] I was bedazzled as I watched the campaign unfold.

Media are agents of governmentality not just because they produce and organize meaning and roles but also and especially because they mobilize collective affective orientations (Grusin 2010, 48–49). The collective affective orientations of Berlusconi's voters preceded the appearance of emotions and rational choice; they impacted viewers before and independently of their rationalization and interpretation of the experience, and they had an impact on their decisions as citizens and consumers. Affect scholars have correlated the deliberate "priming" of the environment in which affective reactions happen with resulting patterns of "deliberation-without-attention and choice blindness" (Massumi 2015, 40). These patterns are typical of neoliberal citizen behavior where the zones of indistinction between affectivity and rationality have become the sites of intervention to exercise control (27–28).

What better proof of this than the Italian study of voters' perceptions showing that, just before going to the polls in May 2001, the characteristics most associated with Berlusconi by the people surveyed were "he is a strong leader" (64.9 percent), "he is enthusiastic" (60.2 percent), and "he is persuasive" (58.9 percent) (Grasso 2003, 2). These qualities were certainly fundamental for Berlusconi's entrepreneurial career, but none of them spoke directly to his capacities as a law or policy maker. They were, however, in line with the profile of the leader of an enterprise party like Forza Italia. The idea of deliberation-without-attention and choice blindness in the context of the electoral campaign, in combination with the concept of mediality, point to how, for 51 percent of Italians surveyed, an important characteristic attributed to Berlusconi was his good looks. Only 38.4 percent of those who answered the surveys identified with his political mandate or that of his party (34 percent), and 25.5 percent and 24.7 percent, respectively, believed in the leader's honesty and capacity to keep his promises (Grasso 2003, 2–3). These poll results suggest that in the background, in the machine-like connections between television and viewers, the interconnected system of perception organs, affective reactions, psychosocial background, and interiority, commonly defined as an "individual," were primed to relate to Berlusconi as a compassionate boss, a successful Casanova, and a father figure (Papì) who could take care of the country rather than as a professional politician with a clear and realistic agenda.[11]

This individuation of Berlusconi's voters unfolded in a milieu that included sociocultural norms as well as institutions and specific media configurations. For example, the syndication of television programming within the Fininvest network did not simply synchronize the transmission of content; it also created a shared time and space, contributing to the collective individuation of a national audience. Technical and policy solutions were crucial for the correct arrangement of elements in a mediascape that structures and individuates. The *individual* and the *collective* were engendered within this governmental, sociotechnical milieu: *individuation*—and indeed *trans*individuation—occurs while the interface between the interiority and the sensing of the individual and the world is developed and managed. From the top down, meanwhile, governmentality is concerned with disciplining, coding, and organizing the mediascape and the television industry's relation to one as part of the audience.

Telestreet's Delirious Milieu

The thread of delirium and creative assembling that started with *autonomia* leads me to Telestreet via Berlusconi. The connection of these apparently disjointed elements detours through Deleuze's distinction between the paranoid and passional regimes of madness: the paranoid is connected to processes of semiotization through codified signs; the passional is connected to processes of subjectivation forging new connections among signs. Deleuze calls these two qualitatively different kinds of madness the "I-will-not-leave-you-alone" of the paranoid and the "leave-me-alone" of the passional. The respective regimes associated with each are mapped onto social formations, where imperialism is associated with the paranoid/coded signifier and unbridled capitalism with the subjective/passional. The former is a process of expansion and coordination of signs while the latter establishes subjects as the agents of capital and detaches bundles of signs from its center (capital) to recode them as needed (Deleuze 2006, 14–16; Demers 2008).

The distinction between the two regimes shows that, even if to many Berlusconi's madness may seem more like a kind of paranoia—a delusion of grandeur—it is, in fact, closer to the passional regime of madness explored in the context of autonomist media experimentation. Hyperbole aside, this seemingly paradoxical relation between ways of exiting the structure and form of capture and control is an important aspect of contemporary forms of neoliberal governmentality. When talking about Berlusconi, it is possible to draw on Deleuze's parallelism to highlight the passional love affairs or orgiastic connections among capitalism's main actors and resistance to them as a struggle over the *differential* accumulation of power, a power that is not a power over *(potestas)* but a power to *(potentia)* (Negri 1998). I showed this with the first nationwide broadcasting strategies and with the politician-entrepreneur aggregate that grew stronger and more powerful as the connections among its elements grew more intricate. Berlusconi's power to recompose the assemblage of his companies like Fininvest and Mediaset, boosting up investors' trust precisely in connection with other events, creates the conditions for such growth. Berlusconi was able to beat the average and accumulate in relation to others (companies and parties) because he acted in an environment where there is topological space to control and flows of signs to harness. The cult of personality was also an important element to skirt around accusations of conflict of interest and always come out as a winner in the voters' eye. Always smiling like in an eighties TV series, Berlusconi and his colleagues have been able to mount countless attacks on the judiciary system, on civil society, and on the new generation of autonomist activists who emerged in the late nineties.

At the same time, this de-lirium, this ability to move out of regimenting structures, merely puts the Italian prime minister on par with most other global multinational powers, which understand the dynamics of power accumulation through capital. Albeit magnified by the rather dystopian Italian example, Berlusconi's relationship to the economy and to the state ought to be seen as an example of *how* power is inextricably linked to capital. The strength of this passional, topological type of capitalism lies in its ability to reconstitute itself as *potentia (constituent power)* while still maintaining a connection to *potestas— (constituted power),* through legislation, material production, and accumulated capital. The force of neoliberal capitalism affects what comes within reach, reordering society through processes that control, shape, and transform opposition. The commodification, structuration, and restructuration of capital unfolds according to a logic that, since the accumulation of power is always relative, compels actors to always try to augment their capital to maintain divisions of power (Nitzan and Bichler 2009, 18). This results in a strong gravitational force that shapes modes of governmentality.

The ability to hack and connect into assemblages is by no means an intrinsically emancipatory process. Then, what does resistance look like and what is the function of media within resistant formations? If neoliberal governmentality acts on its subjects through social subjection, often exercised through socioeconomic discourses and the mediality of television and other mass media, subjectivity becomes the fraught terrain of a struggle that is itself differential. For Judith Revel, resistance is located in the "dismeasure between power and modes of life . . . the dismeasure between exploitation and processes of subjectivation in the very meshes of power itself, in other words, between the management of life and life's power (here, I use power as *potentia,* and not as *potestas*)" (2013, 18). Governmentality from this perspective is about the simultaneity of control and affirmations of liberty and resistance inside the field of governing practices. If, as Revel claims building on Foucault, "power and subjectivation, governance and liberty are indissoluble and, at the same time, dissymmetrical" (18), we can think about this relation as differential—that is, as an ongoing struggle to access and expand control over sites of subjectification, be they television, other spaces of semiotic and cultural production, and in general for social reproduction (media infrastructure, social centers, mutual support networks, and so on). Connective activism is a set of practices of subjectification that engage in this kind of struggle.

The success of Berlusconi's visionary, topological approach lies in his ability to forge new connections and redirect flows of signs, in the same way Radio Alice did and Telestreet has since done. This "folly" finds its source of creativity in the manipulation of signs, not just for signification but also as affective devices that draw on commonsense assumptions about social reality to order and rearrange power. Many of the Telestreettari grew up during the eighties and nineties and claim the language of television as their own idiom to create with. In the affective encounters with the media, whether zines, free radio, *Dallas,* spectacular shows, or pirate television, processes of individual and collective individuation reconfigure. Herein lies the power and importance of projects like Telestreet, and especially insu^tv: in the clash with contemporary forms of capitalist control, experimentation and media tinkering are key to throwing a wrench in the cogs of the communication machine, finding ways to wrest subjectification and social reproduction from the neoliberal-Berlusconian milieu. The delirious creativity of Berlusconi's world and that of Radio Alice and Telestreet may be inseparable but they are not equivalent (Revel 2013, 23). I locate the differential aspect of this kind of struggle in the constituent power of resistance *within and against* neoliberal governmentality, specifically in the neoliberal-Berlusconian milieu.

What follows takes a closer look at how media activism from the nineties onward attempts to constitute itself as *potentia* to tackle powerful social and economic neoliberal assemblages. Here, the growing role of strategic communication and marketing in capitalism is tied in surprising ways to the development of media activist practices that thrive on similar principles. It is important not to lose focus of the material co-constitution of a dominant media apparatus like the one I described here and networks of media activism.

4

Activist Energetics in the Information Milieu

Tens, hundreds, thousands of Aguascalientes, we would say out of habit
from past movements.

—Laboratorio Occupato SKA and C. S. Leoncavallo, *El Sup*

In Genoa in July 2001, internet radio Radio Gap was taken down with a
similar live broadcast police raid that had shut down Radio Alice in 1977.
Radio Alice's groundbreaking use of phone-in announcements had become a coordination tool for protesters, allowing for efficient two-way
communication between the radio hosts and the crowds on the streets of
Bologna, where they were protesting the killing of Francesco Lorusso at
the hands of the police. Similarly, Radio Gap, reporting with Indymedia
from G8 Summit protests, was covering the police killing of Carlo Giuliani.
Such seemingly smooth progression from the free radios in the 1970s to
the global justice movement's alternative media (and little change in police
tactics) easily obfuscates the nonlinear trajectories of twenty-five years
of media-based political organizing. And yet it is important to behold
complexity to fully grasp the emergence of this kind of media projects.
Telestreet, a heterogeneous network of pirate television channels using
both digital and analog hacked technologies, came about in similarly unpredictable ways, within an environment where familiar activist histories
met wandering stories, local events bore the weight of geopolitics, and
economic trends and new alliances bred surprising technical solutions.

Investigating the intercommunication between circulating "energies"
and political invention provides precious insights into the context of emergence of projects like the free radios, Indymedia and Telestreet, whose
seeds and reverberations extend them across time and spaces—before and
after the divergent energies have come together to generate them as specific political assemblages. Importantly, the teeming of contingencies and
reverberations that cut across the narrow boundaries of what self-defines
or is defined as "a movement"—or simply a project—should also remind

anyone interested in examining the impact of activism that questions of successes and failures promote a reductive understanding of how social change takes place. Narratives of successes and failures mostly focus on visible transformations at specific times and in specific spaces.

The achievement of social justice is a long-term endeavor; it spans multiple cycles of struggles and it often exceeds the brief existence of an experiment. Activist assemblages traverse cycles of struggles visibly, sometimes, and in more subterranean ways in other cases. In surprising fashion, they recuperate past histories and repurpose practices as they recompose. This chapter charts *the environment and conditions of becoming* for experiments like Telestreet as they struggle within an information-rich environment, heavily shaped by communication technologies and cognitive capitalism— what chapter 3 shorthanded as the neoliberal-Berlusconian milieu. I move through the stories of other media projects that preceded Telestreet with an eye on complex encounters in order to add new dimensions to the milieu of emergence, or *individuation,* wherein Italian and international movements shaped and were shaped. In many ways, grassroots engagements with technology set the stage for future uses of social networks and media tools, which were quickly absorbed into corporate mainstream tech products. They also offer a view of a proto-networked society before it became a reality for a large part of the world. Some of the phenomena I link with Telestreet and insu^tv are well known, like the communication guerrilla of the Zapatistas in Mexico, Indymedia, the momentous battle of Seattle at the WTO Summit in 1999, and the tragedy of Genoa at the 2001 G8 Summit. Others have almost been forgotten, like the student movement and the renaissance of the Centri Sociali Occupati Autogestiti (CSOA, Self-Managed Squatted Social Center) in Italy that started in 1989. In my account, events, technical infrastructure, and spaces are important conduits for the circulation of different kinds of information that triggers transformation.

Information, here, acts as a structural force. Traditional models of communication that view information as the content of a message tend to underplay the indirect impact of informational dynamics on cultural and political expression, which is shaped as much by information resonance, proliferation, and interference as by events that the distribution of content can trigger (Terranova 2004). This is why, in this chapter, information takes center stage through multiple conceptualizations and roles: it is regarded as a good and a coveted resource in a transforming economy; it is a drive for new architectures of communication; it is psychosocial energy that triggers the reorganization of existing systems and formations (transindividuation). *There is no recomposition of sociotechnical assemblages without information in all these different forms. There is no milieu of emergence without information.*

Tools for Change and the Hacking of Communication Channels

After a decade of activist slumber in the 1980s, following the crackdown on the autonomist extra-parliamentary left, many Italians woke up to a country with a privatized national infrastructure, a weak welfare state, outsourced industry, and the new, more precarious service-oriented economy—a dystopian version of flexible employment that had been part of the autonomist theorization of the refusal of work (Berardi n.d.). With the crisis of communism, for many, the awakening was also a rallying cry for new modes of political critique and struggle. What's more, the deep-reaching economic transformations and the rise of the tertiary and financial sectors had placed a new resource, *information,* at the center of the struggle for accumulation and power. Then, in December 1989, students in Palermo rose up to protest the privatization of research funding and the inclusion of private stakeholders into the university councils, a measure that would allow corporations and the information economy to thrive at the expense of public education. The students also advocated for the right to access free and independent information and opposed Berlusconi's attempts to consolidate his monopoly on the mass media with the help of Communication Minister Mammì (Delisa 2012). By January 1990 the movement had rapidly expanded throughout Italy, taking its name from an undetainable runaway zoo animal sighted at the outskirts of Rome—La Pantera (The Panther). The Panther students declared themselves "political without party affiliation; democratic; non-violent; and anti-fascist" (Delisa 2012). They occupied buildings, self-managed classes and groups in collaboration with some professors, and experimented with available communication channels to reach out to broad audiences. They would also become the first Italian movement to tell its own story through video (Albanese 2010).

With the mainstream media mostly spreading misinformation about the occupations, and audiences recalling a not-so-distant past of political terrorism, La Pantera was so confusing for Italians that some action was

88 · ACTIVIST ENERGETICS IN THE INFORMATION MILIEU

needed.[1] This is when two veteran activists from the 1977 student movement who had become successful advertisers (Ferri n.d.) donated to the students of La Sapienza University in Rome a slogan and a logo (*La Pantera siamo noi!* [The Panther is us!]) for a public relations campaign of sorts. "No one knows where it [the real panther] came from, like this movement that bloomed at a time when there is little space for dissent. . . . And it is also unpredictable, with many faces and it is still hard to pin down its ideology," explained advertiser Fabio Ferri to the newspaper *La Repubblica* during those days (Pucciarelli 2010). The logos, videos, comics, and other media stunts that snowballed from the initial design may have not been everyone's tactic of choice but they certainly succeeded in circulating images of the occupation through what would now be considered memes or viral content.[2] Posters, stickers, and banners turned up everywhere across the country, as they traveled from one faculty to the other. This communication approach was the first of a kind in the history of struggles in Italy.

At that time, I was a high school student joining the occupations in solidarity and being introduced to activism at the Faculty of Architecture of Federico II University in Naples. My own first encounter with this circulating content was a video ad about the real panther on the run. The ad mixed footage of the feline with images of people asking who is afraid of the panther. About the students, poor people, and social justice activists depicted, the male voice-over suggested with a reassuring tone, "*Lui no, loro no . . .* [Not him, not them . . .]," but over the images of people like Prime Minister Bettino Craxi, Education Minister Antonio Ruberti, Fiat owner Gianni Agnelli, and media tycoon Silvio Berlusconi, the voice decidedly declared: "*Lui si, loro si* [Yes him, yes them]." "*La Pantera siamo noi* [The Panther is all of us]" was the punch line at the end of the ad, interpellating audiences to identify with the movement. Many of those I asked could recall the ad but not its origin. It seems safe to assume that it came out of the many experiments that were possible once students could access the expensive technology of some university media labs, and it traveled on VHS tape from city to city. Other slogans on banners, on walls, and at rallies drove home the political message. Students chanted: "*L'università privata, la pantera s'è incazzata* [The panther is pissed off about the privatized university]."

Public relations aside, in activist circles, it was very clear that the image of the panther, which reproduced the logo of its U.S. predecessor, drew a direct connection with the struggle of the Black Panther Party (Ferri 2017) and with the fight against oppressive powers celebrated by rap musicians

Figure 2. Assembly of the Student Movement "The Panther" occupied at SPON—Political Science Occupied Naples, at the Faculty of Political Science of the University of Naples Federico II in January 1990. Photograph taken by Angelo Di Dato in January 1990 in the hall of the ground floor of Via Cardinale Guglielmo Sanfelice, 48—Naples (NA). CC BY-SA 3.0.

like Public Enemy (Philopat 2006). Amid a climate of contamination between mainstream consumer culture, global politics, and imported countercultures, the occupied faculties drew people en masse, from high school students like me to activists from the CSOAs who supported the organizing process. These vibrant spaces, filled to the brim 24/7, offered a gamut of tools for self-run seminars, discussion groups, and experimentation with a variety of communication practices. Out came magazines, radio features, and video newsreels like the *Videogiornale Pantera* (La Pantera 1990). Some of the members of the historical free radio Radio OndaRossa in Rome founded OndaRossa Posse, one of the first hip-hop collectives in Italy (later called Assalti Frontali). The Posse and those who followed inextricably linked the production of this musical genre to the political scene of the Italian social centers (Giurdanella 2014). People sang OndaRossa Posse's "Batti il tuo tempo" (Keep your rhythm / Beat your time period) during the occupations and rallies, as enthusiasm ran high, for the young who had never experienced the thrills of collective action and for the veterans, who had lived without it for a long time.

With the PR campaign, but also with its attempts to control mainstream media messages through tactical interventions, La Pantera entered a terrain of struggle over information channels that would expand significantly in the nineties activist circles. It attempted to create a leveled playing field with the strategic communication and marketing approaches that overtook the communication industries and politics alike. Theories of differential accumulation (Nitzan 1998) are helpful to understand the backdrop of these new practices of resistance. In service-oriented economies, owners can leverage technical change as a tool of power and they can reorganize power directly by buying and selling ownership claims over the information that is produced and circulates while simultaneously capitalizing on the infrastructures that sustain it. Examples of these dynamics today are the struggles against piracy and the battles among internet service providers (ISPs) against net neutrality, where powerful stakeholders attempt to gain an advantage—or even total control—over available information dissemination channels. A fundamental part of the competition among capitalists also unfolds through the constant engagement with the diffusion of information to ensure that messages are not distorted or dispersed. In oversaturated environments, where capital is competing for niche markets to sell products and services (together with the lifestyles that require them and the political discourses that legitimate them), the shorter the message and the faster information reaches its target, the more chances of success. During these struggles to prevail over each other, information distribution patterns and circulating information in the form of short slogans and ever-present logos reshape the informational milieu outside simple channels of communication.

The modulation of signal to noise increasingly takes precedence over the delivery of meaning in this information-rich world (Terranova 2004, 54–58). This is how, as the organization and circulation of information take on more importance for the economy, creative informational practices of resistance establish themselves alongside the rallies, strikes, and blockades to compete for attention. Tactical media stunts and virtual sit-ins (Meikle 2002), the antibranding "culture jams," and "subvertising" (subvert + advertising) campaigns that support corporate boycotts (Klein 2000) gained popularity in the nineties because they enabled activists to target the new enemies, often powerful corporations, with humorous and popular campaigns that threaten their power to accumulate and appeal to a wide public. Some of the seeds for informational guerrilla were planted earlier on.

In the late eighties and early nineties, new technologies met DIY punk ethics at the same time as activists had started to understand the shape-shifting character of capital. Their experiments showed the effects of practices of resistance that repurpose available communication channels (faxes, billboards, internet websites, etc.) and use the familiar language of consumption and advertising to gain visibility in the mainstream media, reaching wider audiences than the restricted activist crowd. During the student strikes, La Pantera pioneered some of these tactics, tapping into marketing strategies and the aesthetics of communication typical of the current phase of capitalism. These experiments catalyzed creations and transformations that exceeded the act of communicating: as information circulated through the new and repurposed information infrastructure, it set off a series of relays between the technological and the social, pushing the limits and options for supporting social change by drawing on technology to develop social practices and vice versa. The new formations that emerged were not only the result of attempts to clear out channels from noise; information was also an attractor for creations that are the outcome of interactions within an information-rich field.

Information as a Structuring Force outside Its Channels: Okkupanet and Networked Activism

When the students of La Sapienza in Rome entered the office of the dean to ask for the keys to the Faculty of Letters, they also asked for the fax machine. After a bit of arguing and some resistance, the dean conceded, "Do you know how to use it?" (Albanese 2010). La Pantera became known as *il movimento dei fax* (the fax movement), named after the internal fax grid they developed. In 1989–90 faxes were essential for the students coordinating actions among universities across the country. Faxes were used to circulate mailing lists with updates on the occupations but they were also critical to break into dominant information circuits and reach government and press directly in their offices. It is no surprise that the dean tried to hold on to his fax machine.

Even more groundbreaking was the appropriation of the Virtual Address eXtension (VAX) computer network in the science departments, which were part of an entirely different, dedicated, cable network. This network was much more powerful than the more common telephone cables used for technologies like bulletin board systems (Botti 1990). The political use of VAX computers from the DECnet grid is an identifiable threshold for the recomposition of the field of Italian media activism. As recounted by Andrea Mazzucchi (2009), one of the students spearheading the effort:

Those of us in Physics [departments] had one more tool [in addition to faxes]: the VAX grid based on DECnet, a proprietary system by Digital [Digital Equipment Corporation or DEC] that allowed us to interconnect VAX and microVAX computers all around the world. At the time, this was space age technology, way more developed than the internet. In addition to performing maintenance and circulating updates, the grid allowed us to use remote hard disks, manage mailing lists, chats and so on. . . . So, me and another nutcase, Simone Botti from Chemistry [department], decided to integrate the fax net with something more exciting. This is how Okkupanet was born.

Okkupanet connected VAX computers into the *infrastructure* of the occupation.

Before Okkupanet was created, DECnet had already become an important point of connection and information exchange with China, where students were protesting against their government in Tiananmen Square. When the government shut down all communication and blocked every source of information about the events, Chinese state censorship was unaware of DECnet, which remained active during the unrest. Every day, the Italian students had cleaned up the messages from their masking headings and passed them on to the mainstream press: "It [Okkupanet] could have just been a techno-elitist experiment but it quickly turned into something different. . . . The students of La Pantera organized themselves into 'commissions,' and I, as the person in charge of the 'Press Commission' was in daily contact with journalists. Probably, some functionary of the Chinese embassy went crazy trying to figure out how it was possible that Italy got such timely updates!" (Mazzucchi 2009). Mazzucchi remembers this event as a trigger for the political transformation of DECnet.

Beyond the transmitted content of the messages, circulating information established a material connection between China and Italy and sowed the seed for further use of computer networks, inspiring the movement to use Okkupanet.[3] The repurposing of VAX computers to discuss politics became a testing ground for some of the features of contemporary social media, enabling horizontal and open communication and the easy archiving and distribution of content. Okkupanet's features were shaped by the prefigurative politics that activists aimed to affirm in society at large: consensus decision-making, diversity of practices, horizontal organizing, and so on.[4] It quickly developed into an active political network where interaction was structured along the democratic organizing principles of conduct of a movement striving to foster participation. According to Simone Botti, the discussion of the practices and potentials for the network went hand in hand with an analysis of the features and reach of the VAX computer network and with a reflection on the needs of the movement.

> At the beginning it functioned as a simple system for email, then the evolution begun. Like a growing organism, first we tried to connect as many synapses as possible, then we started to study "introspectively" all the levels of connection in the physical space of the grid and in the *space of relations*. . . . Okkupanet was put to work for the movement 90 [The Panther], creating a permanent national archive of all relevant documents that came out of the different commissions, and presenting itself as a mass communication tool that is much faster, more flexible and more powerful than the fax. (Botti 1990, 12, emphasis added)

The introspective analysis considered, for instance, the complexity of the levels of communication and how the software and hardware architecture established relationships among users. It examined how power could be negotiated between network nodes and system managers that were located in different university laboratories and had the ability to moderate interaction and exclude users (Botti 1990). The reflections were at the basis of a code of conduct for users and administrators—one that "made explicit its being informatically non-violent" (Botti 1990, 12).

VAX computers had a "phone" command that allowed users to have a "phone call" in real time in the form of a text. This feature fostered a shared language to communicate in a radically new environment that influenced grammar and syntax and allowed for experimentation: the use of real-time chat channels where mundane communication mixed with lengthy discussions about politics, straddling different genres, styles, and registers, was something activists had never been exposed to before.[5] The students involved in Okkupanet discussed its potential for autonomous collective knowledge production, exchange, and distribution, something that will become the focus not only of media activist platforms but also commons-based projects ranging from Wikipedia to archive.org and Aaarg. In the context of the student movement, this discussion extended to the creation of infrastructure for a more participatory relation between the institution and its student body, and more generally for a recomposition of the field of activism into assemblages whose emergent identity is not predicated on flattening out the identity of its components.

> Because [the network] is open to all components, its contribution goes beyond the occupation, becoming a nervous system and a vector for all the actions and reflections that allow us to rebuild the sites of information production as autopoietic systems, rather than as autonomous ones. These systems could retain within themselves a permanent equilibrium among the relations that characterize their identity. These relations, in turn, need to emerge from the contribution of each and every component and subcomponent, as it retains its own [identity] and gets to understand it more intimately. (Botti 1990, 12)

Ultimately, beyond what was achieved at the level of policy, Okkupanet, and the occupations themselves, turned out to be about the ability to create a *space* for new ideas and practices to emerge and provide the *infrastructure* where different components of the activist assemblage could define themselves and their relation to each other autonomously.

The *space of relations* and the *infrastructure* to foster them are both crucial elements in the emergence and recomposition of political formations. Botti draws on theories of autopoiesis to consider the potential of networks to facilitate new activist assemblages characterized by a different kind of relation between its components—heterogeneity.[6] And while the metaphor of a self-regulating system will turn out to be inadequate to conceive of the transformations of an activist field that undergoes constant crisis and reshaping instead of regeneration, Botti's discussion returns us to considering the relation between an assemblage and its milieu of emergence. This relation involves more than space and infrastructure and is at the basis of processes of recomposition that an energetics of movements can foreground.

The experience of Okkupanet speaks to the materiality of information but also to its milieu—the information environment. From now on, and for the remainder of this book, it is no longer Claude Elwood Shannon's information theory but Gilbert Simondon's conceptualization of *metastable* systems and their environments that moves my inquiry forward.[7] To investigate media activism's relay between the technical and the social within an information-rich environment, I conceive of information as a set of inputs affecting metastability, that is, affecting the equilibrium between what is being individuated (the project, the movement, etc.) and its milieu of individuation (the spaces, the events, the economy, the discourses, etc.). For Simondon, information is involved in a process of restructuring and containing systems—technical, biological, human, social—which are always open to new restructuring processes whenever new elements trigger a "crisis" in their structure. In other words, information is a process of *giving form*, which unfolds at multiple interconnected scales, from individual perception to the modulation of social dynamics—all systems that undergo ongoing change.[8] Looking at political assemblages this way, the question is no longer how assemblages *fail* to retain consistency but how they constantly change in a shifting milieu.

In the case of Okkupanet, informational diffusion indirectly impacted cultural and political expression as a series of exchanges between what was technically available, what could be reprogrammed, and the circulating political needs and discourses. I see Okkupanet as an important component of the assemblage that, under the name of La Pantera, set the conditions for a broader recomposition of Italian activism but that also resonated with parallel experiments in other countries. Although it disappeared with the end of the protests, leaving little record of its existence behind, the process of development of this proto-social network as a wide reaching "nervous system" had already provided some information channels and raised important issues about the potentials and challenges of shaping autonomous communication infrastructures that reduced hierarchies within the movement and facilitated participatory decision-making (Botti 1990; Escobar and Alvarez 1992). By shaping language and mobilizing affect, Okkupanet triggered transformations in activists that will influence following media activist experiments. The affordances of the technologies, the emergence of information-based economies, the new targets of struggle, and the needs of movements that were recomposing away from the

96 · ACTIVIST ENERGETICS IN THE INFORMATION MILIEU

structures of parties, unions, and factory floors were all part of the milieu where the technical and the social were entangled at this specific point in time. Okkupanet came of an information milieu and itself was a milieu for new projects, practices, and subjectivities.

This Is What a Milieu of Emergence Looks Like

Despite its cutting-edge analysis of the neoliberalization of the university and some initial victories, La Pantera could not retain its momentum to develop sustainable political solutions to the crisis of education, and therefore it fragmented into new sociopolitical spaces. However, both La Pantera and Sabotax—its 1994 iteration—pumped new energy into political spaces. This change is perfectly summed up in the testimony of a veteran organizer.

> Since the university buildings had become de facto social centers full of activists, after the end of the occupations, many activists were going cold turkey . . . because addiction is not just caused by drugs but also by some experiences. . . . So the CSOAs all of a sudden got really full and were recognized as a driving force . . . also because by then Italian rap was developing, new inquiries and the use of new technologies. . . . Well, many had noticed, and not only on the left, that we were producing something substantial, sometimes even innovative . . . shareable experiments. (Il Duka, qtd. in Philopat 2006, 64)

In addition to the student movement, other events boosted political activity. Police crackdowns on occupied spaces garnered more support from sympathizers when images of the CSOA Leoncavallo in Milan successfully resisting a police siege circulated in the media (Autistici/Inventati 2017, 24). The year 1990 also saw the first demonstrations against the Iraq war that brought more people into the streets.

Space was extremely needed and important for this political renaissance (Bianchi, Luppichini, and Balestrini 1994). The CSOAs, self-run autonomous social centers, were key to relay energies, develop new practices, and foster collective resubjectivation. Some of these CSOAs still function as large-scale infrastructure for education, the arts, cultural production, entertainment, and care.[9] They have been the home base for the coordination of resistance movements ranging from student movements in the first decade of the twenty-first century to struggles against military bases like the Molin in the Veneto region and Muos in Sicily (Piazza 2015, 200–201). Recently, as real estate speculation increases worldwide, CSOAs also function as outposts against the gentrification of the neighborhoods they are located in, supporting movements for housing rights, often in collaboration with migrant justice groups (Mudu 2014). Although CSOAs are by no means strife-free sites, the socialization of political life through activities of social reproduction is a fundamental aspect of the process of subjectivation that takes place as people debate and experiment with forms of deliberation and collectivation that are rooted in anticapitalist principles. In addition to the social centers, scenes developed around radical presses like Shake and magazines like *Decoder* and started discussing hacking, computer networks, and cyberpunk literature.[10] Italy was the first country in southern Europe to organize hackmeetings and set up spaces for hackers—the proximity of these political and cultural experiments brought many facets of hacker culture into activism and radical politics into hacking. The CSOAs often hosted international and national meetings and harbored hacklabs that developed free software, built computers out of recycled parts, and offered courses in computer use and programming (Autistici/Inventati 2017). As the hacking and cyberpunk cultures fed new experiments in the social centers, activists shared knowledge and collaborated on projects and infrastructure during conventions, workshops, and festivals. Technology in these spaces was never a virtual affair but a material, social entangling of bodies and machines.

The first political bulletin board systems came on the scene in the early nineties and were hosted by historical free radios like Radio Blackout in Turin. The connection between old school radio activism and hacking was not coincidental but was the result of an active discursive environment where the potential of communication was constantly being redefined. The European Counter Network (ECN) was founded after a series of Europe-wide meetings of activists in 1989 as a BBS network of national nodes for debate, sharing, and experimentation on the political use of new technologies. The first active Italian nodes of ECN appeared in 1990 in Rome, Milan, Bologna, and Padoa (Di Corinto and Tozzi 2002, 225), all cities with politically active student movements. In 1993 various Italian BBSs like Hacker Art and BITs Against the Empire were networked into Cybernet, an open network for posting political content that linked Italians from the Alps to Sicily. In 1994 AVvisi Ai Naviganti (Avana) (Notices for Navigators) started providing BBS as well as training and discussions on emergent media (244–49). In the same year, a government crackdown on hacking and piracy closed more than 150 BBSs, including the server of Peacelink (Gubitosa and Peacelink 1999). Following this crackdown (the first of many to come), in 1996 Isole nella Rete (Islands in the Net) was created, transforming ECN's BBS into mailing lists for the radical left and functioning as an independent internet provider. Isole nella Rete was one of the first autonomous structures serving internet to Italian activist groups who needed anything from mirroring and anonymity services to listservs and discussion sites. Bridging the digital gaps with analog technology, communication among BBS nodes was often integrated with the help of fax machines, radio, and print media. Hacktivist Snd reminisces: "We felt that it had great potential, so much so that in 1993–1995 we tried to give birth to a parallel experience, a sort of AP of the radical left and a service for the movement's radio stations" (Autistici/Inventati 2017, 34). Zines and bulletins connected to networks like ECN also played an important role, with a circulation unseen since the heydays of *autonomia*. Before they were formalized into the corporate and state institutions of the so-called network society (Castells 1996; Van Dijk 2005), digital technologies were already key to interconnect grassroots activist networks transnationally.

The connection of hacking and political activity was inspired and advanced by many of the ideas summed up in the 1995 handbook *Digital Guerrilla: Guida all'uso alternativo di computer, modem e reti telematiche* (Digital Guerrilla: A guide to the alternative use of computers, modems and telematic networks) published by ZERO! and BITs Against the Empire Labs. The handbook proposed that new technologies can facilitate communication for political change but it also advocated for the creation of public terminals in social centers, infoshops, and bookstores, and the distribution of the same content in print form. Importantly, *Digital Guerrilla* started pointing to the role media activism can play in fostering new forms of sociality: "Such tools are not only great counter-information agencies for traditional militant collectives, they can also give rise to novel community forms" (Autistici/Inventati 2017, 29). This was no cyberutopia: the contribution of tech collectives responsible for the spread of hacking and tech literacy in Italian social movements goes far beyond the circulation of information and coordination; tech collectives were involved in the social reproduction of activists (Serra 2015) away from the corporate mass media and toward the repurposing of media into an interconnected nervous system along the lines of what was envisioned with Okkupanet. This autonomous nervous system supported, protected, and harnessed communication and entangled bodies and machines then as it does, perhaps to a reduced extent, today.

The tech collective Autistici/Inventati, or A/I, was founded in 2001, shortly before the protests of Genoa. Its history is inextricably linked with the Italian (but also international) extraparliamentary left and its political activity both online and offline during this time of ongoing change.[11] It is important to stress how tech collectives like A/I have been performing the work of caring for the political, cultural, and *affective* networks of communication of movements for decades, not only behind the interface but also away from the keyboard, at meetings, in workshops, and at parties. This is because, like other vital forms of affective and care labor, such work is less visible than other forms of organizing, even when it is an important part of the milieu of composition and recomposition of movements. As Maxigas points out in his vivid introduction to the history of A/I, "radical technology collectives build political solidarity and nurture security behaviors within and between activist groups in addition to providing things like email and putting the right cryptographic algorithms in place. . . . Implementation, maintenance and repair is just as important for changing society—or even just technology—as innovation" (Autistici/Inventati 2017, 12–13). Before they take on further consistency in Telestreet and, especially, insu^tv, the traces of practices for connective activism grow more visible here, within these sociotechnical spaces that function as infrastructural points to relay energy.

In terms of a milieu of emergence, we can say that these spaces, events, and practices cross each other to enable a reorganization of the system, engendering new possibilities for activism and for being. Within a vibrant milieu of political action and autonomous cultural production, information technology fed these spaces for experimentation with new lines of subjectivation. The *energy* of the social centers was stoked not just by new technologies but also by maker spaces for printing and building and by new trends in punk, hip-hop, and techno. In the grassroots recording studios, at the independent labels, and in the event venues of the CSOAs, political international styles like hip-hop and reggae were sampled with traditional local folkloric tunes producing exciting new blends of music, like the *etno-beat mediterraneo* (Mediterranean ethnic beats). Bands such as Assalti Frontali and Almamegretta sometimes played concerts for ten to twenty thousand people at rallies and cultural events. They sold equally as

100 · ACTIVIST ENERGETICS IN THE INFORMATION MILIEU

many records. These bands and parties not only functioned as very efficient vectors for the circulation of political messages; they drew young people to sites of politicization and were a source of revenue for the CSOAs and their musicians, who wanted to stay outside commercial circuits.

In the cyberpunk rave scene, media activists often dubbed as VJs (video jockeys) turned to media production outside the party scene. With this strong socially useful basis, social centers opened up to new forms of anticapitalist collaboration and solidarity with other grassroots groups that included fair trade associations, cultural groups, migrant organizations, and farmers markets. Some of these centers have even succeeded in becoming reference points for entire neighboring communities through the institution of services that range from child and health care to libraries and language courses for migrants (Casagrande 2009). In the nineties, cross-pollination was everywhere, constantly *in-form-ing*, networking, and chancing unlikely encounters—linking disparate elements that expanded the milieu and fed the recomposition. As a student during La Pantera and someone who joined in the occupations of the COSAs, I saw many of these patterns of collaboration, knowledge sharing, and political practice emerge before they coalesced in the Italian node of the Indymedia network and then in Telestreet. But before I get there, it is worth noting how this cross-pollination was by no means contained within the nation-state.

Infowars

By 1994 Berlusconi was winning the elections to the football-like cheers of his new party, and Italian students were once again in the streets to protest educational reforms and tuition fee hikes under the banners of the Sabotax movement: "*La rivoluzione non russa* [Revolution doesn't snooze or Not your Russian revolution]" and "Against the financial reform, for work, for the welfare state and the right to study." Further away, the Ejército Zapatista de Liberación Nacional (EZLN, Zapatista Army of National Liberation) had declared war on the Mexican government and on the North American Free Trade Agreement (NAFTA), which threatened its common land and traditional way of life (Castells [1997] 2004, 78). The EZLN was one of the first groups to connect and fuse anticolonial, local struggles with a clearly articulated critique of global neoliberal oppressive economic mechanisms. The novelty of this approach was accompanied by another innovation: guerrilla communication through stories and communiqués that were circulated on NGOs' BBS networks and on the internet. The Zapatistas were able to wage infowar thanks to La Neta, a communication network established by NGOs like the women's group Mujer a Mujer and Servicios Informativos Procesados (SIPRO), which had been looking for more affordable media than fax machines to spread information (Martinez-Torres 2001, 351).[12]

The information war brought the case of the Zapatistas to global attention and fostered a solidarity movement that prevented the violent repression of the EZLN (Wolfson 2014). In particular, the stories of the Zapatista leader—the masked, pipe-smoking Subcomandante Insurgente Marcos—spoke to minority groups all over the world. These stories bridged the gap between an isolated problem in the jungle of Chiapas and global civil society by making visible the direct connections between neoliberal policies and their effects on the territory. In 1996 more than five thousand students, workers, independent journalists, activists, and NGOs from forty-two countries flocked to Chiapas for the Intercontinental Meeting for Humanity and Against Neoliberalism, also known as the Intergalactic Meeting (EZLN 1996).

Despite the difficulty of translating different realities into a common language, the event sowed the seeds for new alliances and networks, facilitated by information technology (Cleaver 1999). The meetings at Aguascalientes also spurred a number of transnational collaborations with Italian CSOAs, which helped set up medical facilities and farming infrastructure (Laboratorio Occupato SKA and Leoncavallo 1995; Pacos & Rio 1997). The Zapatista practices of resistance left an indelible mark on the activism of the global justice movement, while in Italy they also resonated with familiar autonomist and anarchist practices. It is no coincidence that the opening epigraph of this chapter references both Aguacalientes in Chiapas and the past movement of '77. In particular, the EZLN and autonomists shared an orientation toward community building away from state power, and the subversive use of the dominant language to expose power.

In January 1998, in solidarity with the Zapatista struggle, an Italian group of activists, the Anonymous Digital Coalition, called for a globally coordinated Net Strike, that is, a virtual sit-in at five Mexican financial institutions' websites (Anonymous Digital Coalition 1998). The sit-in consisted of continuously clicking on the browser's reload button for the websites to bring down the servers. Within a few hours, the sites were shut down, wreaking havoc among shareholders. Inspired by this action, the Electronic Disturbance Theater, a U.S.-based group of media tacticians

102 · ACTIVIST ENERGETICS IN THE INFORMATION MILIEU

specializing in electronic civil disobedience (ECD), developed FloodNet, a software that sent an automated reload request every few seconds, blocking websites more efficiently. These actions showed how informational guerrilla could be "a source of resistance more powerful than bullets" (Martinez-Torres 1997) and made "swarming" a tactic in struggles for social justice.[13]

Practices of informational guerrilla, including Electronic Disturbance Theater, tactical media, and viral culture jamming, became part of the global justice movement repertoire in the following years, when excitement about the internet ran high and protest on the street seemed to have become less effective. From Mexico to Australia, new experiments with emerging technologies were crucial to stimulate a lively collective discussion on *how* to struggle and in creating resonance among different instantiations of resistance. At the same time, many of the nonhierarchical organizing principles of the Zapatistas and their allies became the backbone for the global justice movement. It is important here to point to Dorothy Kidd's indispensable work, tracing the origins of practices of resistance to neoliberalism in countries of the Global South and, in particular, in feminist and indigenous resistance and community radio. This history has been mostly erased by more North American–centered accounts of the emergence of the global justice movement in the white American middle class (Kidd 2004). The information-rich milieu engendered a global recomposition of assemblages that cut across social formations and provided a series of victories and incredible momentum for social, economic, and environmental organizing—until 2001 in Genoa.

From Seattle to Genoa: The Ups and Downs of Movements

In 2001, when he gave orders to turn the colorful anti-G8 protests in Genoa into a theater of repression, Prime Minister Berlusconi had just won the elections for the second time and was out to set an example for everyone who was watching. And many were indeed watching, glued to mainstream media channels that looped endless images of Black Blocs attacking corporate property. Many others were getting their news from Indymedia's websites, which had become a popular point to access alternative information since the protests against the WTO in Seattle in 1999. From Genoa, free radios coalition Radio GAP and the multilingual entries on the Independent Media Center (IMC) web pages circulated worldwide information about the anti-G8 convergence, the raids at the Media Center and the Social Forum building, the police killing of Carlo Giuliani, the inordinate amounts of tear gas and water cannons, and the brutal beatings of protesters and journalists alike (Indybay 2001). For IMCista Bomboclat, "in substance, the G8 opened the 'era of Indymedia' and with it a completely new political paradigm" (Autistici/Inventati 2017, 69). This paradigm located media activism and infowar at its core and, accordingly, when, only a couple of months later, 9/11 antiterror legislation intensified what Berlusconi had begun with the unhinged repression in Genoa, media activists and organizers for the global justice movement alike were heavily targeted.[14]

Over the years, I have asked many activists around the world what they thought had gone "wrong" with the "movement of movements" that garnered global attention in Seattle: the systematic repression of dissent that followed 9/11 is often at the top of the list but many also mentioned the inability of the massive mobilizations to prevent the Iraq war and "summit hopping" (the habit that activists developed to go from one summit to the other, investing less time in local organizing) as other damaging forces. Organizing large-scale protests requires a high degree of coordination, resources, and labor, and after a countersummit, local activist groups often found themselves depleted of labor power and funds, especially if many had been arrested and were in the grip of the judiciary system. I have also heard countless accounts of how difficult it was to harness the energy that had been generated when a heterogeneous group of people had shared the streets and banners.

Because of the transitory character of the summits, visiting activist groups seldom invested in supporting local struggles, local activists had to focus on the protest planning rather than on their daily organizing, while the hosting process itself often opened up rifts among groups and made it difficult for the movement to grow past summits. The disagreements between supporters of a diversity of tactics, and those opposed to more disruptive direct action, became harder to handle within the movement, suffering of burnout as police attacked protesters and violence took over the mainstream media framing, scapegoating radical groups to justify police repression.[15] Still, this fragmentation by no means signaled the end of coordinated global resistance: (smaller) crowds continue to fill the streets in every city where transnational summits take place (Juris 2008, 161–98). At the same time, more local groups have invested their energies into localized work while thinking "globally."

Many of the elements that made the global justice movement novel also played a role in its defusing: horizontality, in many cases, became "tyrannical" by obfuscating power relations and precluding discussions on hierarchies (Freeman 1970); the intense engagement with information circulation caused information-overload (Wright 2005); and online interaction weighed down face-to-face collaboration between groups (Fenton and Barassi 2011). As the global justice movement grew and changed, Indymedia.org also experienced its ups and downs, in particular in places like Italy, where it grew to an unmanageable size almost overnight after Genoa (Beschi 2005, 94). At the same time, IMC nodes around the world established themselves as reference points in many communities while they could not grow in others (Giraud 2014).

Indymedia Italia is one of the nodes that started strong, and then experienced a series of hurdles to eventually close down in 2012; its erratic trajectory is a parable for the transformation of the milieu of media activism, where processes of recomposition fold in elements and experiences that spanned the multiple sites and histories I have described—from the free radios to the hacker and cyberpunk culture emerging at the same time as La Pantera in Italy and abroad. In this milieu, information and its circulation vectors fed the change at many levels: autonomous information and communication technologies connected a worldwide network of activists and movements, F/OSS powered its digital infrastructure, the architecture of platforms for open publishing translated the horizontal and open participatory principles of prefigurative politics into communication practices, and the production of counterinformational content catalyzed processes of subjectification of the activist and *media activist.*

In this milieu, it is also no coincidence that, initially, many members of A/I were not only involved in setting up the computer infrastructure for Indymedia but also contributed content to it, recognizing that the increased role of communication in political struggle required that they also pay more attention to media activism. For A/I member Bomboclat, "It was during those years that the figure of the media activist emerged. Politics and technology merged, thanks to the glue of the digital possibilities. From the idea of producing alternative media we switched to the idea of being the media. Defining propaganda as everything that comes from television, we created our own concept of media" (Autistici/Inventati 2017, 59). With the emerging subjectivity of the media activist came a variety of conundrums that were often tied to the use of technology itself—issues of inclusion and diversity of voices, control and moderation of newswires and lists, and distinctions between being political activists and/or journalists, among others (Beschi 2005; Autistici/Inventati 2017). These rifts constantly fed information, that is, divergent stimuli that disturbed the equilibrium of the collective and eventually decomposed it into other projects.

Indymedia Italia was particularly involved in covering the trials of people arrested at the protests in Genoa, organizing the Florence Social Forum in 2003, coordinating Media Democracy Day, promoting solidarity with and reporting from Chiapas and Palestine, and, in general, covering political events all over the country (Beschi 2005). Not unlike other nodes around the world, which experienced problems with the decision-making and participation process (Pickard 2006; Wolfson 2014), Indymedia Italia often found itself devising new solutions to solve the challenges emerging from the practice of open publishing, interrelational issues, unspoken hierarchies, lack of diversity in the groups, bullying, and flame wars that erupted on the various coordination lists and IRC channels. Many of these solutions involved creating additional channels of communication, forums, and working groups that allowed coordination in-between the few national meetings. Eventually, they morphed from being a national node in the global network, with collectives working in various cities and publishing on the national site, to being a local network that fed content into a national "aggregator" page, Indymedia Italia Beta (((i)) 2008; ((i)) Italia 2008). For some, like this anonymous Indymedia activist, fostering proximity of bodies was important to reduce the crises: "It is nice to put a face to those loved/hated nicknames from the discussion lists; to look in the eyes of the people you shared autistic nights to update an ftp or simply to hang out in a chat room; to share once in a while not only skills but a bowl of pasta, a beer, a couch to crash on" (Beschi 2005, 176). For ex-Indymedia and insu^tv member Wadada, "These experiments eventually led to the reorganization of the network as multiple citywide nodes to improve collaboration" (interview with Wadada, 2008).

Todd Wolfson (2014) has discussed Indymedia's consensus-based decision-making practices and its decentralized network structure as the two main features that undermined the project in the United States.[16] Although I cannot speak to the specificities of the American cases, for me, the Italian attempts to reconfigure are a testimony to the network's awareness of the pitfalls of technical solutionism to support the decentralized network structure. Having to toggle between the technical and social to prefigure a radical democratic assemblage does not prove the inadequacy of consensus-based decision-making and decentralization but draws attention to the structuring force of information without devaluing human agency. Neither technology nor political practices alone can make movements scalable and sustainable without careful and ongoing consideration of the interaction between these key elements and others.

It seems to me that the loss of strength of the global justice movement and Indymedia was due to a much more complex configuration of their conditions of existence, which included minor differences that were highly destabilizing as well as larger policing and technocultural shifts that seriously impacted these formations.[17] In Italy, as much as in many other non-English-speaking countries, some personalities could be destabilizing more than the structure of the project; moreover, nodes found it hard to participate in the network-wide discussions due to the widespread habit of contributing long posts in English (Beschi 2005, 84). As mentioned, Indymedia suffered a paralyzing repression backlash both locally and internationally, with police raids, arrests, blocking of websites and seizing of servers, and even their exclusion from the news.google.com news sites (Babylonian 2003; Indybay 2003). The protests in Genoa had been the most filmed and photographed in the history of political dissent in Italy, and the trials that followed often used some of this material to incriminate activists. After the Genoa IMC was targeted by police in a brutal raid that left technology destroyed and news material seized as evidence, police continued to take the computers used by Indymedia in 2002 from many CSOAs, looking for audio and video about the Genoa G8 protests (Indymedia Italia 2002).[18] Over the years there have been various attempts to shut down Indymedia and seize their servers in various parts of the world. In Italy, in 2004, 2005, and 2012 there were attempts to shut down the website by targeting its hosts in the United States and Brazil, using a law that allows the state to censor offensive content (Morandi 2005; Indymedia Piemonte 2012). Many of the searches were legitimized by post-9/11 antiterror legislation and have given police a chance to target and intimidate activist groups indiscriminately. In 2004 the Italian Ministry of the Interior's "Report to Parliament on Police Activity, Public Security and Organized Crime" legitimized unlawful seizure of data on servers and police crackdowns on the extraparliamentary left by pointing at media activist groups like Indymedia and Telestreet as potential terrorist threats (Ministero dell'Interno 2004; ANSA 2005; Autistici/Inventati 2017, 89).

Repression takes a huge toll on groups. The final blow for the Italians arrived with what came to be known as the "Italian Wikileaks," when, in June 2012, judges preventatively seized the websites and shut down the more active Indymedia nodes. Starting in 2008, Indymedia had published a series of investigative reports on illegal activities by a Genovese international corporation that involved powerful individuals from the world of Italian high finance, who filed a defamation lawsuit against an anonymous author and the hosts of the article (Redazione 2012). Eventually, Indymedia Italia shut down, drained of energy, resources, and finances, and, sadly, unable to even cover the costs to preserve its own archive. Repression is dangerous for movements not only because it cripples their resources and members but also because it exacerbates internal strife. In 2017 Linksunten, the German node of Indymedia, was unlawfully shut down by authorities following the anti-G20 protests in Hamburg (Knight 2017). They will be dealing with the German judiciary for months, if not years, to come.

Crucially, the growth and diffusion of so-called Web 2.0 and the adoption of social media platforms by many media activists around the world made open publishing less relevant. Although many of these "interactive" web platforms were made possible by the visionary design of the IMC Open Source tech tools, the new, for-profit platforms quickly took over the communication-scape of radical activist groups and NGOs alike (Indymedia Montreal 2016 Convergence Working Group 2017). As new free and ready-made tools made it easy to post content on blogs, set up websites, and add content to multimedia channels like Flickr and YouTube without requiring design and programming skills, there was less interest, energy, and audience for projects like Indymedia. Wolfson's detailed history and analysis of the network seems to hardly pay any attention to these factors that were by no means peculiar to the Italian case, so that, despite his exceptionally vivid account of the project in the United States, readers of his book are left to relegate Indymedia to the historical closet of obsolete media projects. This framing obscures the dynamic transformations of activism and media activism at the turn of the century for which the IMCs were extremely important carriers of a rich history of encounters and collaborations. Moreover, Indymedia was also a vector of innovation whose technology was quickly captured by corporate giants and whose journalistic practices have now been widely adopted in the field. Once new struggles developed, other movements spawned from networks like Indymedia and recomposed around different infrastructures of communication,

108 · ACTIVIST ENERGETICS IN THE INFORMATION MILIEU

sometimes for the better and in some cases for the worse but never without leaving an important legacy for the movements to come. Paying attention to the circulation of energy across these global and local networks of technology, spaces, and practices provides a more nuanced account of the recomposition of the field of activism in its complex environment.

Transition: A Short Note on the Precarity Movement

The milieu I have described was significant for the emergence of new communication practices, and Indymedia was an important threshold after which information production and circulation became modes of resistance in their own right. The final phase of this moment of energetic reconfiguration was more chaotic. In the early twenty-first century many hacklabs were being closed down in a new wave of crackdowns on social centers just as a large sector of the information economy grew around the monopolies of the soon-to-be giants that had survived the dot-com crash—Amazon and Google. At the same time, small tech start-ups co-opted many of the participatory design features of activist platforms (open publishing, blogging, commenting, free hosting of images and video, etc.) into what will become Web 2.0 and social networks (Indymedia Montreal 2016 Convergence Working Group 2017).[19] Blogging became widespread for many political organizations and other subjects that would have otherwise relied on platforms like Indymedia. MySpace appeared as a new site for socializing and kicked off the transition to social media networks, absorbing much of the independent music scene.

Because of the strain the global justice movement experienced after Genoa, groups started focusing on local challenges. In Italy, the energy that had propelled forward the cycle of struggles in the nineties exhausted itself and many movements and projects went dormant, drained by a climate of dissent mostly focused on critiquing Berlusconi. With space and tech infrastructure undergoing reorganization, the information milieu changed considerably. At the level of discourse, a more sober attitude to communication technologies followed the crash of the dot-com economy and placed many media activists on the fence between movement media and proprietary platforms.

In this new climate, the largest movements to emerge were the No TAV, opposing the construction of high-speed trains all over Italy, and the precarity movement. No TAV—*treni ad alta velocità* are high-speed trains—

had started in the nineties to contest the disproportionate investment in an infrastructure project that served few and impacted the health and environment for many. The precarity movement emerged in 2001 around the MayDay network first and EuroMayDay, often focusing on the precarious conditions of workers in the service industry, the exploitative conditions of knowledge production in research institutions and universities, and migrant care work. Its signature colorful protests grew exponentially, especially after the G8 in Genoa, as activists converged on Milan each year and started parades in other cities of Europe. The labor organizers, tactical media artists, radical researchers, and precarious workers of all kinds were interconnected through semantic networking of signs and symbols, message delivery through humorous stunts, media interventions, and the provision of services for autonomous labor organizing. Saint Precario, the patron saint of precarious workers, made its first appearance as a symbol of the precarious neoliberal subject in 2004 thanks to the Rete di San Precario (Saint Precarious Network).

At the head of the MayDay parade one could often see a statue of Saint Precario, in full regalia (a fast-food worker uniform, a call-center headset, and holding a variety of different work tools that mimicked the pose of church statues). The procession used familiar religious symbols to reach out to passersby with a powerful message: "We are all precarious and need to organize together." This shape-shifting figure brought the issue of precarity to debate and helped form a collective subjectivity (Mattoni 2012; Gherardi and Murgia 2015). The processions took over cultural events, factory and call-center pickets, and supermarket chains. As a signifier for a shared condition and as a catalyst for action against the increasingly precarious conditions of life under neoliberalism, Saint Precario stood as the visible face of a set of circulating discourses against the normalization of flexibility and exploitation (Renzi and Turpin 2007). Blazing through the informationscape, Saint Precario reappeared for years on stickers and prayer leaflets (Chainworkers.org CreW 2004), in videos by Telestreet and others (e.g., Obino 2005), in card games and video games, and in drag as a Japanese female designer at the Milan fashion week.[20] The precarity movement condensed much of the communication strategies developed during the nineties to appeal to a wide audience that had no political language as a reference point. As I joined Telestreet, there was intermixing and overlapping among movements: precarity activists, Indymedia, and microtelevisions often covered protests and interventions, and produced fiction around the issue of precarity. The precarity movement built on existing activist networks critiquing neoliberalism and expanded them through a shared popular language, sets of tools for critique, and a web of spaces for labor organizing, education, cultural production, and research that crossed borders and constituencies. Organizers in previous projects joined the movement, bringing with them their experiences and critiques.

Complex Assemblages Demand Multidimensional Accounts

The end of the nineties was an exciting time for movements around the world; opposition to neoliberal policies and the ability to shut down economic summits like the one in Seattle provided great momentum and protests expanded rapidly, with the help of large coordinating networks that worked online and on the ground. Organizers shared their protest strategies and tools as they hopped from one summit protest to the other, from Social Forum to Social Forum, and from Independent Media Center to Independent Media Center. Each site and event was the result of the synergy of local and foreign groups that gave vitality and reinforced the collective identity but eventually also led to burnout and fragmentation. Much happened to this movement that led to its energy drain, even in the brief three years between Seattle in 1999 and Genoa in 2001—too much to discuss here in a satisfactory manner. But if one is to acknowledge the complexity and multiple trajectories of the recomposition of movements, it is also necessary to attend to the materiality of information in its different instantiations. Seen as a set of inputs (social, technical, affective) that impact the (meta)stability of projects, circulating information is what sustains the relation between movements and their milieus of individuation—it is energy that keeps processes of restructuring open. The case of Italy foregrounds some general tendencies toward ongoing recomposition around new tools, needs, and challenges. The recompositions are triggered by a mix of needs, desires, and constraints—they function as in-form-ation.

Ultimately, the lines of development between contemporary activism and projects like Radio Alice and Radio Gap, *autonomia,* and the global justice movement are not of direct filiation but rather comprise a nonlinear process of energy relays and positive feedback between the technological and social realms; among spaces and sites of encounter; and between micro- and macrolevels of formations: from a chat over a beer to a full-blown experiment at a CSOA; from the forests of Chiapas to tinkering with technology; from a free radio to a BBS hosting space; from ravers to media activists; from a critique of corporate capitalism to an attack on Berlusconi's media control; from the streets of Bologna to those of Genoa—where this chapter started. My analysis of the use of technology and reconceptualization of the material impact of different kinds of information has emphasized the relation between assemblages and their milieu of individuation. As I move on to discuss the emergence of Telestreet, it is important to retain this understanding of the metastability of projects that are always only existing in tension between what they already are and what they become as they engage with their outside. When the tension releases and components scatter, one finds their traces where least expected. This, for some, is failure. For me, it is what speaks to how movements change across networks worldwide, and resistance continues.

5

Squatted Airwaves, Hacked Transmission

We no longer have roots, we have aerials.

—McKenzie Wark, *Virtual Geography*

Back now to Telestreet, I can present a network that bears the traces of the autonomist movements of the seventies—traces of Mao-Dadaism, of practices of self-valorization, of *conricerca*, of antagonistic social reproduction and its modes of resubjectivation, of its (partial) connections with the free radios' cultural production and Radio Alice through some of its founders. Telestreet is also located in the humus of the decomposing milieu of the global justice movement and it grows at the same time as the precarity movement—their roots were fertilized by Indymedia practices; tactical media and informational guerrilla; the need to overcome organizing burnout; a strong technological and spatial infrastructure (open-source software, tech collectives, video archives, social centers, hacklabs); inquiries into social reproduction in post-Fordist economies; and desire, intimacy, energy, friendship, and strife, of course. Telestreet picks up some media-making work where others left it, not because the latter failed but because there was a reorganization of the forces and energies in the milieu—some things, practices, tools, and projects popped up elsewhere, for instance, in the pirate TV stations of the squats of Rome, Bologna, and Naples. The airwaves surrounding these spaces were squatted too.

There is continuity but no linear filiation between autonomist media experimentation in the seventies, the global movement that became media visible in Seattle, and those movements that followed. The continuity is important because it speaks to how movements recompose and how change happens over multiple cycles of struggle. It is also important because it draws attention to the becoming of movements within a milieu where forces build and destroy.[1] The discontinuities warn that the recomposition of movements and activist formations is a differential and transformative mode of becoming that is always ongoing; it is not a force of serial reproduction.

The Telestreet I present here is an assemblage that I watched grow, change, and lose momentum in the neoliberal-Berlusconian milieu, as it encountered other movements and fertilized other projects—media connectives, video co-ops, WebTV, and so on. I am witness to the change and I am also one of the countless vectors of its becoming (and becoming no more) because the act of telling a story is a process of subjectivation—and subjectivation is important in the gravitational field of struggle I was pulled into. The environment that generates Telestreet is political and technical but also shaped by economic and policy decisions. The rise of Berlusconi showed how this milieu is tied to social subjection that creates the conditions for power to grow and for specific assemblages to exercise control and govern but also be opposed. In the neoliberal-Berlusconian assemblage, media function as agents of governmentality: media, particularly television, subjectify individuals and collectivities, allocating socioeconomic roles (the consumer) and political functions (the consumer-voter). Groups like Indymedia and Telestreet resist indirect forms of control through media that resubjectify. How do assemblages like Telestreet actually work and what are the processes of subjectivation involved?

Because governmentality deals with *the creation of the conditions of transformation* rather than transformation itself (Foucault 2008), here I focus on the sociotechnical environment and psychic and technical processes of (be)coming together in neoliberal Italy. Three aspects are particularly important: how the neoliberal-Berlusconian subjectivity is produced to govern, the entanglement of the technical and the social elements of the Telestreet assemblage, and how Telestreet sets in motion psychosocial transformations. Here is where the individual, the technical, and the collective come and *become* together visibly. Here is where perception is protagonist— that is, where the ability to become aware of something through the senses connects "the individual" to the technical and the social. Perception is the gateway to the contemporary battleground over autonomous subjectivity. Telestreet hacks into the senses: its technical hacks—across analog and digital components and networks—provide new forms of connectivity that resist the homogenization and standardization of common sense needed for governmental control. But in order to do this, Telestreet also has to set the stage for transformation to happen, reorganizing the media environment, creating the conditions to use its DIY transmission apparatus, and undoing the mediality of television that is dominant in Berlusconi's Italy.

Television works as a governmental machine and its force has to pass through its material circuits before it is sensed. Television technology converts images into a field of varying electronic signals, storing the information in a television receiver and then sending out the signals composing the image. The television receiver reverts the process. Every second, twenty-five frames (or thirty in North America) are created and read as continuous movement, since the human eye cannot perceive fast changes of light and image (Runyon 2009). The connection between the transmission system of the television and the human reception system of the viewer is established via the flow of information in the form of both electronic signals and perceptual stimuli.[2] Watching television fosters connection because it produces stimuli that constantly activate affects—the relational layer that is at the center of individuality (Combes 2013, 30). The relation between media use and sensation (mediality) runs in the backgrounds of the everyday uses of media orienting collective affects (Grusin 2010). This interaction-through-sensation places affective manipulation through media at the center of governmental control strategies (Grusin 2010). Television "primes" the environment in which affective reactions happen, blurring the boundaries between affectivity and rationality (Massumi 2015).

For this reason, the emergence of the collective (transindividuation) is tied to technical assemblages like television that circulate sensory stimuli and relay social practices. Here, technical assemblages individuate too as machines connect with each other (Simondon 1989). But machines are never only technical. Ultimately then, as an individuating "individual" in the (neoliberal-Berlusconian) milieu with its specific brand of television, one (perhaps me watching Berlusconi's electoral campaign) partakes in a multiscale process that intervenes at the level of the technical apparatus of TV but also on the senses impacting sense making, the creation of a shared "common sense," and everyday viewing practices (and leads to Berlusconi's political victory). Telestreet provides an alternative circuit for the sense making of televisual stimuli by recombining technical and social components.

Television as an Apparatus for Interconnection

The sending and receiving of broadcast television images is made possible by assigning a transmission frequency and operating power to a mass media channel, which will be used to transmit video and audio signals, as well as other specialized signals (Hartwig 1995). The signal is carried through space by a wave according to the characteristics determined by the frequency assigned to it. The process used to carry the signal through a higher frequency wave is called *modulation*. Antennas receive the modulated carrier wave of a television station from a transmitter and radiate the signal into space following a designated pattern. After removing all unnecessary signals, a television receiver amplifies and converts the audio and video that will reach the viewer through a monitor for pictures and sounds (Runyon 2009).

This is also how Telestreet's transmission system works, but unlike the mainstream media, which have powerful and standardized broadcasting systems, both transmission and irradiation patterns in Telestreet go through a network of assembled media and different spatial configurations. The Telestreettari and the viewers are plugged into this assemblage. Using Telestreet's DIY broadcasting system, they transmit video material from a source like a VHS or DVD player, or a computer that has downloaded content from a video archive, through a small transmitter to an antenna. However, the DIY antenna connected to the transmitter works as a TV station, relaying the signal to other antennas in its proximity. The "organs" of the Telestreet system—the antennas, computers, mixers, and so on—connect it with other systems, such as the video archive, into ensembles that reproduce its functions but also enable its transformation. The Telestreettari are individuals connected to other individuals and to Telestreet's transmission system, a machine bridging humans and the natural word (Simondon 2006, 262). One can follow the movement of individuation as it transduces from the technical to the social and back again.

Telestreet's transmission apparatus includes a digital component, used in the control room—PCs accessible from an external network, a DVD player, video cameras and other equipment for broadcasting and editing, and an analogical component—consisting of a television and some monitors, the mixer(s) and the device for signal transmission (assembled from an amplifier), a modulator, and the antennas. All components were *repurposed*; they were tinkered with and combined in their specific way in order to maximize the goals of the project: to work at low cost and in the gray areas of legal access to broadcasting frequencies, to adapt to spatial and technical change, and to connect heterogeneous nodes and communities. A section of Telestreet's old website read: "Two computers (not necessarily last generation ones), an amplifier, a modulator, an antenna and a few meters of cable. This is the basic equipment of our Telestreet. It's not necessary to follow high technology and Bill Gates to set up a television station" (Telestreet n.d.).

The DIY transmission system was low cost even in the early twenty-first century: two panel-antennas (30 euros), a DIY power switcher (60 euros), a 12-meter pole (25 euros), a modulator with a 3-watt pilot amplifier (450 euros), a 19-watt signal amplifier (600 euros), and a receiving antenna (10 euros) was insu^tv's initial shopping list. To this was added a gifted Pentium III as an archive, an external hard drive to store the downloaded and produced videos, and another refurbished PC working as a player. Insu^tv then integrated it with a DVD player (50 euros) and a gifted VHS recorder connected by a switch and a mixer to the transmitter (500 euros), and finally two preview monitors (another gift!). After struggling with the black-boxed stiffness of Windows Media Player, the collective was able to switch to Linux software to automate the scheduling and also adopted the free and open-source VLC media player to broadcast 24/7 (interview with Pog, 2008).

The properties of this transmission apparatus emerge when the potentialities of its various technical components solidify and become grounded at the intersection of sociality, culture, geography, and the economy. None of the technical components listed above were originally designed to be part of Telestreet's transmission system, especially the obsolete ones that were donated, but each component's properties could be folded into Telestreet's TV station due to the social and political needs of the project, the geographical proximity of its nodes to networks of support, the availability of components and budget, and so forth. For instance, without the mixer and switcher it would be impossible to toggle between analog and digital systems. These parts were needed to juggle multiple inputs simultaneously, often live in the streets during events or in other makeshift studio spaces in garages, basements, squats, schools, and community centers.

Here is the *genesis* of Telestreet's apparatus: it involves a (temporary) stabilization of the properties of each technical component—what they were initially made for and what they end up doing in combination. In this process the components retain or change their original function. I became involved in a kind of repurposing when I started working for Telestreet, together with the hackers, media makers, and technicians. This repurposing is not so much about recycling and more about allowing for new properties to emerge in connection with the technical assemblage. At a time when some technology is malleable and a lot of it is modular, the concretization of the assemblage is what makes the difference. The process of stabilization is transductive; transformation takes place gradually across scales and dimensions—in this case it is in the movement from the digital to the analog (from the web to television) that concretization takes place. Telestreet's transmission systems broadcast from the internet and other outputs into the houses of people using analog radio frequencies radiating into shadow cones. This movement deliberately counters the common tendency of most technology to transform what is analog into digital, and it leaves noninternet users behind. One of the system's emergent properties is that of connecting, against the grain, what is being separated in the digital divide.

In the individuation of Berlusconi's media assemblage, the syndication "hack" put into relation technologies like VHS recording, analog editing of ads into the shows, broadcasting technology, with the postal services to synchronize programming and bypass national broadcasting restrictions. Not dissimilarly, street television channels place their broadcasting apparatus within areas where stronger transmitting carrier waves are not present— the shadow cones—facilitating the reception and circulation of their own signals. By not conflicting with already occupied frequencies, Telestreet reduces the white noise that could drown its own transmission and avoids getting into trouble for infringing communication regulations. Moreover, using a Berlusconian topological approach to spatial configuration, Telestreet connects all its nodes in a national network via web archive.

At the same time, Telestreet does not share Fininvest's interest in strengthening the reach of its media through consolidation that maximizes capital accumulation. It steers away from the institutionalization and standardization of its transmission system because it is explicitly against the homologation of the practices of its producers and audiences. Even during the campaign to legalize Telestreet, this kind of standardization was never a goal. It is precisely the modularity and flexibility of Telestreet's technical apparatus that makes it powerful. For now, suffice it to say that the project's key modus operandi is *interconnection,* not standardization—and that the social and geographical spaces in which Telestreet activists work constitute the milieu for the concretization of its technical apparatus.

Despite its resistance to homogenization, Telestreet only achieves interconnection because certain features of the transmission system are standardized so that its components can clinch and its properties can be relayed.

SQUATTED AIRWAVES, HACKED TRANSMISSION · 119

I see the standardization in the codecs (short for coding-decoding or compression-decompression) and container formats on the page of each video stored in the NGVision database. Codecs—such as MPEG or DivX— are protocols that standardize the encoding and decoding of the signal and digital data streams as well as the compression of images. Codecs enable video to be uploaded and downloaded regardless of the speed of an internet connection (Mackenzie 2008, 48). Like many other protocols, codecs are usually invisible and only appear when something does not work. A few times, when I tried to play a video, I got the error message declaring that something was missing and needed to be installed—it was the codec . . .

On NGVision, container formats like .avi or .ogg package what is compressed into video or audio formats and make it shareable though various media players. Without shared codecs and formats, video could not be edited or played back on computers with different capacities and software. NGVision's codecs and formats were chosen to enable the broadest spectrum of technologies to read and broadcast video content, preferably using free and open-source software (F/OSS). They are a veritable means to connect the "organs" of a technical individual. So Telestreet's aim is inclusive connectivity. None of the nodes has an interest in forcing users into proprietary formats. The use of these open standards, free software, and public domain technologies concretizes a technical object that is open and interconnective.

As a technical object, the codec itself is individuated through intellectual property struggles and cultural practices like conventions of spectatorship, embodied cognition, and media-historical forms. For codecs to be developed effectively, physical variables—screen dimensions, resolution and color models, network features, the clock rates and memory sizes of the semiconductor, and data storage technologies—need to be considered. Behind Telestreet's television apparatus lies the connective force of codecs, which transmit light, color, and sound on screens calibrated to send psychoperceptual stimuli to the audience (Mackenzie 2008, 54). At this small perceptual scale, a connection is established between the bits of information compressed and decompressed through software and perception. One *enjoys* a Telestreet video on TV in their kitchen because these interconnected components broadcast it to the senses and one is able to appreciate how different it is from what screens on commercial channels.

NGVision was a key element of the Telestreet ensemble until the birth of YouTube and Vimeo. The archive was hosted by Isole nella Rete (Island in the Net), an independent service for the anonymous, autonomous, and not-for-profit hosting of websites, email, and mailing lists born out of the Europe-wide collaboration of cultural associations, social centers, activist groups, and independent cultural producers from the late eighties on.[3] NGVision was created as a peer-to-peer (P2P) platform for sharing video on the internet. It is an open, and open-source, platform for all independent media producers whose work is antiracist, antifascist, and antisexist.

At the technical level, P2P systems, made famous by applications like Napster and BitTorrent, provide a kind of distributed architecture that divides tasks and workload among peers connected in a network where each node has the same relevance.[4] These peers share resources like bandwidth, disk space, and processing power, and make them available to others in an autonomous, decentralized manner, without having to rely on external servers and hosts. P2P sharing cuts costs and facilitates exchange and collaboration among the different nodes of the network in countries with slow and limited internet access. It also makes it difficult for authorities to control the distribution of content.

At the time of its launch, around 2002, the NGVision platform was the gateway to sharing material that could not circulate in the mainstream media controlled by Berlusconi: for example, footage of Carlo Giuliani being shot dead by police at the G8 Summit in Genoa. Because of its properties—its distributed P2P system, its low cost, its information transfer efficiency despite scarce bandwidth, and its open publishing policy—it was incorporated in the Telestreet transmission ensemble. It is thanks to NGVision that Telestreet could function as a countrywide network until other video platforms and faster internet connections became available.[5] In this sense, the network is composed not only of its channels but also of more subterranean distributed networks of (machinic) peers that concretize the transmission system and, for many years, made it possible.

The composition through P2P networks also locates Telestreet within a larger, transnational milieu of hackers and activists bending technology to their social struggle needs. Indeed, some Telestreet events were not simply meetings among local community television stations talking about content production and organization but also supported the discussion and experimentation with available and to-be-developed technologies. People in attendance came from the old guard of 1977 autonomist and free radio activism as much as from hacklabs and the new cyberpunk techno-art, VJing, and rave scenes of the social centers. When I attended the national convention of Eterea II in March 2004, I met tactical media practitioners coming from the Netherlands, Irish lawyers working on the Italian Creative Commons licenses, and media activists with ties to Latin America. At Eterea II, Telestreet was a site of experimentation for new technologies and patches, a project through which to implement practices and tools already developed as well as a place to connect and circulate technical knowledge. The Telestreettari often attended hackmeetings and presented their hacks (interview with Pog, 2008). In this sense, the Telestreet network is deeply entangled not just with social movements but also with hacker culture through a sharing of its infrastructure and a set of skills and attitudes that Gabriella Coleman calls craft and craftiness (2013, 2016).

Telestreet's craftiness—its ability to think outside the box and its willingness to push the limits of technology in pursuit of craft, often beyond instrumentality—has old roots in the hacker milieu as much as in the free radio movement. These roots tie the bending of transmission systems to experiments like the ephemeral television station boicoopTV. In 1998 boicoopTV broadcast the first Italian hackmeeting, asking residents to oppose its imminent eviction from the square where it was taking place (Ludovico 2003). Between 1997 and 1999, closed-circuit television (CCTV) cameras were also set up by video artists at the CSOA Forte Prenestino in Rome to create a TV station during the Overdose Fiction Festival. From the festival, CandidaTV was born—a collective of video artists that joined and supported the Telestreet network and whose members were involved in developing NGVision (Trocchi 2004). Similarly, the adoption of the copyleft Creative Commons license, an alternative system of intellectual property inspired by the GNU licensing of open-source code, also reinforces this connection.[6] The legal implications of intellectual property were often on the agenda of hackmeetings, resulting in the creation of the Italian chapter of Creative Commons, which media producers used and promoted in the NGVision and Telestreet networks. Creative Commons made the legal noncommercial sharing and reediting of broadcast content uploaded on NGVision possible while holding accountable the mainstream media that stole Telestreet footage.

Again, the properties of Telestreet's receiver-antenna-turned-transmitter, the other repurposed technologies, refurbished machinery, and ad hoc software solutions are not those originally intended at the time of fabrication and are concretized in an ensemble within a milieu that is not simply technological but is also shaped by economic forces (e.g., costs), cultural forces (e.g., open source), and social forces (e.g., uses of technology). Such a heterogeneous and DIY ensemble is essential for street televisions, even though its glitches caused many to shut down for good. This ensemble keeps the technical in tension with its environment, ready to be reconfigured according to needs. The process of hacking and tinkering itself is an important one because it creates points of connection between the technical and the psychosocial. Many of Telestreet's transmission systems were procured, assembled, and operated exclusively through the volunteer work of family, friends, and comrades with available hardware and expertise in transmission systems, programming, and electronics. They were a labor of love and friendship. The *antennista* (antenna repair person) from Naples who fixed insu^tv's antenna and the naval shipyard workers who donated the antenna's pole were never Telestreettari per se but were part of a milieu where the discourses on and desire for community media with a self-assembled transmission machine made individuation possible at the collective level. Energy and information transduce through the circuits of Telestreet's DIY assemblage in many ways.

Finally, thanks to a series of international events, Telestreet shared its experience and assisted with the setup of street television channels in countries ranging from postwar Bosnia and Palestine to Argentina, adapting the project to local needs. Some nodes were also part of Transmission .cc, a transnational network of citizen journalists, video makers, artists, researchers, F/OSS programmers, and web producers developing and distributing tools for media democracy and social justice. Networks like Transmission.cc are important spaces where technology is folded into activism. In its reticular interconnection to technologies and spaces, Telestreet created the conditions for further becomings outside its immediate network.

The milieu of individuation of Telestreet's transmission system constantly varied as new ad hoc solutions were developed. An unexpected recomposition was required when Disco Volante TV's contributors and their national and international supporters fought together to reopen the channel closed by the communication authorities.[7] In the year and a half while Disco Volante TV's transmitter was seized, its members and allies continued to produce material, which was then distributed through the web and through local DVD delivery in the community. This configuration expands the very meaning of signal transmission from one of sole technological circuits to a sociotechnical one of a different kind.

The creative recomposition of Disco Volante TV emphasizes the inextricable link of technical individuation with the collectivities it is tied to. It is also a reminder that institutional regulations partake in the individuation of technical objects and concretize the technical properties of the components of an ensemble. For this small node in Senigallia, policy and legislation were also a contested terrain to continue to exist. After a hard-fought campaign, on May 10, 2005, the charges of illegal broadcasting were finally dropped. The judge recognized that "because of its very small broadcasting range, Disco Volante TV does not require a license. This is due to the fact that using a shadow cone in the airwaves, the channel does not create any interferences with other broadcasters or signals."[8] Although this victory did not regulate Telestreet's status as a small-range media transmission system, Disco Volante TV's case legitimized the existence of the network, with its technical solutions, on the basis of Article 21 of the Italian constitution. The article regulates freedom of speech and Disco Volante was able to claim the right to use the language of television to communicate: "There cannot be a democratic place where citizens are not allowed to use a language they can speak" (Disco Volante TV 2003). For Disco Volante TV's lawyer, the language of TV has become a readily available tool for creativity and expression for everyone. The vernacular television language that they can speak through their low-wattage transmission and distribution apparatus stands outside the norm of broadcasting and contributes to distinguishing Telestreet's mediality from mainstream television.

Telestreet's transmission system also has an important environmental component: without shadow cones, the low transmission frequency of DIY transmitters would not have had the power to send images, or would have been shut down by authorities for infringing broadcasting regulations.[9] Shadow cones are the CSOAs of the airwaves. As is the case for psychosocial individuation, the individuation of a technical ensemble is transductive: transformations seep from the small components to the larger sociotechnical assemblage. Shadow cones function as milieus where individuation transduces from the technical to the social. For instance, the shadow cone of OrfeoTv, broadcasting on the frequency of popular music channel MTV, roughly covered the surface of Orfeo Street in Bologna. Here, OrfeoTv's open storefront window beckoned people to stop by, to bring their own videos, and to co-produce, tinker, or simply have a chat. As content was pieced together in its studios, on the street (Janković 2004;

Figure 3. The storefront of Telestreet node OrfeoTv in the historical center of Bologna.

Pelizza 2006), and in collaborations with other groups (Luppichini and Metallo 2008; Angrisano 2011a), the technical stayed concrete because the individual and the collective emerged with it.

I find it difficult to consider Telestreet as a static object of study once all this movement and transformation comes to light. Both the humans and the technical objects in the milieu that generates Telestreet are not constituted individuals but phases in a process of individuation that involves a variety of human, social, and technical actors. All these instances of individuation are concerned with the transformation of modes of existence that seed further transformation. As I describe how technical individuation is neither exclusively technical nor completely social but transduces from one to the other, the technical/social dichotomy breaks down. Information circulates equally across the human and the machine, seeding sensory stimulation and transformation. There is continuity between the hacking and repurposing of technology and the airwaves, and the hacking and repurposing of sociality and collectivity to resist governmental control. I will say more about this in the following chapters.

Telestreet as Community Television: Individuation and Resistance

On a TV set in the early twenty-first century, one of the squatted Telestreet frequencies aired the images and sounds of an election campaign that did not involve Silvio Berlusconi. A series of small-scale political debates had made their way into the phosphorescent cathode tubes of many of the houses in the town of Gaeta, in central Italy. The creator of this street TV channel—TeleMonteOrlandoTV (TMOtv)—Antonio Ciano, claims to be the father of Italian pirate television (interview with Ciano, 2008). He started transmission in 2001, before OrfeoTv set up the official Telestreet network in Bologna in 2002. Ciano immediately joined in and enthusiastically supported a series of institutional attempts to legalize the project with the help of some left-wing members of parliament.[10] I interviewed Ciano in the summer of 2008 shortly after he had won a number of seats in the local council, with his southern Italian federalist party Partito del Sud (Party of the South). For someone like me, investigating the political strengths and radical potential of Telestreet, Ciano's wannabe-Berlusconi attitude was baffling.

His failure in the 2001 local elections led Ciano to set up his own television channel. He described to me how in seven years with TMOtv, which often broadcasts his as well as others' political speeches, the Party of the South strengthened its roots in the town and eventually earned seats in the local administration (interview with Ciano, 2008). This seemingly parallel trajectory of Berlusconi and Ciano had initially led me to search for commonalities in the mediality of their campaigns, but while equating Ciano's modest electoral success story to Berlusconi's (and there are certainly some similarities!), I almost lost sight of some important differences between the two types of media and media moguls. These differences are not differences in the degrees of perfection of mediatized politics; they are differences in the kind of relations between media producers, viewers, and the television assemblage. In other words, they are qualitative differences that pertain to mediality and to the circulation of affects between the technical, the social, and the somatic.

Researching the function of modulation in a transmission system refocused my attention on these crucial differences. Modulation refers to the process used to carry a signal through a frequency wave. In the field of telecommunications and signal processing, frequency modulation (FM) enables the encoding of information in a carrier wave by varying the instantaneous frequency of the wave. In the case of Telestreet, one deals with ultra high frequency (UHF) radio waves in the range between 300 MHz and 3 GHz, and this encoding allows information to circulate through the transmission system and reach its audience, where the decoding makes the images and sounds intelligible to the human senses. Other forms of modulation are also at play in Telestreet's transmission system, for instance during the compression and decompression of digital images and sounds through the codecs as well as in the coding and decoding of information uploaded and downloaded through a modem (literally a modulator-demodulator). But modulation is also key on the human side of the Telestreet assemblage, in the context of individuation, where it underscores the process that gives shape to—or informs—life and beings (Simondon 1964).[11]

In this sense, there is continuity between technological processes of transformation and those in living beings: according to Simondon, modulation allows information and/or energy to come in and out of a system; energy, which is continuous and unorganized, goes through this system and is organized according to the information that also goes through the same system (Miyazaki 2015, 221). I think of radio wave transmission, digital file circulation, the movement between analog and digital formats, *and* human perception as processes of modulation that are ongoing and that couple together many of the components of the Telestreet assemblage. *Individuals are modulated* through successive individuations as the equilibrium of their system is altered and reestablished at various levels of the larger system by sorting out the information received. An energetics of movements considers this aspect of modulation because it drives composition and recomposition on multiple scales.

When I watch—or, rather, what I perceive as an *I* watching—Ciano on television, the stimuli reaching my senses are amplified and resonate between my interiority (the preindividual) and the (transindividual) milieu where signs, symbols of popular culture, discourses on the economy, and social norms circulate. However, my body is constantly immersed in a chaotic flow of simultaneous stimuli, and only some of these stimuli end up producing individuations. This is because the resonance and interference of potentials that preexist "me" when I watch Ciano's political speech *modulate* what will fade before unfolding and what will turn into affects that are felt as an effect (Massumi 2015, 108). The preshaped relation to TV watching, mediality, plays out here differently than when watching Berlusconi. The drama of potential is where affect is tied to modulation and plays out unfelt until bodily reactions and then emotions surface: the scene feels "uncanny," I feel bafflement, I rationalize by searching for differences, I think of how the political show of this DIY mini–media tycoon reminds me of Berlusconi, I make sense of the kinds and qualities of these differences in the absence of spectacular sensory overstimulation, perhaps I turn off the TV, perhaps I walk to their studio, perhaps I write this chapter. . . . The signals and stimuli coming from street television broadcasting modulate affective orientations that produce different kinds of resonances and reactions to television viewing. Rather than immersing a subject into hyperabundant streams of disjointed stimuli typical of the spectacle, the Telestreet broadcasting station modulates a qualitative transformation of the personal relationship to television—an affinity of sorts, bringing television back into the everyday lives of viewers.

In general, I have engaged the medium already before, and independently of, my perception of Ciano's content (Grusin 2010). TMOtv's transmissions reorganize the relation of viewers to television as a medium because they involve the perceptual habits that precede a viewer's engagement with the content of each show. The reinvention of the idiom and practices of television making independently from the models available in the mainstream challenges the audience's habits of everyday media use. Unlike the United States, Canada, and many European countries, Italy does not have community television or open channels, where the gap between the world represented and the reality of the viewers' lives is less perceivable than in professional, mainstream TV. Among the many street television channels, TMOtv came closest to fulfilling the function of community television.[12]

For this reason, it is not surprising that Ciano hoped to legalize the status of his channel and of the network. As part of a nonprofit and volunteer-run community medium, TMOtv members and collaborators were proud supporters and animators of Gaeta's cultural and political life. They produced interviews with fellow Gaetani as well as with the numerous tourists visiting the city and its beaches. TMOtv carried out weekly studies of local food prices; it broadcast local sports tournaments, cultural events, and council meetings. TMOtv also ran live political and cultural debates with politicians and intellectuals on issues that directly affected the area. Like many community television stations, the channel provided its audience with media-making skills, wherever there was interest. Ciano was adamant that they were followed on TV by 60 percent of the population,

128 · SQUATTED AIRWAVES, HACKED TRANSMISSION

which sustained the channel through donations and had often supported it during moments of crisis (interview with Ciano, 2008).

It may be true that Ciano had created his own voters like Berlusconi did, but he did it by harnessing the mediality of street television within the context of Gaeta's local community, its vernacular language, and its desire for different relations to the medium of television. Community TV challenges the unified representation of members of a culture and provides citizens with a voice in the media (Rodríguez 2001; Howley 2010). The stimuli associated with the (production and) consumption of images in community TV stir affective reactions that are modulated, for example, through the resonances between notions and feelings of belonging and recognition, and discourses on membership in a local community, something Italians are otherwise not used to encountering in the glamour of their everyday television watching. Channels like TMOtv were able to affect those who encountered them through individuations that jostle the collective affectivity mobilized by a spectacular mode of publicity that is shared across the country, replacing it with a connection to the televisual medium that taps into the producers' and viewers' personal relation to Gaeta's everyday life. This model of community television that TMOtv pursued is different from the Italian mainstream media; still, it shares with it a fundamental binary separation between producers and viewers, albeit with more openness to input and audience participation. This is community street television as quasi-proxi-vision, one could say.

From Modulation to Connection beyond Community Television

Other Telestreet channels, in fact most of them, also worked outside the mediality of community media, troubling its production processes and positioning of the producers toward the audience. The work of Disco Volante TV exemplifies this altogether different kind of media making—one that, in addition to using a very DIY aesthetics, also centers subjects who would otherwise never appear on television. The Telestreet node Disco Volante TV—flying saucer— was set up in 2003 mainly by people with various disabilities to connect with fellow citizens through programs that focus on local social issues and events, broadcasting documentaries and reportage but also local fairs and cooking recipes. Especially in Italy, where very little if any space is ever opened to different bodies and neurodiverse individuals,

Disco Volante's productions redefined who are suitable people to produce content and appear on the screen in a position of authority. The presence of these self-defined "aliens on a flying saucer" troubles the ableist character of both mainstream and community media; it collapsed dominant assumptions about the abilities of individuals with Down syndrome or paraplegia. My own first encounter with Disco Volante TV producers at work in their studios shattered in a single blow my habituated relation to television making and watching. Disco Volante was also the host of Eterea II, moderating discussions and documenting the event. Especially in this context, it is important to stress that this project was not about taking action for the disabled but about the self-determination of people with disabilities.

My reaction to Disco Volante TV was caused by the short-circuiting of a complex set of background assumptions and relations to the medium of television rather than simply by the content of the program I watched during my visit, an episode of *Barriere* (Barriers). *Barriere* undoes everything I was used to when watching television and is the result of its producers' intellectual interest in experimenting with the purpose and language of television, as my conversation with Disco Volante's editor in chief Franco Civelli confirmed. *Barriere,* a television series written and presented by Civelli, examines architectural barriers for wheelchairs in Senigallia. Civelli, himself suffering from motor and speech disabilities, attempts to move through the town, struggling to cross bridges, enter buildings, or find a suitable public washroom. Civelli presents a jarring account of his experience as a city dweller and television producer who strives to break down both architectural and communicational barriers. His stories use a personal voice that never takes the victim role and adopt simple solutions like paper headlines and abrupt transitions between clips.

Barriere's style is unconventional: in a home-movie-like approach that rejects the polish of mainstream journalism, it presents a new, personal point of view. The language recognizes that television "is unavoidably biased because of the limited way it can frame reality" (Disco Volante TV 2004). *Barriere*'s aesthetic and linguistic choices construct a shared reality that has yet to attain collective existence at the intersection between content and everyday viewing practices. Its production strategies and cultural recoding have effects that go beyond representation, breaking down established television conventions and cultural production codes.[13] *Barriere* affects in a way that is not different from other forms of media experimentation, most notably in the arts, where cinema modulates viewing and perceptual habits, rearticulating lived experience (Deleuze 1986). Still, when the experimental register is brought into the television genre, the effect is amplified.

The *expressions* that challenge dominant codes and perceptual habits cannot be reduced to an unexpected, mediated encounter with a disabled person's perspective. I read the work of Disco Volante TV and other channels with a comparable approach as challenging aesthetic norms and, through that, perceptual habits. The low horizon of a film shot from a wheelchair, the movement of a camera held by someone who moves differently, modulates a kind of free-floating sensibility that is not simply attributable to the encounter with the subject in the video (Shaviro 2010, 5). I relate this conscious attempt at expanding the narrative and aesthetic possibilities of the medium with a tradition of Italian experimental and underground media art. The work of Alberto Grifi, one of the foremost Italian experimental video artists, was often referenced during Telestreet's meeting in Senigallia. At the same time, Telestreet is directly linked to media experiments like the installation *Minimal TV* by a group of Tuscan video artists working in the mid-1990s. *Minimal TV* deconstructed the medium of television through performances that exposed television's hidden mechanisms, changing the programming according to the viewers' wishes and broadcasting to a small group of households using local cable TV (Ludovico 2003).

In addition to pushing TV outside its genre and coded, standardized aesthetics, Disco Volante TV was able to establish a relationship with Senigallia's inhabitants and with the authorities, using productions like *Barriere* to catalyze social events and develop templates for architectonic accessibility in the town (Renzi 2006). Once this relationship with politicians attracted the attention of the mainstream media, the Disco Volante TV team quickly ascended the Olympus of mainstream journalism, collecting national awards and broadcasting on satellite. *Barriere* received the prestigious national Ilaria Alpi award for journalism.

Nevertheless, Disco Volante's explicit rejection of mainstream media's canons is more than visible in an exchange between Franco Civelli and the Ilaria Alpi award ceremony host, who, handing him the plaque, asked him whether his bias as a person with disabilities got in the way of objectivity.[14] This rejection has nothing to do with a need to adapt to the constraints of low-budget, grassroots media making: as Civelli disavowed any claims to objectivity, he was careful to underline that individual points of view are favored in his work as a way of finding value in diversity and heterogeneity. At the same time, Civelli underscored Disco Volante's vision of television language as a tool to communicate within and outside its community, without claiming a privileged position for the producer over the audience and without needing to produce spectacular content to retain viewers.

Disco Volante TV's presence in the community, the use of TV to bring about change in the town, and its battle for survival when its transmitter was seized tell a different story about television, even as a local, community medium.[15] The work of Disco Volante TV laid the ground for new aesthetic language, genres, and making and viewing practices, engendering new compositions of bodies and technology—veritable systems for the circulation and modulation of information and energy. These practices of media making that create the conditions for new individuations are a source of resistance to governmental control because the individual and collective emerge through resonance between the personal and its environment, through aesthetic experiences that target the sensorium, unleash affective reactions, and then produce emotional responses. Affect is what triggers the ongoing reconfigurations, yet affect is not the content of what is transmitted through the broadcasting system; rather, it creates an exchange between individuals and media technologies that is distinct but not separable from the information exchanged in the interaction (Grusin 2010, 114). Modulation regulates the circulation of information and affects across systems—it connects from the technical to the collective through the sensory. Crucially, affect always escapes complete capture and its surplus remains as potential for resonance. This is one of the ways energy transfers and cross-pollinates movements.

Processes of individuation are subtle, pervasive, and, undeniably, facilitate insidious forms of control precisely because of how diffuse they are across multiple scales of psychosocial reality. The work of channels like TMOtv and Disco Volante TV is an example of how the modulation of affect is not just a process harnessed in order to govern populations top down through the mainstream media but also one where collective actors can hack into the circuit breakers of affective circulation and trigger individuations that resist governmentality. Many Telestreet nodes harnessed a sense of familiarity, interactivity, and participation when their transmissions tapped into a discursive field of street television, community, and locality, as well as opposition to Berlusconi. This hacking of the relationship between media and perception cannot take place without an intervention into the arrangement of the components and into the concretization of technical systems—modularity, interconnection, and inclusive connectivity instead of standardization and gatekeeping—that circulate affects and reshape the mediality of television. Technological experimentation, software development, and tinkering with hardware are fundamental and yet the notion of hacking, here, includes both practices of technical tinkering and the reorganization of the collective relation to media. *Craftiness* shines on more than one level.

The practice of repurposing media is built on the fusion of craft and craftiness, functioning as a driving force in the hacked sociotechnical assemblages that take on consistency as they *connect* different media ensembles, individuals, and groups. Telestreet's resistance becomes more meaningful as one recognizes its ability to hack into television as a medium and shape an environment wherein precognitive and noncognitive stimuli trigger different individuations. When hacking the senses, Telestreet's activists hack into "common sense," understood as the shared meanings, languages, and practices that connect audiences to television's content and mediality. From here, it is possible to expand on how the recomposition of (socio)technical systems fosters certain activist assemblages, types of repurposing, and practices of connective activism. The case of the longest-standing Telestreet node, insu^tv in Naples, will be the site to flesh out my provocation.

6

Subjectivity, Therapy, Compositionality in the Porous Spaces of Naples

Each generation must discover its mission, fulfill it or betray it, in relative opacity.

—Frantz Fanon, *The Wretched of the Earth*

In the unique localities and temporalities of insu^tv's Naples, I encounter a minor history of resistance within a minor history of Italian movements: a *minor minor* history with something that is hard to put to words but that goes back centuries and feeds the coming together of groups. It feeds their falling apart too. This something, at times ephemeral or nebulous, is not just a thing between a *we* or an *us (our thing)* but also the very thing that allows a movement to take shape and reshape. It is that which creates or breaks the social fabric, connecting groups with each other, providing distance and closeness, empathy, solidarity, and indifference. It makes friend, comrade, and frenemy in the face of adversity.

I can find no better word for this something than *porosity*—the porosity between groups that makes the difference between a crowd and an assemblage. This is a term already embedded in the history of Naples. Walter Benjamin described the informality of the city and creative make-do mentality of the Neapolitans as a kind of porosity, where adaptability (not a choice but a necessity) allows for new, unforeseen constellations. Benjamin observes that in Naples, "the stamp of the definitive is avoided. No situation appears intended forever. . . . Porosity results . . . from the passion for improvisation, which demands that space and opportunity be preserved at any price. . . . Porosity is the inexhaustible law of life in this city, reappearing everywhere" (Benjamin [1924] 1978, 171). In the contingency that Benjamin describes, anyone familiar with Naples can recognize not only the tumultuous character of the fabric of the city but also the constant awareness of time and space that Neapolitans have developed to navigate it.[1] This awareness is environmental—it keeps one tuned into the milieu of changing potentialities. This awareness is embodied because it is sensorial, only perceivable at the level of affective exchanges, functioning as vectors of individuations of people and collectivities in an environment teeming with energies that thrust people and things toward each other and then apart. The intensities make the social and spatial boundaries porous—like the spaces Benjamin describes. The activist field also reflects this. Alliances between groups form and dissolve. The assembling and decomposition leave traces that take on intensity elsewhere, carrying the imprint of the past in people and groups.

In Naples, I often hear discussions of *how* groups *could retain porosity* to scale up struggles for social justice. Neapolitans ask as organizers what I also ask as a researcher: What lures us, them, and us again into proximity, making porosity among groups possible? What kind of *compositionality* makes the social fabric political? What keeps groups together in the activist field, or what forms of connective activism could do so? There is value in considering the becoming of groups in relation to each other, as the *I* keeps connecting to the world; there is value for theory and for practice. Sometimes, focusing on the relation between groups is even more insightful than examining what happens between one specific group and constituted power because it reveals how the psychosociality of the activist is itself a terrain for organizing and building momentum.

As I relay here the tales of my *compagni*, I traverse the political past and present of the city of Naples, following for a while its restless movement that constantly recomposes and layers the city's spaces and temporalities, porously. Insu^tv is possibly the longest-living Telestreet channel, outliving the network by many years. Its longevity is the outcome of its having made media that brings groups closer to each other, to engender new capacities. Over the decades, historical, economic, and social changes in Naples have led to different approaches to the effort of retaining porosity, from inquiries into new terrains of struggle to the creation of spaces to come together, from yearly festivals to periodic conventions that network groups, from coordination bodies for grassroots groups to psychosocial therapy through media production. This may not be unique but it stands out in the history I have encountered.

In this context, the expression "activist field" is not entirely apt to describe a system of microrelations that forms the basis of political interaction because an activist field, as it is traditionally thought of, constitutes a collection of groups that mobilize on the basis of a stable identity. Porosity is produced by ongoing microsensorial and microsocial exchanges that individuate activist groups *and* their field into compositions that are set in motion or changed by staged events and by crises. Identity is only part of what pulls people in the same field of forces. I found out in Naples that what makes the activist field into an assemblage is how groups come into connection with each other (or not) through these microexchanges. Because each group constitutes an extension of the individual/activist (not just the sum of the preconstituted activists), the lines of differentiation in the activist field do not run directly between the individual activists and society but first among activist groups.[2] I propose to think of the activist field, with its microexchanges, embodied awareness of time and space, and different degrees of porosity, as the social body of the activist, to which she relates through a system of values and beliefs that inform her relation to society as a whole.

Porous Pasts

It is March 17, 2001: Naples is hosting the Third Global Forum. There are government representatives from forty countries, multinationals, and other institutional bodies, like the Organization for Economic Cooperation and Development and the World Bank, eager to discuss e-government and electronic security. At the Faculty of Architecture of Federico II University, the autonomous research lab on the third floor of Palazzo Gravina is bustling with students. Since a group of students claimed and upgraded these abandoned rooms in 1995, there has been space for meetings and to study in groups; there is a screening room, a small library, a sound archive, a dark room, and computer labs with video editing suites— something rather hard to come by for the many who cannot afford this expensive technology.[3]

All these years, the TerzoPiano Autogestito (Self-Run Third Floor) has been the training ground for many activists investigating the social and architectural transformations of Naples's urban and industrial spaces. TerzoPiano has filmed hours of videos that document the *inchieste metropolitane* (metropolitan inquiries), barefoot research projects exploring the effects of the shift from industrial to postindustrial economies in Naples, spotting the abandoned spaces in the old industrial areas, and mapping the arrival of migrants who squat them. The results of the inquiries have contributed to the collective and autonomous organization of nonprofit

136 · SUBJECTIVITY, THERAPY, COMPOSITIONALITY IN THE POROUS SPACES OF NAPLES

political and cultural initiatives (debates, screening series, exhibitions, meetings) where not only students but also workers and the unemployed "can study and exchange knowledge autonomously from the official trajectory of education" (TerzoPiano n.d.). TerzoPiano collaborates with social centers, collectives, environmental and housing rights movements, and independent media. On this day in March 2001, some of these students and many of their national and international *compagni* are running the Independent Media Center that covers the Third Global Forum. In previous years, they had experimented with different communication tools, and now they are wielding their cameras like weapons. In a few minutes, they will feed into the projector the footage collected during the clashes with the police that have taken place only three hours earlier. They will screen them in the baroque court of the building. In the audience are journalists from independent and mainstream media waiting to hear what the activists have to say.

Many in the audience have come to this press conference because they contacted the Global Forum authorities through cloned versions of the Organisation for Economic Co-operation and Development (OECD; in Italian, Organizzazione per la Cooperazione e lo Sviluppo Economico [OCSE]) websites. In the spirit of tactical media, the sites look identical to the original but redirect visitors' inquiries to activist groups impersonating the organization (Rete No Global and Network Campano per i Diritti Globali 2001). Aside from a few subtle subversions of the text that present the OECD as protecting the vested interests of multinationals at the expense of developing countries, the websites look legit.

Once discovered, the OECD prank will attract a lot of attention to the protest, while very little is known about the Global Forum event itself. The media activists' mobilizations call out what they see as the Global Forum's uncritical championing of technology and profit, the commodification of life through biotechnologies, and the colonization of the free internet, constantly threatened by multinational consolidation and by repressive measures in the name of security (Rete No Global and Network Campano per i Diritti Globali 2001). The journalists present are interested in what motivates the thirty thousand protesters once again flooding the streets. After Seattle, Prague, Davos, and other contested summits, people seek to understand this new wave of political dissent. As the images of police brutality appear on the giant screen, the journalists film them and transmit them live on the national and international news. The media exposure will force the government to start an investigation into police action—an unforgettable victory but one that will not be repeated at the next big protest.

Months of information campaigns and debates on the Global Forum issues have preceded these events and they successfully brought people together because they used information as a weapon and as a channel for coalition building. Groups came for the info sessions and returned for the organizing assemblies.[4] Now that the forum has ended, media tacticians are supporting those on the street with even more interventions, like a net-strike against the online trading company Fineco to block its financial transactions. The very long line outside the universities' computer labs gives away the low-tech solution: for hours, the volunteers click manually on the browser reload button to bring down the servers hosting Fineco's website. Media attention is directed onto many strategic sites in the rest of the city: *in-fest-azione* (in-fest-action) blocks traffic with allegorical floats about economic globalization down the streets. There is an invasion of a McDonald's with living goats and chickens. The in-fest-action then concludes with an organic food feast outside the fast food store.

I can sense pride and excitement in my friends' voices when, one after the other, they tell me a version of this story. All the members of insu^tv who were in Naples in March 2001 start narrating their media activist initiation story with this event, a moment in time when the sense of purpose and the strength of community were felt vividly. This Global Forum represents a particularly important point in the coagulation of Neapolitan activist groups, and in the growth of media activism. Like similar threshold points, it is a door into the present of social change in the area. The forum etched itself in activist memory for its successes but equally for its police brutality, which foreshadowed the events of Genoa. Neapolitan organizers call the protests at the Global Forum *le quattro giornate* (the four days), harkening back to the historical four days of uprising during World War II, when Neapolitans chased the German army out of the city before the American troops arrived (Rete No Global and Network Campano per i Diritti Globali 2001). In this sense, the Third Global Forum is also a door further into the past, because Naples's activist memory folds in old and new worlds, the multiple histories, cultures, and social realities that make them, the hard struggles for bare survival of a unique part of the country with a history of exploitation, and a strong identity rooted in autonomy and informality.

A Minor Minor History of Struggle

The tales of struggle I hear take me way back into the past. They spin unexpected connections and remind me that Telestreet in Naples is even less about challenging Berlusconi's media empire than it is in other cities hosting Telestreet channels. For Neapolitans, the Berlusconi regime is just the mediatized and spectacular upgrade of the same old story of the looting of public funds and relentless economic accumulation in the hands of the powerful, be they politicians or the Camorra. It is the same old story about those who maintain and even exploit the century-old, widening economic and infrastructural gap between the north and the south of the Italian peninsula. The history of this harbor city—one of the first European metropolises—goes back many centuries, to colonization and revolts, to provide a simple explanation of the structural problems that affect life here.

Despite the often-paralyzing hardships, the more than three million inhabitants densely populating Naples and its outskirts sit on a rich history of creative social and political struggle that informs the becoming of movements more than elsewhere (or at least more visibly). This is a history that does not have a unified narrative and subject but a patchwork of events, sites, and political residues; it is chaotic and peculiar, and it shapes political action in subtle ways. For most observers, the memory of this history is hidden behind the countless tales of crime, stereotypical laziness, criminal inclinations, and picturesque urchin folklore that dramatizes the representations of Naples. However, it is felt by many others as it haunts the old industrial sites and the port, the working-class areas, and the many pockets of informal and black economies. It is also present in what it produced: groups, housing, jobs, and so on. Among the most recent episodes, the networks and actions set up during the cholera epidemic in 1973 and after the devastating earthquake of 1980 not only stand out as exemplary moments but also pave the way for the Third Global Forum struggles and the Faculty of Architecture's TerzoPiano media activist incubator. They are an integral part of insu^tv's genesis.

In a city where no support ever comes from institutional politics, autonomy seems the only possible answer to instigate social change. The unemployed and underemployed—the so-called reserve proletariat—coordinated in the early seventies and eighties, forcing the government to create "socially useful jobs" *(lavori socialmente utili)* and legalize many grassroots interventions that dealt with the cholera and earthquake emergencies (from garbage removal and disinfection to reconstruction). So-called autonomous

SUBJECTIVITY, THERAPY, COMPOSITIONALITY IN THE POROUS SPACES OF NAPLES · **139**

"lists of the unemployed" were created to bypass the patronage system supported by the Christian Democratic Party in power and were used to secure training programs and jobs, without having to go through political back doors (Festa 2003). The groups and committees that emerged in the seventies, especially the Movimento Disoccupati organizzati (MDo, Organized Unemployed Movement), had such strong footing in Naples's various wards that in 1980, within three months of the earthquake, they were able to squat twenty thousand empty dwellings to house the victims, leaving a slow and disorganized government with little else to do than legalize the occupation. In 1986 the City of Naples officially allocated "The Ship Sails" (Le Vele) of Scampia and Secondigliano to the victims of the earthquake. These large brutalist housing projects inspired by Le Corbusier's *unitès d'habitation* in turn have now become the site of more struggles against housing precarity and criminality in an area of social and economic neglect (Festa 2003, 391).[5] When I asked Raro from insu^tv how he first got into politics, he told me he had grown up playing at the housing weekly meetings, which he attended with his parents (interview with Raro, 2008).

I discover more porosity between past and present. Many of those present at the Third Global Forum are tied to or inspired by the work of groups like Movimento Disoccupati organizzati to address these local systemic problems while they also oppose global economic forces. But before I circle back to the climax of the Global Forum, I want to explain how my interviewees try to make sense of the events leading up to it by talking about the trials and errors to foster porosity in the nineties. This is when issues of political subjectivity and social reproduction take center stage in our conversations. The student movements of La Pantera in 1990 and Sabotax in 1994 are two moments they mention because the energy and porosity generated needed to be spread, once the university occupations ended. The restructuring of the economy to immaterial and service-based production, with its changes to the social fabric, had dispersed the potential subjects of struggle, once concentrated in the factory. The new collective actors of the student movement took their work outside schools into the community, looking for the "eruption of subjectivities" of the "new forces" in the style of the seventies' *conricerca* (Armano, Sacchetto, and Wright 2013).

Many felt the need to look once again at the social fabric, searching for points of continuity between different mechanisms and levels of socialization and diffusion of resistant movements (Alquati 1975, 225). Projects like TerzoPiano Autogestito sought to understand the new microconflictual level of everyday struggles, the new targets of such struggles, and the trajectories of communication among struggles in order to channel what had been generated. A new wave of occupations of the social centers provided a kind of an answer to continue building momentum, to articulate new social needs and solidify resistant traditions and behaviors. In these newly occupied spaces, minor histories and new insights flowed into processes of individual and collective self-valorization to sow the seeds for more critical mass in future struggles (Palano 2000).

The question of retaining porosity was, in essence, a question about how to compose a field of collective individuation that supported strong ties among groups. In the new CSOAs like Tien'A'ment (1989), Officina 99 (1991), and the Laboratorio Occupato SKA (1995), groups took up the issues of the redistribution of social wealth and the disengagement from the pressure of labor time through the concept of a guaranteed income. This return to older tools from *autonomia* was the direct outcome of a political analysis of the new territories of struggle in a city where precarity reigned more than in the rest of Italy. It was also an attempt to create new connective energy. For almost a decade, these CSOAs tried to build relationships among their constituents, among each other, and with the surrounding communities, with different degrees of success. In 1998 a three-day forum produced a long document *(il documentone)* mapping out groups in struggle, intervention points, and communities to work with, leading to a series of collaborations and actions in support of migrants, the unemployed, and people on the verge of homelessness, especially the elderly. The document aimed to "rebuild the political subject in relation to other subjects" (interview with Sara, 2008).

Piece by piece, and layer by layer, I assemble a collective narrative and an analysis of the ripening and difficulties of a movement (of movements) that, by 2001, not only counted thousands of sympathizers in the streets but also welcomed an unrivalled number of participants in the organization of events and activities—with coordination assemblies bringing up to one thousand people in one room at a time. In addition to the spread of the global justice movement, a diffused sense of disillusionment with the center-left government of the city contributed to this growth because the election of progressive mayor Antonio Bassolino in 1993 had slowly eroded what was left of the formal and informal models of welfare precariously sustaining much of the local population (Festa 2003, 394). The struggle against neoliberalism brought into conversation unlikely allies—

from Catholic groups against debt to the Disobbedienti, from unions to fair trade associations—that were able to use consensus-based deliberation to organize large protests and campaigns (Andretta 2005).[6]

The impasse following the Third Global Forum and the G8 in Genoa became a new moment that called for a reflection and reorientation. As Alfio eloquently puts it: "When the connective energy dissipates, Naples discovers its own fragmentation, the deep-rooted social divisions. The city is described as porous due to its historical and urban characteristics but also, especially, when there is enough energy for processes of connection. Without that energy, all that is left are the different forms of geographical and social confinement" (interview with Alfio, 2008). New emphasis needed to be placed on coordinating different groups while preserving their autonomy and heterogeneity, something that had yet to prove sustainable outside sporadic moments of catalysis around specific events. Porosity is always messy and slippery because, at the microlevel, it is spurred by the energy that feeds collective individuations. How does one intervene in these complex, multilayered, tiny interactions? For some, porosity needed to be fostered by reshaping the relations and exchanges between groups. They went looking for ideas in unexpected places.

Near Colonialism, Porosity, and Political Consciousness

Antonio Gramsci called the set of problems affecting the south of the Italian peninsula *la questione meridionale* (the southern question), referring to the striking economic and social disparity between north and south. Gramsci's popular analysis has framed the political economic account of the impoverishment of the south in postunification Italy (Gramsci 1995). I grew up in Naples and am familiar with this reality and its description. Still, I was not quite surprised when, in more than one conversation, people told me that, instead of Gramsci, they read Frantz Fanon's *The Wretched of the Earth* to understand social problems in Naples. The struggle for social equality in this part of the country has resembled one of liberation from distant occupying powers that deplete the area of resources, exploit the labor force in sweatshops and in risky criminal activities, pollute the environment, and swap services for votes and favors.[7] It is Fanon's insights into the colonized mentality that attracted my friends' attention.[8]

Fanon maintained that psychiatry is socially constructed and therefore plays a role in controlling populations. This position led him to denounce

142 · SUBJECTIVITY, THERAPY, COMPOSITIONALITY IN THE POROUS SPACES OF NAPLES

psychiatric institutions as part of a colonialist system that fosters a false sense of self, overdetermined by the experience of colonization. The Martiniquan psychiatrist studied how French colonial powers in Algeria shaped the value systems of the colonized and how this influence shaped in turn the very same strategies that resist colonization, especially in the cultural realm. For Fanon, the psychological blockages and dependency on the oppressor typical of the colonized complex produce either negative or positive identifications with the oppressor, and therefore, assimilation or self-isolation become the only two possible outcomes of the same kind of alienation (Fanon 2004, 15–17, 51). Ultimately, Fanon's work not only underlines how colonial hegemonic forces inflect counterhegemonic practices but also emphasizes the need to escape this vicious circle through conscious efforts to retain or reshape the value systems and social models that affect the emergence of subjectivities.

Fanon was certainly not writing for white activists in a near-colonial context, but *The Wretched of the Earth*'s focus on the psychosocial dimension of resistance helps many Neapolitans understand how the relations among disadvantaged groups—from migrants to the unemployed in the southern regions—sustain the economic and cultural gaps between the two areas of the peninsula. The colonized complex Fanon identifies, where one internalizes the inferior and/or criminal image and identity molded for her by more powerful others, has its analogue in Naples, where the southerner's genetic and cultural makeup—hot-bloodedness, laziness, and cultural backwardness—is flagged as the root cause for social problems in the country.[9] Centuries of discrimination and stereotyping lead the exploited southern Italian to "suffer" from low self-esteem, which prevents many from working toward self-determination.

Under the neoliberal conditions of diffused precarity, the near-colonial mentality of the southern Italian doubles up at the intersection of old imposed identities and neoliberal individuation that trumps collective agency and depoliticizes the gap between the haves and have-nots. This double articulation of identity is not lost on those who are trying to make sense of a changing field of struggle: neoliberal discourses celebrate individualistic entrepreneurship and, in case of crisis, reroute the causes of failure onto the individual: they fragment the social fabric. In one of our conversations at insu^tv, Alfio reminded me that, for example, the 2008 financial crash was often blamed on the greed of buyers rather than on the banking and financial systems that financed their debts. At the same time, the institutional and governmental classifications regulating migrants and refugees worked in tandem with the mainstream media panics, spreading fear about ethnic, racial, and social others to seed isolation (interview with Alfio, 2008). Migrants and southerners (migrants themselves in the north of the country) easily become the scapegoats of both politicians and fellow Italians at times of high unemployment and austerity programs. At these times, when groups are pitched against each other, the intersection of the near-colonial and neoliberal vectors of individuation intensifies the isolation and fragmentation.

Francesco, an activist at the CSOA SKA, also uses Fanon to explain the degree of resistance against cultural enslavement and the level of opposition to the value system that is imposed by what he describes as colonial powers (Festa 2008). Whether one agrees with the accuracy of its framing, the analysis leads to calls for sustained attention to the "porousness of political conscience" (Festa 2008) that can cut across sclerotic forms of resistant subjectivities to engender autonomous practices of self-determination for groups that include the unemployed and underemployed, the migrants (who often come from former, real colonies), but also others. A porous political conscience for Francesco means that it is subject to constant re-shaping along external cultural, symbolic, and social, as much as economic, forces. So, when it comes to scaling up against old and new forms of control, some activist groups in Naples not only consider the relations between the powerful and the oppressed but also and especially how subjectivity shapes the relations among dissenting groups. For many migrant and local activists, including those at insu^tv, social cohesion must be rooted in the agency that comes out of self-awareness, and in the *porosity* between groups. Fanon in Naples reveals attempts to update autonomist theories about self-valorization and subjectification that are still too focused on labor and the factory in a new reality where the vectors of oppression are much more intersectional. The Neapolitan readings of Fanon also reveal the almost invisible strategic importance of *transindividuation* that gives shapes to the political fabric of society.

In connection with this thinking and its attendant experiments, the capillary work of unemployment lists, grassroots committees, and social centers is not merely a strategy to organize on the territory but is also the outcome of the mobilization of different social meanings through embodied practices that attempt to gain agency by developing and sharing resources and knowledge that speak to a collective porous conscience. Moreover, if protests

144 · SUBJECTIVITY, THERAPY, COMPOSITIONALITY IN THE POROUS SPACES OF NAPLES

and convergences are moments of eruption around which groups temporarily can come together in consensus (Andretta 2005), it is the social-therapeutic experiments of activist camping holidays and other cultural events like the yearly movement festival Adunata Sediziosa that strive to retain a diffused porosity by attending to friendship and intimacy.[10] This is by no means always successful but it is an ongoing effort that takes different forms at different times. Around these readings, collaborations, inquiries, friendships, and conflicts, the activist field constantly recomposes its shapes through microexchanges that forge and retain connections.

Local Media and Psychosocial Therapy in the Gray Zone

To say that organizing among groups always ran smoothly even during the planning of the Global Forum and other events would not only be false but would also be counterproductive for anyone who sees self-critique as a necessary political practice. As is often the case, contentious elements in the discussion and organization of the event included the divergent attitudes toward direct action and ritualized violence, which required considerable negotiations (Andretta 2005). In Naples, the conflict was encapsulated in the debate over the communication strategies and the logo of the social forum: Pulcinella, a traditional Neapolitan *commedia dell'arte* character wearing a gas mask and wielding a baton. For many civic associations and independent trade unions, the aggressive connotation of the image did not reflect the attitudes and strategies they were about to take to the streets. Conversely, the choice of a spokesperson for the unified movement to convey its message to the mainstream clashed with radical principles of horizontality and self-representation at the basis of many organizations involved (Festa 2003, 399).[11]

The coordination of large events was successful enough to offer a considerable degree of shared understanding and contamination among diverse groups, which was hard to retain when translating an ephemeral collective identity into more localized strategic directions. Between 2001 and 2003, much of the porosity holding the Neapolitan movement together started dissipating. The events of 9/11 unleashed a wave of repression that exacerbated the burnout that many already felt after the Third Global Forum, the G8 in Genoa, and the demonstrations against the Iraq war. The distance among groups that had been bridged grew again. With the connective energy gone, the illusion of having come closer to creating functional

SUBJECTIVITY, THERAPY, COMPOSITIONALITY IN THE POROUS SPACES OF NAPLES · 145

internal and network dynamics for collective struggle also disappeared. Even the more radical, autonomist groups distanced themselves from each other as the "*area antagonista*" revealed old fractures and opened new cracks. It is probably easier to grasp the friction between social centers, associations, NGOs, and unions than the fractures among autonomist groups. Steve Wright (2007) wisely quipped that, although the different theoretical positions among autonomist Marxist frameworks may be reflected in the Italian movement itself, anyone with personal experience will find this only an imperfect explanation.[12] Félix Guattari and Antonio Negri (1990, 91) have pointed out that any process of recomposition also carries dogmatic and sectarian elements from old stratifications, which threaten collaboration from inside and complicate the articulation between immediacy and mediation, tactics and strategies established through multilateral and practical relations.

In any dissenting formation, beyond political hard lines there are flows of energy that run deeper because the sense of belonging to a group is a dimension of an individual's personality. This means that what makes up a group is an assemblage of individual tendencies, instincts, beliefs, meanings, and expressions—what I call here *personality*—and that affect the emergence of a group itself, much in the same way individual beings are engendered. If the sense of belonging is still tied to affects and discourses that cannot be recognized in the "new" group, a "crisis" of belonging ensues and conflict can grow. To tackle these blockages, Félix Guattari and Franco Berardi call for practices that set in motion new, unforeseen a-signifying chains that were previously hindered by established meanings, obsessions, social and linguistic norms, and "communicative double binds that generated neuroses and the pressure to repeat" (Berardi 2008, 131; see also Guattari 1995, 70–71). Enter media activism again.

Starting from the mid-1990s, debates on the use value of communication and experiments with media had been frequent and emboldened by the contribution of La Pantera and Sabotax. In Naples, various radio projects, magazines, and newspapers like the internationalist magazine *Blue Line* (1997) and the independent press sheet *Infoaut—Agenzia di comunicazione antagonista* (2000–2001) (Infoaut—Antagonistic communication agency) had appeared on the scene. If the Global Forum itself was not so important on the international map of global meetings, its successful use of electronic disturbance tactics and independent media reporting had indeed raised awareness about the city and its problems: "All in all we created the event, betting on this chance to give Naples and its contradictions the center of attention for a few days, as Seattle and the global justice movement had done elsewhere before us" (anonymous activist, qtd. in Festa 2003, 408).

Despite its successes, for the activists organizing the forum, media activism was a tool for information circulation rather than a mode of struggle per se. Radical movements often see cultural activism and even media activism as collateral activities that support more "serious" forms of organizing. For this reason, there was hardly any debate about how media activism could be a political practice in its own right; some even felt that it could be a trap for militants.[13] As Indymedia Italia was set up in September 2001, in Naples, members of TerzoPiano and other media activist groups started a sustained reflection and coordination of media work in the city.

Many believed that it was critical for a project of social change that truly addresses the needs of the local groups to develop inclusive practices of participation because groups were scattered around the territory and only became visible during moments of contestation like the Global Forum. What's more, the inclusive practices had to center around communication: "There was a desire to leave the extreme left discursive ghetto and set up a web of relations that could harness the heterogeneous groups emerging from the recomposed social tissue of the area" (interview with Alfio, 2008). In other words, the kind of social therapy required to retain porosity could build on more creative uses of media (interview with Sandro, 2008; interview with Wadada, 2008). Many of my *compagni* tell me about their conscious search for media tools and strategies to harness the energy generated during catalyst events and retain porosity. Each in their own way was captivated by the potential of grassroots media for new forms of political work.

When OrfeoTv in Bologna published the Telestreet manifesto and called for a meeting, a few from Naples drove up and came back inspired by an idea that upgraded the joyful experimentation of Radio Alice to contemporary means of mass communication—television and the internet.[14] For Aurelia, also thrilling was the ability to use her work skills as a media maker for politics (interview with Aurelia, 2008). Pog too thrived on bringing his hacker skills to the repertoire of political practices when he joined insu^tv, initially to switch the transmission system to Linux (interview with Pog, 2008). It was not hard to find kindred spirits to start the experiment in Naples, though at the beginning it was harder to recruit women among them.

Soon after the initial success of Indymedia Italia, it became clear to many Neapolitan media activists that the internet was insufficient as a channel for independent communication to reach different strata of society, separated by a considerable digital divide, especially in the poorer south— online communication alone cannot foster porosity. Various newspapers, the IMC-affiliated pirate radio station Radiolina, and insu^tv were born in 2003, as attention moved to the needs of local groups.[15] Both insu^tv and Radiolina shared the same antenna and workspace and were part of Media Indipendenti Napoletani (MINA, Independent Neapolitan Media)—a coalition of autonomous media collectives pushing for a more local approach to media activism, one that would be adopted by Indymedia Italia after its "reflection pause." Local media could use more accessible language and technology to reach a wider audience that was not computer literate and was outside the restricted circle of activists.

Most members of insu^tv had been involved in the mobilizations for the Global Forum and Genoa in 2001 and had previously been part of other cultural production projects like the TerzoPiano, *Blue Line,* some free radios, and the IMC. For them, opening up communication to those who did not identify with the radical language or practices of the movement was one of the reasons they gravitated toward the Telestreet model. Some also described a "gray zone" of the movement where people decided "not to decide" whether to be part of one group or the other (interview with Sara, 2008; interview with Wadada, 2008). For them, it made no sense to go back to before the connective experiments of the Third Global Forum, which they considered successful. The soon-to-be members of insu^tv (insulini) were interested in the communicational and social therapeutic potential of media activism—one that had been present in projects like Radio Alice—that was encapsulated in the Telestreet model of proxy-vision and that had also been theorized by Guattari in his work on postmedia.[16] This model offers the reference points for individuations and microexchanges that are less conducive to a crisis of belonging.

Compositionality and Collective Individuation

In the late eighties and early nineties, the introduction of new technologies, especially computers and the Minitel, had inspired Félix Guattari (2012) to imagine an era when the interactivity afforded by media could resubjectivize enslaved and docile mass media audiences. Guattari was interested in how the creative engagement with media multiplied processes of subjectification, which were otherwise fixed by capitalist media's subjective modelization and by traditional psychoanalytic models.

Even though they never met, Fanon and Guattari shared a training in materialist psychiatry with Jacques Lacan, Jean Oury, and François Tosquelles. They both denounced the role of psychiatry as a tool for governmentality (Greedharry 2008, 112). Moreover, Guattari's (1995) therapeutic practices reject the role of language, typical of traditional approaches to subjectivation, and focus on aesthetics and ethics instead.[17] For Guattari, affect reaches into the interiority of the individual—the preindividual level constituted in life lived, social experience, and microexchanges— during esthetic encounters that can take place in connection with autonomous media experiments. The insights of Fanon and Guattari, and the autonomist tradition of media experimentations and antagonist social reproduction I discussed in previous chapters, inspire and inform the media production work of insu^tv. This work can be seen as part of a project of liberation first and foremost from subjugated subjectivities and fossilized political identities. It cuts through the diffused (and often unarticulated) memory and awareness of time and space in Naples; it is directed at images of inferiority and articulations of agency that connect isolated individual struggles but also at the expression of a porous collective subjectivity that finds strength in its ability to entangle groups. In general, art and other aesthetic practices are conducive for this kind of work (Guattari 1996, 106), but for insu^tv, it is the video cameras and transmission system and the environment they can shape that defuse the tension between bodies and produce the energy for collective individuations.

It is no coincidence that the first experiments with insu^tv were based in places with a strong history of struggle outside the social centers: the roofs of the Ship Sails of Scampia, with the support of the Coordinamento lotta per la casa (Committee for Housing Rights), and in the old historic district of Forcella. In these spaces, the camera guided territorial inquiries into "the needs of the neighborhood," literally taking the camera and boom mic into the houses and small alleyways to ask how one lives in Forcella or how one wishes to improve Scampia (Wadada, qtd. in Stein 2016). In these places, cameras usually hide the face of a journalist scooping the drama of Camorra casualties—they swoop in and never return.

Those at insu^tv quickly became familiar faces, trusted because they created events to bring neighbors together in laughter and dreams: "We went into the houses to do an interview and then tuned their TV to our channel, telling them when they would be on. . . . Through word of mouth we became quite popular. . . . People loved our shorts and spoof ads because they were funny" (Sandro, qtd. in Stein 2016).

During its first couple of years of existence, insu^tv built methods and *"momenti di condivisione,"* moments of sharing—through making, finding each other on the TV screen, and watching together at open-air screenings—moments that foster collective individuation: becoming together by sharing.[18] The fun aspect of it was not just a therapeutic and easily relatable way of communicating with an audience but also an important aspect of connecting with each other as media makers (interview with Aurelia, 2008; interview with Pog, 2008). The humor set this kind of work apart from that of militant organizing, which all too often is based on self-sacrifice, gravity, and inward-looking language. It was easy to see the impact of this kind of media making on the groups collaborating with insu^tv (interview with Pog, 2008). Humor, of course, but also joyful experimentation can be more successful ways of bringing groups together across social and political divides. They can be psychosocially therapeutic, and in this sense political. The extraparliamentary left of Naples recognized the value of the work of insu^tv, which ended up with its studios at the CSOA Officina 99, chronicling different events and struggles for years to come.

There are specific processes that undergird collective individuation that are somewhat counterintuitive but are key to understanding the formation of critical masses beyond allyship and coalition building (which of course are crucial in movements). Overall, individuals feel integrated in the social whenever their social individuation does not conflict with their personal individuation because an individual's system of beliefs is not necessarily always structured, even if it underlies interaction. The system of beliefs is not structured as long as there is no need to consciously articulate a sense of belonging to the group. This means that, although it is one of the ways one tends to make sense of groups, the articulation of political beliefs and identities among activists is the manifestation of a moment of "crisis" rather than the basis of an activist group's emergence and persistence. *Crisis* here is a neutral term that refers to a moment of intensity in which something begins to take place as a response to an event, in certain cases resulting in

150 · SUBJECTIVITY, THERAPY, COMPOSITIONALITY IN THE POROUS SPACES OF NAPLES

the feeling of not belonging. As a system of relations that mediates between the individual and the city at large, the Neapolitan activist field presupposes a passage through smaller groups of reference/identification, the different activist and community groups—NGOs, various autonomist projects based in social centers, local neighborhood and community associations, migrants coalescing around cultural cooperatives, organized workers and unemployed coordination committees, Cobas, unions, and so on.[19] Porosity is present in situations where individual beliefs (opinions) and collective beliefs (myths) that characterize the group (and relate it to the outside) can circulate while the activist who has to structure and define her belonging to the group can do so in a way that is intelligible to the out-group (Simondon 2006, 171–75). In the case of internal conflict like the discussion of a diversity of tactics, the individual has to redraw the line between in- and out-group.

A psychosocial therapy model for porosity depends on the ability to restrict or extend the boundaries between the in-group and the out-group while still allowing productive encounters—for instance, it is about the ability to come into composition by repurposing media making. The individual tendencies, instincts, beliefs, meanings, and expressions (the personalities) that make up the group can come together through the desire to experiment with media more easily than when debating political positions. In this sense, as a psychosocial therapeutic experiment, insu^tv is not a solution to smooth protest organizing but a project that fosters a culture of porosity and socializes different kinds of social reproduction that preexist and support recomposition. This is not a totalizing process nor an all-encompassing solution but a way of tending to the activist field. At times, this kind of work offers an opportunity to support or accompany the valorization of subjectivities that happens in other activist spaces like the CSOAs.

From a strategic perspective, this model for porosity is about *compositionality*—the semi-intentional orientation of heterogeneous groups in an effort to scale up social struggle by emboldening intercommunication and co-individuation. Compositionality in the activist field deals not so much with an arrangement of established relations (as in the case of alliances between groups) but with the ability of different groups to come together in a porous way. Compositionality *as a strategy* is the conscious, social therapeutic practice of creating or retaining porosity among groups. To look at the process of becoming of groups and the exchanges that are enabled among them means to consider the individual and her group as in tension with the environment (not as terms in relation to each other), and to work from that tension through an ethico-aesthetic approach to media making.[20]

The work of Fanon and Guattari pointed to alternative approaches to therapy that experiment with processes of subjectification, away from hardened reference structures (which cause psychic impasses such as paranoid group subjectivity): "the invention of new analytic nuclei capable of bifurcating existence" (Guattari 1995, 18). As I joined the team, the ins and outs of this therapeutic model became visible and the contours of a practice of connective activism, not only among individuals but also among groups, more compelling.

7

Insu^tv, Media Connective

> We are a media connective, not a collective.
>
> —Nicol* Angrisano, motto of insu^tv

I am driving through the central station zone, or at least this is what Neapolitans once called it. This overcrowded crisscross of trains, bus terminals, stores, and vendor stalls now goes by Chinatown. The area morphed fast and furiously, with Naples's port stocking more than three million tons of legal and illegal, mainly Chinese, merchandise that then spreads throughout Europe (Saviano 2007, 7). Most shops here are now Chinese-owned and they are surrounded by street markets where the rest of the migrant population makes their daily ends meet. Surveys estimate at least 120,000 to 130,000 documented migrant workers have settled in Naples (Direzione Generale dell'Immigrazione e delle Politiche di Integrazione del Ministero del Lavoro e delle Politiche Sociali n.d.). Naples and its province host 56.4 percent of the entire migrant population of southern Italy because of its location, the services and businesses available, the work opportunities, and the port and the railway that connect to other parts of the country. One in four migrant workers lives in Naples, and they have transformed its social and economic fabric.[1]

On this particular evening in 2007, I am driving to meet up with insu^tv—this motley, friendly crew of social workers, teachers, designers, doctors, architects, journalists, researchers, tinkerers, media makers, and students with a background in political organizing. We have a planning meeting, but with the vendors and shoppers gone, the eeriness of the area disorients me. I stop my car to ask a sex worker if she knows how to get to the CSOA Officina 99 in the industrial area behind the station. "Of course honey, I'll take you there if you drop me off to work. I'm Anna." During the brief drive, Anna talks about her life as a trans woman in the area but I am left to wonder why she knows the kids from the social center. When we get close to Officina, her clients are waiting impatiently and we have no time left to chat.

The CSOA Officina 99 has not changed much since it was squatted when I was in my late teens. The building crumbles, the ceiling leaks, and even though the city council has entrusted the large building to the activists who run it, no one has enough money to maintain it. Nevertheless, for almost three decades, the youth of Naples have congregated in this old industrial structure dancing to the tunes of 99 Posse and other indie bands in the crowded concert hall, discussing politics and culture at meetings and performances, recording music, programming free and open-source software (F/OSS) in the hacklabs, or sharing food and wine on the massive roof terrace. Many friendships, loves, and alliances were shaped or broken in the graffiti-tagged rooms of Officina 99. One could write almost thirty years of Neapolitan activism history by peeling off the layers of colorful posters and flyers that cover many of these rooms.

Some things I notice are different: there are the TV headquarters with a control room, a large space for live events, a music recording studio for bands, a radio studio, and an open kitchen for collective cooking. Cables network everything, so that when other groups are not using the facilities, creative television making has free rein. The control room piles up all sorts of technology, DIY rigs, refurbished PCs, digital cameras, mixers, and so on. I notice what is on air from the monitors: children talking about their ideal neighborhood. The shaky camera tells me it is probably the product of a workshop in a school. On the PC screen, I see how Soma, the media player I heard so much about, automates the programming through a system accessible 24/7 from outside the studios.

Insu^tv's Pog, together with a hacker from Milan and a Greek exchange student, cleaned up the mess of clunky proprietary players from the refurbished computers and brought the transmission system into the twenty-first century of F/OSS during a hot, beachless summer. Originally Soma operated pirate radios and the team proudly showcased the results of the crafty mod at a hackmeeting in Palermo (interview with Pog, 2008). Apart from not relying on proprietary software, and having made the broadcasting system much more reliable and efficient, Soma also offers the possibility of inserting a message crawl at the bottom of the screen. This is how viewers learn about upcoming events and find the information to contact insu^tv staff. Radiolina, the local radio transmitting from Officina 99, also uses the same platform to broadcast its radio shows remotely.

On Officina's roof, the tall antenna irradiates insu^tv and Radiolina waves into east Naples. Over the years, insu^tv developed relations with broadcasting specialists for technical support and many local commercial TV channels and pirate radios have also donated surplus technology.[2] The Cooperativa Megaride built two very tall antenna poles for insu^tv using sailing boat masts. The donation acknowledged the media activists' support after they documented the workers' successful occupation of a shipyard that led to a takeover of their reckless boss's bankrupt business. Now, with this broadcasting system beaming a signal of quality as good as any other local channel, insu^tv offers its transmissions to thousands of viewers in the central and eastern areas of the city. Because Naples has the highest population density on the Italian peninsula (21,586.3/square mile), this microbroadcaster potentially reaches more viewers than any other channel in the Telestreet network. Indeed, for many in the audience, it "looks good" but the insulini—or like the neighbors call them, "the television people"—are still surprised when they are stopped in the street and complimented. With so much on their plates from the production side, they have little time to wonder about the size of their audience. Some insulini do not even get the signal in their homes and have never watched the programs from the comfort of their sofa.

As I spend more time at Officina, I realize that it is not only the physical place that has changed. On a random afternoon, I open the door to *signora* Franca, a middle-aged lady who has come to bring us cake (and wants to help clean the place!). Franca and many of her friends live in the neighborhood and have become comfortable with the social center during a wave of protests against a proposed dumping site in an old tobacco factory around the corner. People from Officina were involved in the protests, and the squat became a meeting place for the neighborhood. Some of the residents still come here after they celebrated their victory against the dumpsite plans. I sense the difference since Officina's golden age, when the Neapolitan youth flocked to its overcrowded events from all parts of Italy but the social center struggled to root itself in the neighborhood. Now, the events no longer pack a crowd because newer social centers are easier to reach. At the same time, Officina has won the trust of many in the neighborhood, who appear more comfortable frequenting the place.

Some of the neighbors show up at a cinema downtown to watch the videos on gender freedom in which they also starred. We are showing a series of shorts during Maygay, a festival on gender and sexuality insu^tv has co-curated.[3] This is one of the many public events that expands and solidifies the ties between groups that met when producing media. The audience of insu^tv find each other in public. In the DIY TV studios, at the meetings, on the streets, and at the public events, the insu^tv community and its members, including myself, become together while they meet and participate. The interactions that drive this becoming mature in the collaborative media making and in the repurposing of technologies, of familiar languages and television formats. Through the practices described below, repurposing facilitates myriad psychosocial connections that are therapeutic and inform an ethical attitude that gives the project its political force.

Domenica Aut: Connection Machine

Locals come to Officina to be a live audience for the TV shows, especially *Domenica Aut* (Sunday out). *Domenica Aut,* insu^tv's most popular format, is a talk show that takes place on a Sunday, usually once a month or every two months, depending on the other projects running simultaneously. The show involves studio guests, video features, live entertainment, and theme cooking of food to share with guests and audience. For those familiar with Italian popular culture, the title itself already points to the idea behind the show. *Domenica In* (Sunday in) is a mainstream Sunday afternoon show that, since time immemorial, has kept entire families glued to the screen with music, dance, games, and comedy (and a lot of *veline* [a certain kind of showgirl] in bikini). Insu^tv's show is about a Sunday *out* but also about *aut*onomous Sundays (and no bikini unless it takes place on the beach).

Domenica Aut repurposes a familiar format, with some of its tropes and symbols, to create a space for unfamiliar encounters among participants. The show is an occasion to carry out new inquiries, to investigate and discuss the problems plaguing local communities. As people come together they become more than just an audience. Unlike a TV audience, where the viewing experience is mostly isolated, the participatory character of *Domenica Aut* sets up an environment where individuals and groups become familiar with the technical process, share ideas, and experience the show in relation to one another. In some cases, the collaborations also kick-start new initiatives that address what has emerged during the inquiry.

Sitting on the benches of Officina at an episode kick-off meeting, pizza and pen in hand, the insulini choose the episode's topic: this time we are looking at the effects of new antidrug legislation on the local territory. We research the threads that lead into the local communities and establish contact with key stakeholders to define a point of view and collectively produce the show: there are drug users, lawyers, legalization advocates, public health specialists, centers for addiction and mental health, possibly a drug dealer, and chocolate—lots of it—for the in-studio chef. The next meeting is with some of the stakeholders to decide how to structure the show, what to give priority to, whom to invite as experts in the studio, what to cook, how to execute the interviews and minidocumentaries, and so on. This episode will become *In^sostanza*—a pun on the word *in substance*, which, in Italian, can mean both "in the drug" and "in essence." A couple of months later I will be involved in planning "Onda su onda" (Wave upon wave), an episode on/with the Anomalous Wave, the 2009 student movement opposing the reform and privatization of the education system. "Onda su onda" will be produced together with the Neapolitan students organizing the protests (insu^tv 2009b).

During my first weekly meeting at insu^tv, I also find out that Anna knows Officina because of a *Domenica Aut* episode on sexual freedom. The episode involved, among other things, a series of inquiries about and interviews with local sex workers. The members of insu^tv who drove around on the mobile clinic with nurses and social workers had used the night visits to popular cruising sites to chat with the sex workers. They invited Anna and her colleagues to participate in the show and to come to a screening of *Mater Natura* (Andrei 2004), a local independent movie on transgendered people. The interactions had established enough confidence that, on the night of the screening, Anna and a few others even brought a copy of another movie that a French filmmaker had made about them, contributing to the programming.

For insu^tv, *Domenica Aut* is "the first television show that invites you to turn the television off" (insu^tv n.d.). This two- to four-hour-long program asks you to leave the house, meet the groups involved in the production of the show, and come to the studios to "enjoy the *smells,* and *warmth* of television" (insu^tv n.d.). Smells and warmth: the choice of words could not be more unusual and at the same time spot-on to describe the multisensorial relations that inhabit the studios during a show. The cooking, the music, the mock ads and short videos that liven up the breaks, the heated discussions among audiences and experts, the relaxed environment: all contribute to a unique sensory experience of television. In this environment, one easily finds a member of the audience rolling up cables, holding a boom mic, or chopping tomatoes.

In a media environment where closed industry standards and protocols govern most chains of signification, *Domenica Aut*'s openness to experiment with alternative visual languages and with the terms of engagement of media making fundamentally reframes the function of television. Crucial for this purpose is also the practice of *inchiesta* (inquiry) tied to autonomist tradition of co-research. *Domenica Aut* provides in essence a tool to probe the changing territory—paying attention to forms of conflict, social needs, practices of dissent, and solidarity—using media. The goal of producing a TV show and the twist of involving groups in the process of production add a joyful and fun dimension to an otherwise common militant practice. *Inchiesta* is a collaborative epistemological practice that, while it unfolds, informs the emergence of alternative subjectivities, devising new modes of subjectivation and setting up a web of new connections.

I knew *Domenica Aut* from watching the episode "Citta' e Periferia" (City and suburbia), where insu^tv brings together civic associations working in Scampia, notorious for its high unemployment and criminality and for one of the recent bloodiest Camorra feuds (fictionalized in Matteo Garrone's movie *Gomorrah*). "Citta' e Periferia" explores another face of Scampia in the work of local community art projects like the Gruppo Risveglio dal Sonno (GRIDAS, Awaken from Sleep Group) and Voci di Scampia (Vo. di.Sca, Voices of Scampia). Lounging on green inflatable armchairs with the orange and yellow backdrop of the studio walls, Asterix introduces eighteen-year-old Rosario Esposito La Rossa, author of *Al di là della neve: Storie di Scampia* (Beyond the snow, stories from Scampia) and founder of Vo.di.Sca.[4] Esposito La Rossa recounts his youth in Scampia and his frequent close encounters with death at the hands of the Camorra, and describes the self-run projects that young people are developing to cope with the social trauma and police repression. At the bottom of the screen crawls insu^tv's text with the title of the show and an invitation: "Naples center and periphery: the informal metropolis tells its story—Initial notes from an inquiry into the real city—Scampia through the voices and stories of its inhabitants—To participate, come to Officina 99, Via Gianturco 101" (insu^tv 2006). A video that Vo.di.Sca produced during a workshop with insu^tv follows Esposito La Rossa's interview. Afterward, the audience discusses with GRIDAS how to stimulate social involvement using street art and carnival allegorical floats and masks (GRIDAS n.d.; insu^tv 2006).[5]

Vo.di.Sca's youth had also participated in an *inchiesta*: as they made videos about the area, revealing the mechanisms that govern their lives, they gained a better grasp of what it means to think about solutions.[6] It is no coincidence that autonomist researchers have often framed co-research as a mode of organizing in itself. Moreover, the critical engagement with technology and this collaborative mode of knowledge production facilitate a shift *from product* (counterinformation) *to process* (coproduction). This means that the production-based research supersedes content-driven practices where independent information is one more product to circulate, that is, consume. Insu^tv and its collaborators engage the affective, connective, and creative potential of working together to make sense of issues that directly implicate the groups involved. People who usually do not encounter each other are not only in the videos and on the stage but also in the audience that participates in the debates. With all the different stakeholders, the making of and participation in the episodes of *Domenica Aut* trigger the temporary reconfiguration of group boundaries to their outside. Difference is effaced but it no longer forms the basis of the interaction because the process of making displaces the identity-based posturing of those involved. The mediation of the *inchiesta* via the camera, editing, and viewing screens sets the focus of interaction on the process of collaborative making around issues that directly affect everyone. Thanks to this mediation, groups can interface with each other in a more organic way. My random encounters with Franca and Anna and the planning of *Domenica Aut* confirm what I heard from the *insulini*. Over the years, *Domenica Aut* effectively linked people: *Domenica Aut* is a means, or better a *machine* (Guattari 1995), to engender connections.

In *Domenica Aut,* but also in other activities like the media literacy workshops, the technical objects of media production cease to be hypnotic or an easy source of marvel for the uninitiated. Instead of simply functioning as a tool for the production and circulation of information, technology—once demystified, hacked, and reassembled—entangles individuals and their environment. Anyone who has been behind a camera knows that the experience of filming is not purely visual and that what stands beyond the screen is also *felt* through other senses. Sounds, smells, heat, fear, and excitement, to mention a few, are often part of how an individual perceives her environment through the LCD viewer. In this process of mediation there develops a synergy between a diversity of elements that come together as the affects that ooze from the warmth and smells of filming together clinch across the disparity of information. Then, what only holds potential at the level of the preindividual becomes something felt in

Figure 4. An episode of the live TV show *Domenica Aut* organized with local communities by insu^tv in Toronto, Canada.

the collective. More precisely, the video camera and the other objects for editing and screening propagate a new field of relations and relay the process of individuation between individuals and their transindividual milieu.

The cabled spaces, the transmission technology, the exchanges among the people, the food, and the affects all converge in a process of individuation of the TV channel and broader community outside dominant signifying chains. The chains of significations replace the mainstream media's overstylized, sexualized discourses and images so distant from everyday experiences. In the proxy-visual space of sensorial and bodily mingling, the making together and the watching redefine the role of TV and its studios as a space for conviviality and collective reflection. In this sense, *Domenica Aut* is a theater of collective individuation where technical objects like the cameras and the transmission apparatus literally *mediate* between individuals and their environment—and among groups—instituting and developing a relation; technical objects partake in genuinely creative activities. The *repurposing of technology* is *immanent* to these processes of collective individuation; technological innovation itself cannot be seen as separate from other processes of individuation—and from broader processes of change.

As part of a psychosocial therapeutic approach to collaborative media production, insu^tv repurposes both technical objects, like video cameras or transmission technology, and the autonomist practice of inquiry to break down group boundaries and preestablished modes of communication. Officina's space brings the TV studio closer to home, where the interlocking of technology and sociality, not the TV apparatus alone, creates a machine for connections. The connection machine fosters porosity that seeds transformation in the larger activist field from the smelling, talking, hearing, watching, and tasting by the individual through a collectivity that spills outside the studios. The connection machine runs on *repurposing*— and repurposing as a political strategy to generate energy is in excess of the reuse of technology or the appropriation of televisual language. It functions at a higher level of the system. I am moving across layers and levels of repurposing here, in a transductive manner. More on this soon.

Media Coproduction and Its Reverberations

In July 2010, insu^tv and fellow Media Indipendenti Napoletani (MINA, Neapolitan Independent Media) member Radioazioni supported GRIDAS during a series of protests and initiatives to retain the squatted building that had housed the project for thirty years. The collaborative initiatives that included floats, music, and dancing in public squares convinced the local administration to give in to GRIDAS's demands and grant access to the building. I have seen and heard about these kinds of reverberations from collaborations between insu^tv and other groups often. Some of the stories are indeed very inspiring.

The episode "Citta' e Periferia" could not ignore the presence of immigrants who live so close to Officina 99, especially because, during the production phase, a sudden wave of police repression started targeting the street markets that migrants run near the railway station. With some support from insu^tv, a group of Senegalese migrants was able to produce a video inquiry that identified in a new urban development project the root cause of the crackdown. Within a few weeks, the Senegalese recorded interviews with the *ambulanti* (itinerant street vendors) and drew out unseen connections between the destruction of cultural diversity, the displacement or elimination of businesses with regular permits, and social problems like homelessness and unemployment. The symbolic power of a camera helped the migrants initiate a conversation with the authorities that led to the discovery of plans to gentrify the area. The plans did not include a consultation with the local migrant population, which has been a constant presence for more than fifteen years. The video inquiry screened at a public meeting between three hundred migrants and the authorities and was received by the city council representatives with promises to include the migrant population in the urban planning of the area.

The collaborations with migrants over the years have taken various forms, from media literacy workshops for filming and editing to incorporating them in the stable programming. Both Radiolina and insu^tv have had migrant-run projects, especially news in different languages. After the initial project on the persecution of street vendors, the *TG migranti* (Migrant news) was, for a while, a regular show at insu^tv. Unfortunately, because of fast turnover of the crew (migrants often have to chase work opportunities around the country), this project could not be sustained. Even during the video-editing course I attended with a new group of immigrants, it was clear that it is hard for them to honor their commitment due to their precarious life and work conditions.

For insu^tv, practices of knowledge sharing and training are key, and in some cases, the energy generated during the media literacy workshops has enabled insu^tv production practices to reach a different level of collaboration with groups and communities. These efforts have solidified in the feature-length documentary *Una montagna di balle (Wasting Naples)*. Starting from 2005 (with a *Domenica Aut* episode), insu^tv followed the evolution of the garbage emergency plaguing the Campania region, where Naples is located. By 2008 the seriousness of the crisis had turned the entire area into a worldwide spectacle of monstrous heaps of garbage, equally horrifying Italian and international publics. The source in a nutshell: a fourteen-year-long state of emergency declared to cope with the garbage crisis periodically removed avalanches of waste taking over the streets for months on end instead of addressing the problem in a sustainable way.

The longer version of the story includes the fact that, in addition to this ineffective treatment of legal waste, since 1994, the areas surrounding Naples, Caserta, and Benevento have been the illegal burial ground of toxic waste from the industries in the north of the country. Over and over, independent investigations have pointed to the collusion between the business sector, the government, and the Camorra, but this link is hard to break because low waste disposal costs make production prices low and make small industries competitive transnationally, boosting the Italian economy. Legal and illegal waste has been dumped and buried in hidden, cheap, and unsafe landfills with devastating consequences for the surrounding territory and for the health of the population. The situation is so dire and the incidence of cancer so unprecedented that international science journals discuss the high levels of toxicity in the region with expressions like the "death triangle" (Senior and Mazza 2004).

Overall, the business connected to the management of waste, ranging from transportation and storage to incineration and energy production—which also involve receiving government subsidies—offers such high profit that any sustainable and environmentally friendly alternative has been sidestepped by reckless for-profit policies. However, as garbage turns into a commodity traded in the stock market (insu^tv 2009b), the level of conflict between a desperate local population and the authorities rises. The conflict climaxed in the large mobilizations of 2008–9 only to end with the militarization of areas handling garbage, violent police repression, and the legal prosecution of the protesters. Insu^tv attempted to "open a crack in the official version" about the garbage crisis ("Campania" 2009), through inquiry and media support of the protests.

The crew was able to report on the mobilizations at different sites but also train groups in the more isolated communities to produce their own documentation of the protests that were being silenced. In the summer of 2008, together with MINA, insu^tv ran a twenty-four-hour media center in Chiaiano to cover the ongoing mobilizations. The Chiaiano woods are one of the few green areas in Naples, and its inhabitants had barricaded the entrance to the provincial park to prevent the construction of a landfill. For two full months, the woods in general and the media center in particular became a round-the-clock site of coagulation of many groups involved in the struggle. We were the only source of reliable information available to the citizens, and we were also a place for meeting, strategizing, and socializing. The connections among some groups and people became so strong that, when we were forced to dismantle it, the inhabitants from the area would not let us go without promising to be back.

This bond is emblematic of an entire period of struggle where people, often completely new to organizing, met each other, shared knowledge, and fought against repressive and violent policing. They experimented with alternative forms of governance, like the self-organized recycling site that the population of Gianturco and Officina 99 set up in January 2008 in the old tobacco factory to stop the opening of an urban dumpsite in an already heavily polluted industrial area. Citizens set up new organizations like the regional coordination body for waste management and for the public management of water in an effort to have a voice in the debate (Zanotelli 2009). During these protests, communities became more familiar with activist practices, from sit-ins to culture jamming, and I with the new emergent activist scene, which was meeting in the streets once again. In Naples, garbage became the new battleground; as a new cycle of struggles swelled up, groups involved in other environmental struggles around Italy came to visit and expressed solidarity.[7]

All throughout the crisis, independent media was a key counterpoint to the national news' racist representations of the southern mob. For the Italian brand of environmental racism, the spatial management of garbage in the region is inextricably connected with the special management of people through the localization of dumpsites at the "spatial, economic, social and political margins of society" (Petrillo 2009, 14). The "abnormalization" of the population in popular culture and in the media is the oil that makes the governmental machine run smoothly. Superstition, violent inclinations, restlessness, self-destructive drives, pointless revolts with no political claims, irrational aggression, and rage are the basis of current stereotypes and assumptions about the south in the same way they were in the past (18–19).[8] The process of categorization and division that applies to the *terrone*—the dirty southerner—and the migrant alike easily becomes a discursive component of governmental assemblages that solidify during crises to justify the call for a state of emergency. These assumptions combined with more modern claims about the Not in My Backyard (NIMBY) syndrome engender a formidable discursive field that leaves no space to critique destructive political decisions.[9] In 2008–9 Naples, Frantz Fanon had Michel Foucault as his sidekick in many discussions about the forces and power relations sustaining the conflict. Independent media became the medium to tell this story.

In fact, it was very easy to deny the political validity of the work of all the committees and associations whenever politicians and media could mobilize these near-colonial racial discourses about the south to point behind the protest to "natural" effects of a sort of pathology, as well as to the archaism and potential criminal motives of the protesters. I heard these explanations every time I was away from the sites of organizing, even from my parents, southerners themselves. For those who participated in the media center, and for those watching its coverage, the construction of the narrative about the crisis cut across dominant binaries between modern incineration technologies and the antimodernity of the protester—but also across the opposition between the rational government and citizen and the irrational revolting masses reappearing from old folkloric tales. The self-portrayal of the communities in resistance was all the more powerful because it was immediate and unmediated: it used Mogulus, one of the first livestreaming technologies, to broadcast to television.[10]

For those who had access to the live feed, Mogulus created an affective link between the viewer and those in the street (Renzi and Langlois 2015; Thorburn 2015). It did not just cover the police brutality; it also broadcast the cultural initiatives and debates taking place at the media-center-turned-TV-studio. Mogulus was also fundamental in providing a shared framework of understanding in a context where the depoliticization of conflict in the mainstream national discourse and the racialization of these protests had had the effect of isolating and pitching one community against the other. Elise Thorburn (2014) has demonstrated how critical use of streaming technologies can engender sociotechnical assemblages that function as nodes of counterpower and provide the space for the construction of subjectivities in the streets. The circulation of alternative forms of knowledge, and the collaborations that started around networks like MINA, aimed to offset these centripetal forces fragmenting the resistant social fabric.

The mobilizations against the garbage crisis had different effects in different parts of the region. In cases like Gianturco, groups were able to stop the government and affirm political subject positions otherwise denied to the protesters by institutional politics (Petrillo 2009, 118). The Italian army brutally suppressed the blockades to defend Chiaiano's woods and many other attempts to protect citizens and environment. In 2009 Prime Minister Berlusconi inaugurated the first of many incinerators planned for the region and imposed an information ban on waste management, turning the waste management into a secret sector of social services.[11] The repression and the construction of an incinerator cleared the streets of angry residents and garbage alike. With the end of the protest cycle, the communities and groups insu^tv had trained came back to insu^tv with more than five hundred hours of footage, asking for a documentary that told that story. This was a turning point for the group and a moment when the connection machine shifted into turbo gear as it experimented with a new model for collaborative documentary production. The method relied on the direct engagement and participation of groups and individuals interested in the production of what became *Una montagna di balle,* or *Wasting Naples.*

Among the techniques used to include groups in the production process was open space technology (OST), which allows scalable self-organizing work among large groups of people to narrow down an initial open agenda to more focused work (Open Space 2016). Though the method mostly serves the corporate world, insu^tv was able to repurpose it with the help of a *compagno* who had received OST training. OST effectively assisted short-term discussion and the decision-making process needed to produce an initial film sketch. After the OST session, the group posted all the material assembled on a blog to build a chronological history of the events and compare the video footage with the texts produced.

The second phase of the production process called upon the same communities for a crowdfunding campaign and soliciting professional contributions for the production of the film: screenwriting, music, research, and so on. Many more people joined insu^tv as producers through the crowdsourcing site Produzioni Dal Basso (Bottom-up Productions). The final cut that insu^tv edited provides an accessible narrative thread in the voice of well-known actor and environmental activist Ascanio Celestini. "Here the state of emergency is another form of government; they should teach it in political science: there is monarchy, tyranny, democracy . . . and emergency!" (insu^tv 2009b), jokes Celestini as he narrates the story of *Wasting Naples.* This seemingly light-hearted joke reveals the question guiding the documentary: "What if 'living in a crisis' was just someone's strategy to make profit?" (insu^tv 2009b). The fairy-tale structure that frames the inquiry into the garbage emergency makes it intelligible to the audience, who would otherwise be overwhelmed by the plethora of reports and interviews with experts, community workers, and those affected.

Despite the fairy-tale trope, with the typical evil characters and heroes that belong to this genre, *Wasting Naples* presents a multilayered analysis of the relationships among government, the media, the eco-mafia, powerful corporations, and poisoned areas, crops, and inhabitants. Beyond its local value, as a connector, *the documentary* brings garbage into a critique of capital, to see where it intersects with other issues. It delivers a map of the relations between the governmental assemblage behind the waste removal economy. Of course, most of the information was already available but no one had brought it all together, not even the judge involved in eco-mafia investigations who, at the cinema premiere, declared (somewhat pompously) to the press that he "will follow up on the evidence presented to the audience" (Chetta 2009).

Upon completion of the documentary, every coproducer who participated in the process received a copy of the film. The distribution process was key to continue tapping into the connective potential of *Wasting Naples* thanks to various steps during which the film circulated around the communities involved and a wider audience in the form of DVDs (or other digital formats), screenings, special events, and online streaming. DVDs and other digital copies were released under the Creative Commons noncommercial license for easy sharing, and on the same day of the release of the documentary one could already find it on popular torrenting sites.

In the grant-writing jargon of insu^tv, the aim of the method used for *Wasting Naples* is to produce a film that "1) Activates co-producers' participation, strengthens internal community ties and involves new individuals outside of the target communities; 2) Gathers the resources necessary for the completion of the film; 3) Instils into everyone involved the feeling that they are an active part of the production process."[12] During the screenings, *Wasting Naples* was used to generate discussions, organize forums, support campaigns, or forge new ties among groups. The insulini participated in public screenings and events organized by third parties both in Italy and abroad. The film, subtitled in multiple languages, screened at film festivals and at cultural institutions. Following two large sold-out cinema premiers, *Wasting Naples* had more than 150,000 views online, nearly 300 public screenings (of which 25 were abroad), and was broadcast on Current TV and Sky Italia satellite channels. A copy was included in the package handed to the European Union special rapporteur leading an independent investigation into the garbage crisis (ami 2010).

Wasting Naples circulated so far and wide because it offered a rare insight into a complex and opaque state of affairs that was made relatable through powerful images of solidarity, determination, and in-depth analysis. It was

168 · INSU^TV, MEDIA CONNECTIVE

also so successful because it had the solid support of the communities involved in its making.

We Are All Nicol* Angrisano:
Co-individuation and Compositionality as Becoming Together

In *Wasting Naples,* the self-representation of the communities proliferates the coproduction process using poetic language to string the stories together. The narration exploits the tension between the loving tone and images of Naples and scenes of police brutality, government neglect, and environmental devastation. Violence and frenzy mark the garbage emergency and yet the police beatings, expropriations, and army incursions do not drown the voices that speak directly to the viewer. Even though the film aims to expose the reasons for the crisis and break the silence about the opposition to local waste management, the documentary also celebrates the strength of the population challenging a de facto occupying army and talking back to the mainstream media racist representation of the southerner.

In the months of production and postproduction, I witnessed the individuation of *a* collectivity unfold in the larger milieu of the garbage crisis. The process was not merely narrative and discursive but embodied, transindividual, and *mediated* by the documentary assemblage (its technology as well as production methods). The connections among groups became more porous as people encountered and recognized each other at the workshops, filmed on the street, attended the OST event, contributed to and donated to the crowdsourcing campaign, turned up at the premiere, and hosted events and debates. In this context, the production of the *we* in Celestini's fairy-tale-esque narration transformed *Wasting Naples* into a choral narration that spilled out of the screen. The support and networking of the documentary contributed to its narrative, kept the energy high, and encouraged the sense of being part of something. This ongoing individuation stretched across groups rather than within a larger group.

The bio of Nicola Angrisano, the collective pseudonym used to name the director of insu^tv, nods to this process.

nicol* angrisano broke into the mediascape one day in 2003. This mysterious and charismatic character perpetrates guerrilla communication actions to free the infosphere. nicol*'s stomping grounds are the Neapolitan airwaves. In 2004, leading a group of media activists, s/he powered the first transmitter, sending an interference signal, cracking the monotonous and smooth surface of the mediascape. This is how insu^tv was born: a Neapolitan pirate television broadcasting in a shadow cone of the S19/UHF frequency. For five years, insu^tv has been exploring the surrounding territory, and together with various social movements it inquires into and traverses different experiences. During the production of the documentary *Wasting Naples,* on the local garbage crisis, nicol* has been contaminated by the experience of the communities hit by the events, thereby reinforcing the assemblage of affinity groups and individuals involved in direct narration of reality. nicol* angrisano stands for a multiplicity of visions and perspectives, it is a hybrid form: it uses a lowercase letter because s/he refuses the concept of authorship; s/he takes the asterisk to inflect for all genders. Nicol*'s is a collective—a connective—identity of a group of media activists radically searching for different reading cues to transform simple narrations into tools of struggle and liberation from the yoke of mainstream disinformation. (Toronto Free Broadcasting 2009)[13]

Insu^tv chose the collective pseudonym nicol* angrisano in 2003 in the artistic and activist tradition of nom de plumes like Monty Catsin and Luther Blisset. In particular, the Luther Blisset Project that started in Bologna in 1994 and spread to various cities spawning a series of pranks, radio shows, and publications critiquing and embarrassing the mainstream media for five years was very much on insu^tv's founders' minds when they started the pirate TV (Alfio, qtd. in Stein 2016). As Marco Deseriis discusses in his study of Luther Blisset, the choice aimed "to obfuscate both the identity and number of referents"; it connected activists to a historical knowledge of struggles and enabled them to fold that knowledge into contemporary tactics (2015, 3).

Deseriis defines names like Luther Blisset as *improper* in the sense that they are not attributable to a circumscribed domain and therefore do not facilitate a process of subjectification based on the proliferation of difference. Instead, improper names mediate processes of subjectification as users recognize each other in the name and their heterogeneous utterances and actions are brought into the same discursive space. Furthermore, Deseriis traces a shuttling between heterogeneity and homogeneity, totality and difference. Improper names express this shuttling when they function as a milieu where the singular and the multiple, the individual and the collective engender each other in the process of sharing an identity (Deseriis 2015, 3–4). The nicol* angrisano bio recounts an origin tale in fantastic actions and heroic deeds—breaking into an enclosed mediascape, doing guerrilla to free the infosphere, finding allies, etcetera. This framing contributes to mythmaking and lends symbolic power to those who claim nicol*'s deeds and productions.

At insu^tv, each of us has been Nicol or Nicola, to attend screenings, curate events, give lectures, make movies. There were even a few perfectly delirious moments where nicol* angrisano achieved the impossible— being a multiplicity granted the gift of ubiquity. Nicol* was in many cities and countries at once. Nicol*'s event profile pictures were always ambiguous; the hotel check-ins were furtive and hilarious whenever film festivals booked rooms under the award-winning director's name. One time, a distracted scholar even published a study of insu^tv that described the director as a real person. The improper name was a powerful way of becoming together, embodying a tradition of intimacy and media making that traveled through decades of Italian media activism from Radio Alice to tactical media. In the toggling between the individual and the collective the ties became stronger, increasing the potential for new connections. In writing this chapter—or perhaps even this entire book—in fact, the process repeats itself. I write as Nicol, with nicol*, for a Nicola that is always more than the sum of *their* parts.

Deseriis emphasizes how improper names work toward the production of a *common* (Deseriis 2015, 214). And while the improper name's relation to the common enables me to highlight the value of relationality among individuals, the capacity of individuations to transduce across layers of the social outspreads this relationality, through technical objects, to the wider field of transindividuation that occurs around the garbage crisis and projects like *Wasting Naples*. I shift the emphasis now from collective assemblages of a shared alias (that is, relationality among humans) to connective assemblages of collaborative filmmaking to think in terms of connectivity and porosity, or compositionality *that includes technology*. After all, "we are a media connective, not a media collective" *is* nicol*'s favorite political statement.

An Ethics of Connection

As a connective, insu^tv always holds its potential to mutate in interaction with its environment. Each connection with other bodies and objects, each new project, each recombination of elements prompts a new individuation. In essence, the group conceives of its work as creating resonance by giving priority to acts that extend beyond themselves to become contagious—to affect and relay through the pleasure of being and creating together. This approach—a kind of ethical conduct—guides insu^tv's actions, redefining the direction of politics at a moment of stasis in Naples. Insu^tv's ethics considers how every individual act can also *inform* collective becomings to generate critical mass. It evaluates actions and ideas in function of their potential to tap into the sociality of politics to foster social cohesion that is conducive to political action. Importantly, more than a chain of individual acts that are separated and spontaneous, a web of acts nested in the coproduction practices triggers the collective individuations, which can resonate with each other while the activists address social, political, and economic issues. As a system based on difference (rather than identity), the individual is always in precarious (metastable) equilibrium and continuously individuates.

Simondon discusses how accepting and engaging the metastability of certain structures—that include the individual—is at the basis of an ethical comportment toward oneself and others: "Ethics is the sense as well as the direction of individuation, the sense of the synergy among successive individuations" (2006, 229). This approach to ethics as an openness to affect and be affected (Deleuze 1988; Spinoza 1992) is integral to connective activism where the repurposing of media thrives on a desire to come into composition because people are eager to work together on projects that weave their interests and concerns together. Insu^tv's ethical comportment offers some ways of using collaborative media making to break down the signifying chains that rigidify interactions, and that social norms and political ideologies unavoidably crystallize. This is due not simply to discursive practices but to a myriad of affects, perceptions, and memories that impact the openness and closure of systems like groups or individuals, as seen with *Domenica Aut*: "The value of an act is its breadth, its potential to unfold transductively" (Simondon 2006, 230). Insu^tv's set of (changing) engagement practices indissolubly connects the experimentation with social relations to processes of individual and collective individuation.

These practices inform the connection between individuation and politics because it is at this ethical threshold that it becomes possible to *repurpose the social field for politics through media production.* In this sense, I argue that insu^tv repurposes ethics for politics, at a time when politics badly needs to be reinvented.

Metastability is unpredictable, and the last years at insu^tv have posed a challenge to the sustainability of connective activism. As energy circulates, circuits may fry. The question I am now concerned with has to do with what happens when assemblages destabilize and decompose. Can this ethical attitude support recomposition?

8

De/Re/Compositions, in Process

Appropriate the communicative channels in order to talk about other things (and not just anything), modify semiotic production in strategic moments, make care and the invisible networks of mutual support into a lever for subverting dependence, practice "the job well done" as something illicit and contrary to productivity, insist upon the practice of inhabiting, of being, a growing right.

—Precarias a la Deriva, "First Stutterings"

In 2003, Scampia, an area of social marginalization with high symbolic value even before the recent bloody Camorra feud, experienced insu^tv's first transmission. The pay-per-view decryption card that the novice team added to the Telestreet transmission apparatus reconfigured the function of television from the roofs of this troubled landscape, and so it birthed a powerful assemblage. Once more, it was just a simple hack: from the roof of *le vele,* a dystopian social housing shaped like the sails of a flotilla, the test signal beamed a match of home team Napoli FC for free to an ecstatic audience of football fans.[1] Ma.gi.ca TV, soon-to-become insu^tv, seized the break during the match to broadcast its own locally produced content. Ma.gi.ca TV, literally a magic TV, captured the power of *Ma*radona, *Gi*ordano, and *Ca*reca—hero players for the viewers and earthly intercessors between the blissful glamor of the sports entertainment industry and the boundless passion of the local-audience-made-protagonist. Much of the homemade videos transmitted, indeed, placed the inhabitants of the Sails of Scampia at center stage, where they could recount their dreams of public space and football fields for the local kids. From that roof, the makeshift antenna's signal functioned as a conduit—a vector to relay the energy of the pirate television assemblage to its outside (a magic pirate flag, one might say).

The antenna emitted electromagnetic waves connecting bodies and resonating through them. Its signal traversed the inhabitants of Scampia and moved around them, transforming them into components of the transmission circuit (Munster 2014, 153). For Japanese media activist and artist

Tetsuo Kogawa, this is "bodiness," a feeling of presence through interconnection of air and airwaves where "bodies can communicate in the resonance." In bodiness, "resonance does not exchange information but synchronizes between bodies" (Kogawa 1999). This is because communication, for Kogawa, is not about the transfer of information-as-content; it is about "structural coupling" and "emotional resonance" (Kogawa 2000). Communication is about transformations that take place across bodies; it precedes linguistic utterances, and transformations unfolding via the communication of stimuli—that is, information in a Simondonian sense— have indeed to do with energy.

This lingering image sprang to mind many years ago when I read the email on the Telestreet listserv announcing the appearance of Ma.gi.ca TV: an antenna beaming energy, turning the area it reached into an experiment of gatherings. Electromagnetic communication is *energetic* and energetic signals move through transmission in roundabout ways (Barad 2011; Munster 2014). They reach bodies, turning them into transducers for energy that reorganize the field of watching and the meaning of the game. That energy was circulating through the sensory apparatus of the viewers and the pirates. Connecting the bodies to the signal-turned-images-and-sounds gave consistency to the insu^tv assemblage. That signal germinated from seed to expression when it came into contact with attractors like the football match—in so doing, it harnessed the potential energy that can trip *meta*stable arrangements such as the habituated relation to watching football. The signal beaming from Scampia precipitated the possibility of resonance (Massumi 2002, 34, 74).

Energy is what makes matter take form. As this book approaches its end, I call attention to the bodiness, the structural couplings, and the emotional resonances Kogawa describes and insu^tv expresses so well. Again, I draw attention to energy. One cannot think about individuation without considering the energetic potential of a system. Insu^tv morphs as potential energy accumulates and triggers transformations across fields (Scott 2014, 43). Energy is generated in interactions, hacks, collaborations, and signal transmission. Repurposing requires energy. Energy pushes disparate human and technical elements together but also apart. Energy is not always "positive." Energy is implicated in the circulation of stressful psychosocial stimuli as much as in the disaggregation of social formations.[2] There can be surplus energy thrusting in different directions and causing friction and interference. In these last pages I examine the resulting re/de/compositions.

The interventions that produce the political are always contingent and therefore ongoing. For philosopher Alberto Toscano (2012, 92), political formations materialize when the larval presence of divergent energies comes into communication. Telestreet and insu^tv, in all their metastability, gained consistency as many divergent energies flowed into formation around a transmission hack in an environment of media monopoly and technopolitical experimentation. For a long time, as long as they replaced one another on the roofs of Scampia, then Forcella, and then Officina 99, those antennas were relays of energy channeled through the groups involved in the making and watching of pirate television—*Domenica Aut, Wasting Naples,* instant docs, public events, and so on. That energy brought people together and kept them connected, individuating and seeding almost imperceptible transformations. Much of this changed when Italy moved to a digital broadcasting system in 2010 and there were no available airwaves to travel through. As the energy of the activist field started petering out again, after the financial and garbage crises, the social centers of the airwaves were vacated too. Insu^tv had its own ups and downs, its points of stabilization—but especially destabilization. The transmission hack no longer works and insu^tv is reconfiguring, slowly. Its currently lopsided assemblage is pulsing, contracting, and expanding, sending low-intensity signals that travel in roundabout ways; sometimes they do not go far, and sometimes they do.[3] Like the good old electromagnetic waves that are locked out of the Telestreet transmission system, the energy that insu^tv can emit into the world today needs to traverse new technical and social thresholds to take on renewed consistency, perhaps even under a different name.

The Bifurcation of Connective Activism

In January 2010, Italian broadcasting switched from analog to digital, obliterating pirate analog UHF transmission for a viewership newly equipped with digital TV decoders. Never had Italy transitioned more smoothly and efficiently; with Berlusconi pumping out state funds to his cronies to replace the antennas with digital receivers (Fontanarosa 2006), the potential and functioning of insu^tv shifted, equally fast. Insu^tv launched an ambitious project in 2009, energized by the connections forged through its work: Assalto al cielo (Assault on the sky) brought together media and grassroots organizations in and around Naples to rent a digital frequency and set up what would be the first open community channel in the country. This channel would give "voice to the cultural alternatives in the region, to environmental and anti-racist struggles, to bottom up democratic experiments and to social movements" (insu^tv 2010a).

In Campania, the region around Naples, most television frequencies belong to commercial channels—often owned by the Camorra—and grassroots organizations lack legal and affordable access to broadcasting frequencies. Since Italian legislation does not even offer the model for community television, the groups and their lawyers looked into European Union directives on community media and into international examples to build their framework. Assalto was an unprecedented and bold experiment, which, in its connective potentiality, intended to set up and amplify a community of viewers and users for social, cultural, and political projects, and to create a participatory production circuit as well as a participatory structure to guarantee financial sustainability. The project also included a parallel frequency for community radio, drawing on the experience of local free and pirate radios (insu^tv 2010a).

If successful, Assalto could have elevated media activism as a practice of autonomous collaboration to an unprecedented scale. The project scaled up the ideas about connectivity that started insu^tv, which envisioned this community channel as a collective effort rather than the enlargement of insu^tv itself. In that sense, the goal was to shift from a geographical area of neighbors to a deterritorialized community of affinity groups—a daring effort to expand the connective potential of media making (interview with Sandro, 2015). Unfortunately, Assalto did not work out for a series of reasons that the insulini, with hindsight, partly blame on not having recognized the changing field of action, and partly on bad timing. The launch of the project coincided with the climax of the financial crisis, when austerity politics effectively killed or paralyzed many of the organizations in the nonprofit sector that would have been involved. Lack of funding, precariously existing commitments, and even a long stint of bad weather that sabotaged a grand three-day open-air fundraiser put an end to any dream to build a channel that would have needed extensive resources for its programming. During this moment of instability the two directions that had formerly coexisted—the connective documentary and the *Domenica Aut* proxy-vision format—forked.

The documentary *Wasting Naples* was a huge accomplishment but also a colossal effort. The many decisions to make it, the responsibility toward the communities involved, the travel, the interfacing with the world of mainstream media, and the energy poured into Assalto all took their toll on the group. Some members had to move to different cities and countries; some had to take breaks for family reasons, reducing their willpower, enthusiasm, and ultimately their contribution. As new people joined, the dynamics of the group further reconfigured. Above all, the switch to digital broadcasting changed the circulation of energy through the assemblage, the energy it emanated, and the energy that fed it. And change the technological apparatus did, now organized less around spaces like the studios and formats like *Domenica Aut* and more around video distribution networks and online sites. Changing were many of the practices and processes of production. Changing were also the ties between the group and communities. I saw and experienced these changes working with the insulini often remotely on Skype, wikis, shared docs, and email; during the long weekly planning meetings, the grant writing, the editing and event planning; and through the visits and projects in Italy, Canada, and Germany. Such change was not inherently bad but it was certainly not as good as a much-needed rest.

One of the things that had struck me about insu^tv when I joined was that, unlike many other groups I had worked with, there was a generosity and light-heartedness to the activists that made this "work" an extremely pleasurable experience. A joyful attitude cheered insu^tv's meetings and defused friction while still allowing for confrontation and disagreement.[4] "Joy, fun, tears, humanity, a desire for contamination and experimentation"—these are the elements that, as Wadada reminds a podcast audience (Stein 2016), characterized nearly a decade of spontaneist connective activism.

Foucault wrote that one need not be sad to be militant (Deleuze and Guattari [1972] 1983). Insu^tv was a case in point: members' sense of humor and cheerfulness was contagious and made collaborating with others easier. Remembering an old autonomist song from the seventies, "Lavorare con lentezza e leggerezza" (Working slowly and lightly), Asterix once told me, "If this becomes a task, then it will stop working." Sara added, "Insu^tv works because it can die any minute." These beliefs do not suggest a lack of commitment. The commitment is to the possibilities of an assemblage that needs to change once its productive potential is exhausted. Metastability as commitment means that rather than being ready to walk out the door and close it behind, this attitude translates into openness to innovation without seeing mutation and external influence as threats to the insu^tv assemblage.

The insulini examined the causes and potential effects of change in order to make decisions based on functionality, without betraying any personal or collective values. The latter orient the project; they do not define it. Already when I was in Naples in 2007 we organized focus groups and other kinds of reflection inquiries to understand how to grow the assemblage, how to streamline production and innovate technologically. During these self-analyses, we discussed how to better couple the process of collaborative production with recruiting new members, started an investigation of how to incorporate Moglus livestreaming into more of the programming, and brainstormed how to mobilize new available technologies. The idea of Assalto came out of reflections like these.

Of course, when the conditions of existence changed and the internal and external pressure and workload mounted, the joyous attitude dwindled. Until the end of TV broadcasting, interaction centered around the process of collaborative production rather than on the discursive negotiation and articulation of an identity for the group. With the antenna gone, what changed along with the flow of UHF frequencies was also the fact that there was less need to all work on common formats, and parallel projects pulled people in different directions. The molecularization of projects offered less opportunity to partake and share in the satisfaction of a collective final outcome: "The lack of sharing/partaking [*condivisione*] seemed to take away meaning and direction [*senso*] for the group" (interview with Fedina, 2015). More and more conversations about the collective orientation of the group filled the meetings.

As fragmentation returns individuals to themselves, there emerges a need to constantly reproduce the process of collective individuation at the discursive level to make up for the lack of closeness during the actual work and planning. I saw a strong collective subjectivity crack under the weight of overwork, rants, nagging, and finger-pointing. Group *cathexis*—the concentration of mental energy on one particular person, idea, or object—and fragmentation changed the energy feeding the group as the obsessive refrain about collective identity replaced collective making, only to cause estrangement. Nevertheless, the breaking of the antenna with no use in fixing it, the switch to digital TV, and the move of many of us away for work did not discourage numerous attempts to consciously recompose, some more effectively than others in this erratic milieu.

Connective Documentaries as Movement Tools: The Question of Distribution

Genuino Clandestino (The genuine clandestine) (2011a) was the next experiment in large-scale connective media making. The project documented and networked the farmers, breeders, shepherds, and artisans who faced off the agroindustry economic paradigms to support traditional and local knowledge. After a chance encounter with a farmers' association at a market, insu^tv followed the evolution of the local farmers' movement, coproducing the documentary as a way to bolster organizing. *Genuino Clandestino* retraces the birth of this movement from the first farmer collectives in Bologna to the national meetings in Rome, Perugia, and Naples; it exposes the dynamics of the food market and how farmers resist industrial farming collectively. *Genuino Clandestino* supports the voices and work of the *clandestini* with information about the food industry, economic development, labor issues, environmental protection, and access to soil and water. In a country where direct distribution from farm to table still amounts to more than 10 percent of the market, the phenomenon portrayed is far from marginal and "these local realities and the evolution of collective upheaval emerge from this coral narration" (Angrisano 2011a).

The crowdfunding platform Produzioni dal Basso distributed the documentary all over Italy through farmer networks that organized public debates and food tastings. This collaborative production and distribution process made the documentary into a tool in the repertoire of the movement. *Genuino* was successful because "the people supporting it felt it was their own" (interview with Fedina, 2015). In this sense, the format and production process that started with *Wasting Naples* proved to be a very effective tool to spread awareness while bolstering a social movement. Large-scale connective documentaries are successful when those working on them can tend to the connections they foster and to the production and distribution process—they are energy and resource intensive. For this reason, it is hard to work on them with a small team, or when commitment is discontinuous. Shorter forms of documentaries are better suited for low-intensity production times.

In January 2010 I received a very frustrated email from the insu^tv listserv: "We are screwed . . . apart from insu^tv, basically no one moved their asses, not even in Calabria!!! There is only someone from Cosenza. Talk about independent media . . . we are really screwed here . . . there is a media coverage desert . . . can we handle this???" Some insulini were coming back from Rosarno in the far south of the Calabria region, after an impromptu trip with little economic resources and a borrowed car that broke down on the highway. Still, the thirty-minute documentary *Il tempo delle arance* (Gone with the oranges) (2010a), ready for screening only eight days later, is a visually powerful, unmediated documentation of the eviction of five hundred migrant workers from an abandoned industrial site. On January 9, 2010, following a riot against the latest attempt to shoot dead some of the migrant workers hired to pick oranges from the orchards, local inhabitants trapped the migrants to make sure they would be deported, threatening them with bats and guns.

In the midst of the pogrom, the extreme close-ups of the angry and shocked African men speak directly to the audience. They not only denounce the shootings, the exploitation, and the racism but, above all, they blame and criticize the media for fomenting the hate. With no faith left in journalists who depict people of color as "troublesome, destructive, and as cannibals," they accuse the corporate media of thwarting their political and media visibility. "The root of the problem is . . . the Rosarno people are killing us! . . . But Italians don't know, because you, the journalists, don't tell them! So now, we take you the journalists and the Rosarno people as the same, because when we speak the reality to you, you don't tell Italians! So now Italians are taking us as the rioters," says one of the men interviewed in front of a wall on which someone has spray-painted in English: "Avoid shooting blacks" (Angrisano 2010a).

Il tempo delle arance draws out the savage racism of some as well as the double standards of others, who need cheap labor to propel Italian oranges into the global economy. At the same time, it exposes the contradictions that are at the basis of a war between the poor and other minorities, pointing to the conditions of exploitation under which migrants have to live and work—often providing an intersectional analysis of how race plays out in the Italian and European economies. In this short documentary there is no voice-over. The close-ups of the people speaking, the guided tour of the migrants' appalling living quarters, and the images of the police escorting the convoy speak for themselves, leaving the viewers to grapple with their emotions.

Members of insu^tv were involved in various kinds of collaborations with media activists around the world, from Gaza to Rojava, chronicling struggles and drawing connections among them. Attention to migration issues peaked as the Arab Spring and the violence that followed it brought ever more refugees from countries like Libya and Tunisia to the shores of Italy. Some of the insulini traveled to the island of Lampedusa, where many boats were docking and lifeless bodies were being washed ashore. They traveled to Tunisia to produce in-depth inquiries into the immigration phenomenon—often long before the mainstream media.[5] Many of these inquiries are rendered in what insu^tv calls "instant doc," documentary shorts on news neglected by the mainstream media that are produced over a few days to dig into the root causes of a current issue.[6]

Insu^tv has covered the attacks on migrants in the country: the forced evacuation of one thousand Moroccan workers in San Nicola Varco near Salerno (insu^tv 2009c), the murder of seven African workers by the Camorra in Castel Volturno, and the subsequent persecution and deportation of migrants by the authorities (insu^tv 2008), among others. Often, these instant docs are used as a starting point for discussions and for organizing events. Like other instant docs—for example *Lampedusa Next Stop* (2011b) and *Via Padova è meglio di Milano* (Via Padova is better than Milan) (2010b)—*Il tempo delle arance* was screened all over Italy at festivals and political events. It won best documentary at the festival Doc/IT and reached other countries in Europe, starting with Spain and Germany, where people are also organizing around migrant solidarity.

Although they are not produced collaboratively, instant docs are structured and distributed tactically, repurposing the films themselves (the files as well as the projection setting) to support organizing around specific issues. In certain ways, instant docs repurpose media once they are circulated within the movement through the contagious practices of screening, reflection, and mobilization. The events circulate energy across the available infrastructure of social centers, festivals, and community events, which become conductors as the instant docs are repurposed to mobilize action. Without being overly optimistic about the power of video to change the world, the discussions and use of these documentaries as visual inquiries form part of an *infrastructure* for organizing. It is no coincidence that some of the more successful media activist projects in Italy at the moment deal with the creation of distribution networks and autonomous digital infrastructure to cut through the information and video glut.

Insu^tv's collaborative documentaries and instant docs are supported by Open Distribuzioni dal Basso (Open DDB, Distributions from Below), an on-demand library for independent documentaries, film, books, music, experimental cinema, and inquiries licensed under Creative Commons.[7] The platform promotes emergent, independent authors; it builds "spaces of encounters and knowledge sharing between authors and online users in order to foster collective debates and harness content (public screenings, pitches, festivals); . . . construct networks and connections between independent productions in Italy and abroad; . . . experiment with modes of support based on new economic relations and gift economies."[8]

This kind of project exists as part of a newer radical media infrastructure responding to the current challenges and recompositions of media activism, where distribution quickly becomes a dominant concern once the resources for production are available.[9] In an environment awash with independently produced content, revealing the hidden sides of a story hardly mobilizes viewers: the targeted distribution of platforms like Open DDB ensures that the videos produced effectively circulate among audiences, and that producers are networked and connected to their viewers. *Distribution infrastructure* is a key component in recomposing media activist assemblage around new practices and networks of mutual support.

Proxy-Vision on Social Media

I had left Naples again at the tail end of the garbage crisis, when the direst effects of the 2008 financial crash and the politics of austerity forced movements to reset their priorities, campaigns, and modes of struggle. In the following years, as precarity dug its dirty nails even deeper into the fabric of the city, there developed a large movement for housing rights, alternative care and education infrastructures (e.g., childcare, assistance to migrants), and cultural production. Naples saw hundreds of occupations of houses for homeless families, students, artists, activists, occupied theaters, and cultural centers, in some cases benefiting from a somewhat sympathetic administration under the new mayor, Luigi de Magistris. The housing rights movement in particular has made strides as a diverse network of activists, working-class families battling precarity, homeless people, students, the unemployed, and migrants. Among the most active groups is Magnammce o'pesone (Mop)—a Neapolitan dialect expression meaning "let us eat the rent check" and referring to the choice many people have to make between paying rent and eating. Naples is experiencing one of the fastest gentrification rates in Europe, an acceleration that digital platforms like Airbnb.com have visibly facilitated. Between 2015 and 2016 the number of apartments rented to tourists through Airbnb has grown a whopping 219 percent (Gervasio 2018), making housing in the historical center and around other UNESCO-designated heritage sites inaccessible to its former inhabitants. Mop aids families who have received eviction notices, offers legal services, has anti-eviction squads to protect vulnerable individuals, and organizes protests and occupations.

Some insulini are directing their energy to this movement. Insu^tv was also involved initially in the occupation of the Asilo Filangieri (in 2012), a large sixteenth-century school building in the historic center of Naples that now functions as an autonomous, co-run cultural center and space for artists and workers in the culture and entertainment industries (interview with Iasus, 2015).[10] Here, the insulini seeking to update formats like *Domenica Aut* collaborated with the artists and cultural workers of the collective La Balena on the talk show *Stalking Asilo* (2014). Unfortunately, *Stalking Asilo* did not receive the same attention nor did it achieve the same connective potential of *Domenica Aut* for a variety of reasons. Noteworthy was the lack of audience in the room that diminished the power of proxy-vision and left a product unsuitable for distribution on the now popular social media platforms: "It was a lot of work but without appropriate distribution channels; no one was watching it. Officina had a community whereas here the community had splintered on social media. I realized that that kind of product only works if there is community, otherwise no one watches it because it is not a format that works well online" (interview with Sandro, 2015).

Stalking Asilo was a 50/50 collaboration with art professionals building a production center at Asilo Filangieri. Unfortunately, the project did not pay enough attention to the necessary distribution channels and to the production *processes*—something that insu^tv had tended to when making television at Officina 99. Additionally, the high degree of professionalization and the expectations of many of those involved were hard to match with the DIY character of *Domenica Aut,* thriving on connectivity rather than aesthetic finessing.[11] To make matters worse, some technical glitches with the recording apparatus lowered these standards for one of the episodes to the point of being unwatchable, while the face-to-face event could not garner enough traction because it had no social basis: "We were too tired to optimize our efforts and poured so much energy in a project and left none to distribute it, causing people to lose interest. . . . The first episode still had a good audience but once we eliminated it to make the production

Figure 5. Members of insu^tv direct an episode of *Stalking Asilo,* at the occupied cultural center Asilo Filangieri in Naples. Courtesy of insu^tv.

more practical, we could not find a purpose for the show and no one watched it. What's the point if no one watches it?" (interview with Fedina, 2015).

The issues taken up at *Stalking Asilo* were certainly timely—precarity and gender, among others—and yet it was harder to feel connection during the show. Repurposing could not work in a context where objectives and processes were too disjointed, and connection in the space was a little contrived; *Stalking Asilo* continued only for a few more episodes, generating some content but no excitement for the already overstimulated online audiences. Perhaps, *Stalking Asilo* also repurposed television—its genres and medium—for the internet at the wrong time: its potential audience had already swapped their tether to the TV set for one attaching them to their smartphones, tablets, and computers. A DIY talk show on social media lacked the tantalizing character of the new flashy video formats, Instagram-curated images, and targeted, bite-sized content. These factors held the videos within the group boundaries of the established constituency of Asilo Filangieri.

Users of social media tend to be grouped together according to algorithms and design criteria that seldom map onto the heterogeneity of the social fabric of the city.[12] Corporate social media networks are organized by proprietary, for-profit algorithms that work along the hardly porous principle of homophily (Chun 2016): customized selections keep users within their networks of friendships and media consumption habits and it is usually hard or expensive to tap into different content distribution flows.[13] Beyond enjoying the random viral amateur YouTube video, viewers have quickly gotten used to high production standards, which render the DIY character of homemade television underwhelming and perhaps a bit too vintage to like and share online. Importantly, the quantification habits cultivated on corporate social media have also impacted the relation between the media produced in other contexts and the energy it generates: "Social media make you think that you have to have tons of likes and hits. We didn't use to really think about this but now people ask themselves what all the work is for when only fifty people watch but you get two-hundred and fifty likes for a selfie" (interview with Sandro, 2015). Many *insulini* mention the metric-driven character of media consumption today, even when they propose a variety of solutions.

Insu^tv de/re/composition unfolds in a milieu where producing and managing content are increasingly complex (Alfio, qtd. in Stein n.d.), and corporate social media platforms like YouTube and Facebook are ubiquitous among organizers. Many of these new relations to technology impact the media activist field and its relation to activist and community groups. Younger media producers, often alone more than in a group, have taken to reporting about rallies on the street with their live feeds.[14] In previous years, this activity kept media activists embedded within social movements and established reference points between activists and audiences. The nature and simplicity of the new technology allows individuals to work alone. An army of solo live streamers has joined the front lines to chronicle protests all over the world, in some cases going viral and tapping into different networked audiences; "the lack of TV apparatus made it impossible for insu^tv to get into people's houses" and narrowed the audience (interview with Sandro, 2015). Live streamers mostly reach a very select public.

It seems that movement communication in Naples today is tied to specific projects and is less concerned with forging larger alliances and collaborative networks to retain porosity. Radical filmmakers are seeking to build a shared distribution infrastructure to circulate their films while citizen journalists and independent media tied to social movements seem mostly tied to proprietary and readily available platforms. In this sense, even when organizing is in full swing, the circulation of information seldom spills out of its own insular (platformed) channels: "We entered a new phase. Insu^tv had lost the role of those taking a video camera to the street because now there are many micro-web channels. We don't have that role anymore" (interview with Sandro, 2015). This molecularization transpires in the new media landscape of individual or small cells of media activists; it seeps into intergroup relations.

Networked social media are active agents that carry with them an associated milieu that reproduces and organizes the functions of technology. Their vectors of enclosure and molecularization can be found in the architectures, interfaces, and discourses promoted and their larger interoperable assemblage of networks—you can read a Facebook post that takes you directly to a blog, then tweet the YouTube video embedded in it, and so on, all within interoperable and interconnected spaces of control (Langlois 2014; Renzi 2015). These processes join individual and machine through a flow of affects productive of habituated gestures, serialized acts, and, in many cases, hollowed-out notions of participation and solidarity. Simultaneously, they interpellate individuals as entrepreneurial subjects through precoded roles and functions as reporters, protesters, moderators, and voyeurs at political events. Platform users are not simply subjectified as producers and consumers of information; they are simultaneously turned into relays of information and data, generating energy that often only circulates online and that feeds the corporate system.

A sociotechnical assemblage that is too reliant on corporate media platforms built on for-profit homophilic logics holds a limited capacity to adapt and recompose. With Simondon, I have insisted on framing the question of technology as part of an account of co-constitutive relations among organic and nonorganic beings where technical individuals also individuate thanks to a generativity that leaves them open to innovation and new compositions. Jonathan Zittrain's definition of the internet as a "generative technology" that can be coded for new uses that are in turn sources of more innovation exemplifies how individuating technology works (Zittrain 2008; see also Deseriis and Renzi 2014). As a given technology branches out, its functions are defined in connection to its users while retaining the openness for further change.

Telestreet's television technology too was generative, and it individuated with every new hardware and open-source software hack or appropriation of available platforms. DIY technical solutions, hacking, and the rigging of old and new media engineer new social connections. Each reuse, fork, customization, and expansion in Telestreet and insu^tv generated production and transmission technology that reshaped the project with its attendant proxy-vision and connective approaches. Each recomposition with these technologies was generative of new relations that modulated individuality and collectivity. The co-constitution of the *I* and the *we* took place in this milieu of humans and machines where desire and affects flow and generate energy in the process of collaboration. Proprietary platforms cannot be hacked or modified and thus they limit the scope of repurposing within activist assemblages.

The black-boxed platform-based media infrastructure and molecularized activist practices affect the field of potential for resistance and the spaces of intersubjectivity that emerge around media—important aspects of a connective activist practice. In addition to providing alternative sources of information, insu^tv's connective and proxy-vision models had forged new relations among communities and strengthened those that already existed. As media technology in its effective functioning changes, insu^tv's connective potential weakens. This is because the collaborative and lengthy production processes of insu^tv are no longer necessary if a single individual can use a smartphone or small camera to produce video, post it on their own YouTube channel, and promote it on their social media networks. The ties forged during the process of media making are crucial for connective activism more than the fact that insu^tv reported on protests and events.

The physiological reactions taking place in a social media user's body generate plenty of energy within a mediascape where flows of information trigger processes of signification that hyperconnect users, interfaces, hardware, fiber optic cables, data and metadata, and so on. Still, individuations that technical objects mediate are by no means intrinsically emancipatory; on the contrary, they may entrench habits and semiotic processes that subjectify and enslave simultaneously (Lazzarato 2014).[15]

The platforming of activism through Twitter, Facebook, YouTube, Instagram, and the like has had an impact on the technological generativity, practices, and psychosociality of activism. My analysis shows that, currently, corporate social media platforms work against the power of proxy-vision because they replace the technical objects that Simondon says are the "support and the symbol of that relation that we would like to call 'transindividual'" (1989, 247). As the technical object changes, so does the milieu of transindividuation, reshaping the relationship between the physical, biological, and psychosocial. The decomposition of their DIY assemblage and recomposition around proprietary platforms have resulted in a repatterning of the transindividual milieu that molecularizes collectivity, even when it appears more networked through technology. In the context of connective activism, repurposing needs to support the conditions for collaborations that scale up political action by fostering more porosity. For this reason, rethinking the modes of connective activism requires that one pays close attention to technical objects whose function and potential for hacking is still in the process of emerging. This rethinking for recomposition can only happen in combination with an inquiry into the changing fields of struggle. Ultimately, the connective potential that propelled insu^tv's TV model for years emanated from the interaction of the practices and processes I discussed. It would not be a cutting-edge new direction of production alone but the recomposition of the entire assemblage that would allow insu^tv to go on generating porosity.

Changing Technologies and Social Reproduction

Insu^tv's first signal had come from the roof of a housing complex in Scampia, thanks to the support of the local Committee for Housing Rights. This collaboration ties housing as a site where fundamental unpaid labor for the care and reproduction of the social takes place in another site of social reproduction: the airwaves where communication happens. Autonomist feminists like Mariarosa Dalla Costa, Leopoldina Fortunati, and Silvia Federici identify reproductive care and affective labor as key components of the persistence of capitalist systems: this labor produces the workforce and is hence integral to the reproduction of capitalism (Dalla Costa and James 1975; Fortunati [1981] 1995; Federici 2012). Communication and language are important elements of social reproduction because they are attached to the worker's living body (Deseriis 2015, 146). As communication takes on more space in private and work life, it too becomes fraught terrain. Networked communication technologies in particular are important aspects of the reproduction of the social: "As much as the foods we eat, the beds we sleep in, the love we make so too are communicative technologies elements that permit the quotidian replenishment of human beings and of labor power" (Thorburn 2016).

The monetization and surveillance of affects, fears, desires, love, and friendships has come to the attention of those who research the contested role of communication in information-based capitalism (Terranova 2000, 2014; Coté and Pybus 2011; Scholz 2014). Black-boxed platforms possess a kind of generativity that is proprietary and captures communication acts into networks of value extraction. The impact of networked media platforms on individual and collective habits is considerable, in the sense that networked media platforms subsume and monetize time; they orient individual and collective desires toward immediacy and instantaneity and away from the affects, perceptions, and emotions of belonging that come from the touch and empathy of sharing spaces, of making and hacking together, or of having to work out differences and affinities (Serra 2015). For Fulvia Serra, we are seeing an erosion of intimacy and the enclosure of the social relations that are necessary for reproducing one's own identity and the collective identity of movements. The process of enclosure of shared spaces of production and of social relations "can be redefined as a process that aims not only at the accumulation of capital and resources but, more importantly, at creating political paralysis and dependence, reducing workers' ability to negotiate and cutting off the possibility of freely accessing forms of self-sustenance" (Serra 2015). These new platforms conform to and transduce the individualistic logic of neoliberalism even in the activist field where, for instance, online the visibility of campaigns often becomes more relevant than long-term investment in communities on the ground.

The collaboration between the Committee for Housing Rights in Scampia and insu^tv—and later on its connection to the new housing rights movement—draws attention to some of the ways groups subtract the spheres of social reproduction from capital through the occupation of housing and the airwaves first, and then care for the spaces they have created. In the case of the Committee for Housing Rights, since the initial occupation of twenty thousand housing units after the 1980 earthquake, the committee has fought to improve living conditions—and therefore life lived—in the buildings, while insu^tv has developed technological solutions and collaborative production processes to support alternative forms of sociality. Both cases are not just reminders of the importance of thinking about social reproduction in struggles for justice; they also and especially call for a discussion of the unpaid and unrecognized work of care to keep movements going.

Silvia Federici has pointed out that "political movements that fail to create new forms of social reproduction are destined to be reabsorbed into

190 · DE/RE/COMPOSITIONS, IN PROCESS

the mechanism of the capitalist system" (qtd. in Serra 2015). Two insights from my fieldwork are worth emphasizing in connection with this warning. First, at a time where communication has become an important site of struggle, media activism needs to involve more projects and practices that wrestle the sphere of communication from processes of overproduction and redirect them toward social reproduction within movements. Second, it is important to recognize the strategic importance of sustenance, care, and affective work within movements to allow porosity, healthy interactions, and scaling up. This may require a reconceptualization of what is considered political work.

Withdrawing social reproduction from the capitalist machine becomes an act of resistance in its own right at a time when regimes of ownership and control that enforce fees for or restrict access to basic necessities "enclose the material conditions of life, making it virtually impossible to reproduce ourselves and each other free of waged work" (Armstrong 2012). Amanda Armstrong and Rada Katsarova call the forms of resistance and autonomous organizing that develop skills, resources, networks of mutual care, and forms of collective governance insurgent forms of social reproduction (Armstrong 2012; Katsarova 2015). The austerity regimes instituted in many countries after the 2008 financial crisis seem to have multiplied the insurgent forms of social reproduction that strive to build the commons.

The struggle for survival that swallows migrants and locals alike, as they find themselves in need of spaces and strategies to nourish the body and mind, comes front and center wherever austerity policies rule, when white supremacy and xenophobic populism take over governments. In Naples, new experiments are adding to decades of fighting for housing, setting up autonomous crisis management infrastructure, independent unemployed movements, and spaces for cultural production. The work of insu^tv cannot be considered in isolation from these and other transnational and local movements. With social media use informing new habits of communication and resistance that increasingly fragment and molecularize, few still recognize the political potential of collaborative/connective work to oppose the monetization and fragmentation of social relations—a key component in the capitalist reproductive sphere today. I consider, with autonomist feminists, connective media activism an insurgent mode of social reproduction, especially because it fosters intimacy and social ties (Serra 2015)—what many in Naples have called porosity for a long time.

In this sense, insurgent social reproduction is entangled with the concept of repurposing the social for politics.

The story of Italian media activism, how one of its deviant ramifications started with abnormal uses of radio, reached for the internet, and eventually birthed Telestreet and insu^tv, is a reminder that collectivity and connectivity—sociality—whether face to face or mediated, are not intrinsically political but need to be politicized. The move from the social to the political is a conscious one that requires putting into relation and communication the larval energies that traverse a specific social field. Political energetics—as an ethics of connection—involves engaging metastability *as such* and fostering "the event-invention which crystallizes into a new configuration" with potential to transform again (Toscano 2012, 92). I think again of the beaming and bodiness of Ma.gi.ca TV in the hacked milieu of Scampia's passion for entertainment and what is in common. Experiments like the ones I have described can be key sites where the work of social reproduction and the care for collectivity take place because they hijack existing relations of production and reproduction.

As I write these final pages, insu^tv has been meeting again to tie up some loose ends. In the past few years (2013–18), when production slowed down and the directions of the collective were unclear, a few of us talked about the legacy of insu^tv and the necessity to create an archive. The opportunity to work on this has come with the development of a new international cooperative network for social justice and the testing of new F/OSS decentralized technology for archiving and collaboratively editing video.[16] Both initiatives are part of a larger context of experiments for bottom-up welfare and the creation of infrastructures rooted in the principle of the commons. It is not surprising to me that, in a network that strives to build alternative financial infrastructures, including a fair crypto currency, one of the tools developed is a platform to support video archiving. Memory is a key discursive and affective component of the process of collective individuation, as well as an important resource to develop new practices of resistance.

Social media's ephemeral feeds and short attention span hardly valorize collective memory. As Asterix pointed out during a meeting in 2014, many young people today come to activism through social media, not through social spaces like the CSOAs, youth groups, workplaces, or schools. For this reason, they are excluded from certain kinds of conversations, knowledge exchange, intellectual investigations, and intergenerational contact that shaped struggle in the past decades—and that engendered important frameworks and practices in reaction to older ways of doing politics (e.g., decolonial, intersectional, antiracist critiques of old feminisms or labor organizing). Storytelling about the political past and collective knowledge gathering and dissemination are part of a practice of care and social reproduction that need to be preserved as political tools. This is especially the case if they can be mobilized to support processes of co-individuation.

At this juncture of new forms of resistance to neoliberal immiseration and to the hyperconnectivity of enclosed communication platforms, it is still unclear what connective activism can look like. In this context, the question for activists but also for engaged scholarship becomes one of how to *understand* and *facilitate* the composition of new assemblages that attend to the specific ways in which the technical, the social, and the somatic interlock as much as possible outside the enclosure of individualizing systems. Some of the formats that Telestreet and insu^tv developed and some of the concepts I present herein may be taken up and repurposed in a different context. Most likely it will not be insu^tv that rethinks connective activism and media repurposing for the future, even though production continues. Others will have to develop new concatenations of social forms, knowledge, and technology to "build forms of social solidarity that are capable of re-activating the social body after the long period of its isolation and subjugation to competitive aggressiveness" (Berardi, qtd. in Hugill and Thorburn 2012, 213).

Epilogue

Repurposing Is How Connective Activism Happens

To think of subjectivity "in terms of the milieu" is not a matter of theory.

—Isabelle Stengers, "Experimenting with Refrains"

The milieu is the stage for a dance of individuation that seeds the conditions for both resistance and control. At each step, assemblages form. Their specific composition of heterogeneous elements is a formula to wield power. Never should one believe that connections and connectivity alone will save us. Silvio Berlusconi, a master connector, has much to teach us here (chapter 3). Who would have thought?

The movements that became visible in the 1990s, from Chiapas to Seattle, took on powerful configurations in Italy as they connected to local student struggles, the work of the social centers, and hacker scenes (chapter 4). If the free radios in the seventies had set a precedent for creative media activism (chapter 2), the nineties may be considered a golden era for technological innovation that gave momentum to political organizing, from informational guerrilla actions to Indymedia, from electronic disturbance theater to tactical media. It is during this period that forms of connective activism came to the surface. The fax machines of the occupied universities, the integration of the fax grid with the VAX computers from the science labs, the spread of bulletin board systems supported by the free radios, the development of open publishing online platforms—all of these are, in their own ways, examples of repurposed media for connecting people in novel ways. Through the lens of connective activism, organizing that involves the appropriation, design, or recombination of technology modules expands the field for thinking about social change and developing new practices of resistance (chapter 1). Telestreet gave more consistency to these practices, while insu^tv dedicated them to creating porosity among communities.

Repurposing as a practice has surfaced at different times and in different contexts from these pages: the reuse of discarded technology; the hacking

193

of old and new technical objects like antennas, transmitters, and the internet. In Telestreet and insu^tv, television as a medium for entertainment is repurposed for activism; activist spaces are repurposed for studios; the airwaves are taken over as public space; *inchiesta* is repurposed for subjectification. Repurposing for connective activism best describes the work of insu^tv, and it is, I believe, the reason why insu^tv still exists today amid all the change (chapter 6). But repurposing would not be a particularly compelling, and useful, concept if it was limited to finding a different use for what is already available. I have been most interested in outlining the various ways in which *repurposing can create the conditions for collective becoming and the formation of activist assemblages.*

The ethico-political value of repurposing lies in its potential to tap into coproduction and commingling to give sociotechnical assemblages a new force for politics—a *repurposing of the social* that harnesses encounters and events to care for movements (chapter 7). In fact, if the subject is a necessary but not sufficient condition for politics (Toscano 2012), the repurposing of media sows a seed for the creation of more powerful, heterogeneous collective formations. *Repurposing gives purpose to transindividuation—*that is, it sets forth or directs certain kinds of becoming, ways of coexisting among groups at a time of fragmentation and polarization in the social fabric. Crucially, this potential is not containable in the agency of the individual or group but lies in the ability of human and technical individuals to come together through various forms of connective activism. Repurposing harbors political potential in its ability to foster *re*composition—that is, to configure new relations among hacked media, activist practices, and collective needs.

Technology today plays a major role in shaping resistant formations and, in this sense, it has agency, to use an old-fashioned word. Technical individuals like Telestreet's transmission apparatus individuate: their properties emerge when the potentialities of various technical components solidify and become grounded at the intersection of sociality, culture, geography, and the economy. Technical individuation is a process that is at the basis of the becoming of contemporary activist formations (chapter 5). Telestreet's and insu^tv's technical components are themselves conduits of individuations that transduce across electromagnetic waves and sensory stimuli. As these stimuli circulate, they trigger reactions that are folded into already stratified relations: social, cultural, and so on. New habits and ways of thinking come to life. For example, Telestreet's proxy-vision model of collaborative video production engaged audience and producers alike in a process of sense making, which was couched in an alternative web of practices. The ensuing individuations involve a kind of connectedness that is simultaneously productive of new collectivities and of their subjectivities.

It takes a certain awareness to reveal the implications of technology for people and the social field (Simondon 2006, 251–53). This means that to foster stronger political formations it is necessary to inquire into the potential, the actual properties as well as the dangers of what comes into composition and connection. Insu^tv's efforts to keep the activist field connected and porous are rooted in an understanding of how video technology and production practices tie the groups involved in media production and consumption with the different communities that are engaged in each project. The surplus energy that is generated in this process becomes itself a point of contagious relay. For instance, the connective force of *Wasting Naples* did not end with its release but intensified with it: the hundreds of events organized around the film reached past the Italian borders to the rest of Europe and North America. To all of them, nicol* was invited to speak about the struggle and the filmmaking but also to coproduce new projects.

In Naples, individuals and groups collaborated and co-individuated without having to position themselves according to rigid identities (chapter 8). This interaction forged long-lasting ties because, as autonomist researchers remind us (Alquati 1975; Borio, Pozzi, and Roggero 2002), the collaborative process of knowledge production is itself a mode of subjectivation and organization. In cases like this, the mediation of certain modes and objects of inquiry keeps material and discursive practices as close together as possible by focusing on the interaction and collaboration that each project triggers rather than on defining a position of the individuals involved on the social (identitarian) grid. Insu^tv's work shows the impact of nurturing stronger collective actors from the co-individuation of the groups with a media-based model of social therapy. Despite the sadness of seeing an exciting project slow down, the story of insu^tv is not sung to the sad tune of violin music but is meant as a call for others to continue to experiment with alternative forms of social reproduction, rethinking media activism along, or beyond, these principles of connective activism that refuse to fetishize corporate, participatory platforms.

Energetics of Movements

"Telestreet was a TV for witnessing while we were a form of resistance—this is why we endured," said Sandro of insu^tv in one of our interviews in 2015.[1] As a form of resistance, insu^tv's function was connective at a time of post-Genoa fragmentation; it dug its roots in the movements it came from while also broadening its reach among local cultural, environmental, and migrant organizations. With the ushering in of corporate social media, witnessing as a mode of media production has become more widespread. At the same time, activism that attends to social reproduction has invested more in rebuilding the social, educational, and economic infrastructure that austerity politics have destroyed. Activist assemblages are not stable: they are *meta*stable; they are constantly reshaping as new components are added and the energy circulating through them changes. The decomposition of a certain kind of movement media assemblage and the emergence of new ones presents an opportunity to reframe how we study media in relation to cycles of struggle.

A study of media use from a perspective of movement energetics focuses on how media ecologies and social ecologies are entangled in complex ways, instead of taking for granted the adoption of specific technologies. The concretization of technical ensembles itself has less to do with ready-made technologies and more with hacking, tinkering, and exchanges between bodies and technologies as they come together and transform each other. It is important to document the sources of energy (or passions, to paraphrase Anna Tsing [2005, 216]) that carry the seeds of assemblages.

Media scholars are starting to recognize the value of the less tangible components that make social movement media what it is. In his article on memes and Occupy Wall Street (OWS), Jack Bratich builds on the work of Guattari, Goddard, and Negri to think of OWS as an ecology of media and of practices for subjective production that involves the movement of desire and reasoning. For Bratich, all too often movements are treated as episodic eruptions that should be gauged by their measurable achievements and decomposition instead of elaborating "the mechanisms that *persist across* and *connect* them" (2014, 66). Citing Amador Fernandez-Savater's ideas, he proposes to think about climates rather than movements to account for the milieus that can trigger the condensation of certain desires and ideas at specific periods in time: "a climate can facilitate an emergent body politic's passage from social movement to social rest, and back again. What are the mediating mechanisms that operate in this moment of social rest?" Bratich asks (2014, 70).

An energetics of movements focuses on this capacity for transformation while overcoming representations of monolithic movements: to understand the capacity of media ecologies to constantly change, one must consider the energetic potential of the system, that is, one must think about (trans)individuation, also at the moment of decomposition, when groups cannot preserve their psychosocial stability—and traces of their presence scatter elsewhere. From Radio Alice and tactical media, through raves and bulletin board systems, to Telestreet and insu^tv, I have shown seeds that were crucial to understand how divergent energies came into communication. My threading and weaving of them attempted to pull together some of the many lines that condition political invention across cycles of struggle—across climates. I have also considered other parts of the infrastructure for activism (CSOAs, hacklabs, protests, networks, etc.) because they are part of a milieu where seeds germinate.

A focus on transformation can tell more about the value of activist projects than any assessment of their failures, especially if it brings with it concepts and tools that evolve elsewhere. The focus on energy—among people, groups, and technical objects—and transformation develops a way of discussing activist projects' capacity (and perhaps need) to change rather than their efforts to remain the same. For this reason, this study of the de/re/composition of Telestreet and insu^tv does not give it a shape by imposing a specific narrative but rather reads its history and presence diffractively (Barad 2014), pointing to the value of connective activism as a tool and an ethics to engage the present. Ultimately, the focus on compositionality and connectivity of this book opens up the space to expand the role of co-research to inquiry into the potential of movements to change—in so doing it provides a different angle to study mediated practices of resistance.

Currently, a variety of movements are developing alternative governance models, supporting migrant rights and tackling economic crises, climate change, and social emergencies. Strong autonomous media infrastructure that bolsters the burgeoning movements are mostly absent.[2] Make no mistake, networked media technologies are present and visible. Corporate social media in particular afford wide and immediate reach through the interlinking of different platforms and it would be careless not to recognize their important contribution to political organizing. Twitter allowed the residents of Ferguson, Missouri, to bypass the mainstream media to denounce police brutality and grow the Movement for Black Lives (Jackson and Welles 2016); #IdleNoMore started as hashtags and led to stronger alliances between indigenous peoples and settlers to protect the climate across two continents (Coates 2015); Facebook livestreams the killing of unarmed black men like Philando Castile. Corporate social media provide free and technically stable environments to circulate information without having to rely on independent coders and costly infrastructure (web hosting, data storage, video streaming, etc.).

How does contemporary mediated activism function in the larger activist field? What can media activism do today? What does the available technology afford or prevent? For researchers and activists alike, the challenge is to understand the current formations in dynamic interaction with the wider activist and nonactivist milieus, to discern what compositions engender new forms of agency, and to develop studies that relay this knowledge in a way that can also be mobilized back into movements. The new activist mediascape is heterogeneous, networked, and yet fragmented. It combines corporate and alternative in a variety of ways. It is therefore harder to grasp by looking at the use of the technologies that facilitate communication and information circulation because these only tell us a partial story, one of double binds with corporate media, or of futile resistance against the media giants with small and underappreciated autonomous tools. To keep exploring the relation between activism and technology, *it is time to declare that there is no more alternative media; there are only alternative media assemblages in ongoing recomposition.*

Finally, in terms of looking at the recomposition of movements, the inquiry into media (medium is also a translation for the French word *milieu*) that are part of an infrastructure of transindividuation poses the question of whether media need to be necessarily technical objects, with wires and chips. What can researchers contribute to the field of media studies by broadening the focus of the study of media for social change? Infrastructure is receiving much needed attention nowadays. Deborah Cowen discusses the value of *social* infrastructures that are built, material, and lasting. She invites scholars to look at this kind of infrastructure because it is future-oriented; "it is assembled in the service of worlds to come" (Cowen 2017). I add, it circulates energy. What kinds of media in their broadest sense function as activist infrastructure?

Connective Research

My approach to studying media and its practices diffractively brought together a variety of ideas—autonomist feminism and political thought; the philosophy of science of Gilbert Simondon, Karen Barad, Donna Haraway, and Isabelle Stengers; the work of French philosophers who influenced autonomist thinkers and activists alike. I read their insights through one another, looking for small differences that matter while retaining an awareness that the frameworks and apparatuses that I use to understand what I study co-determine what I can see and how I can describe it.[3] I wrote with the political intent of showing the power of repurposing and connectivity. Guiding this intention is an understanding that ethics is about taking on responsibility and accountability for the lively relationalities of becoming, in which researcher and communities alike take part. To say it with Barad, ethics is about working through the entangled materializations of which we are part and recognizing that responsibility is about our ability to respond and take into account the response of the other who is entangled with what we call self (2007, 70). In my case, it is not just that this book would not have existed without my encounter and learning with Telestreet. It is that I would not be the person, activist, and scholar that I am if I had not gained so much from co-individuation with the *compagni*, from holding a camera and seeing the world through its lens. How one acknowledges this debt in research and gifts in return is a question that needs to be posed again and again with each new inquiry and context.

What my research showed me is also that this kind of inquiry cannot happen without a constant commitment to including collaborators in the production of knowledge, which requires patient translation of ideas, needs, and constraints in both directions, without taking on frontline work; holding space for other voices; and resisting the academic urge to speak on behalf of activist and community groups. Power relations in knowledge production are messy and cannot be ignored, even and especially in co-research environments. Leading the way in this approach are visionary feminist, queer, black, and decolonial thinkers who are reconnecting the practice of knowledge production to the purpose of engaging the world beyond prevailing strategies of control: extraction, mystification, generalization, objectivity and objectification, claims to universality and scientificity, among others (Harney and Moten 2013; Haraway 2016; Simpson 2016). During my research and the writing of this book, I have been fortunate enough to encounter people and situations that made me *feel* and *imagine* (Stengers 2008, 57), *and* held me accountable for my privileges.

History and patriarchy have made it hard, especially for female-identifying subjects, to make claims about feelings and imaginations without being discounted as knowledge producers. Nevertheless, insofar as there is a politics of knowledge, it is necessary to think about the production of subjectivity and the work of social reproduction that binds together, that entangles researchers and researched—a politics of knowledge that teaches us to feel, imagine, learn, and respond. With insu^tv, I learned to repurpose research as an ethical mode of being an activist *and* a scholar. In my fieldwork and media practice I often observed how research could help develop effective strategies of respectful and productive collaboration. *Connective* research forges ways of being together that, hopefully, do so with care because "no such event, no such production of subjectivity, is good per se" (Stengers 2008, 58). Like many other "participatory" processes that neoliberalism celebrates, co-research without an ethics of connection can be just another method of knowledge extraction.

Feeling and imagining certainly smack anathema for a "legitimate" approach to media studies and social movement studies, but I contend that the kind of psychosocial and ethicopolitical entanglements I have discussed can be an *a/effective* entry point into understanding the energetics of social and media ecologies. When mobilized, the research I performed here and encourage others to produce can generate new possibilities for relaying energy through the activist milieu. How we come to a good understanding of one another and how this understanding shapes our movements are, in my opinion, questions that are entangled. We can start answering them simultaneously by setting up a research process that foregrounds listening, collaboration, experimentation, and recomposition. Thus, inspired by the processual and circular approach of co-research, the body of knowledge I present can be rediscussed, verified, and enriched through future experiments that make it more useful (Borio, Pozzi, and Roggero 2002).

Following the initial step of posing the question of Telestreet/insu^tv in terms of learning and experimentation developed through co-research and immanent critique, we can continue to look for the conditions and potentials for organizing networks of solidarity between academics and activists that modulate (rather than isolate or oppose) and embolden a radical politics for social justice already taking place. In this sense, networking and connecting existing practices of resistance both builds upon and recontextualizes the work done so far while addressing new problems to be formulated collectively. Building connections among activists, organizations, and individuals is not simply a matter of naming a condition; nor is it a matter of creating a concept that might provide a point of theoretical connection: it is in the actual process of making, or embodying, these connections that new practices of sociability emerge.

Acknowledgments

This research project, spanning almost fifteen years, owes less to my determination and much more to the inspiration, trust, encouragement, and collaboration of the many, many wonderful people I encountered along the way. Their generosity, friendship, and wisdom sustained me all along and will stay with me during future projects.

The precious insights, patience, and curiosity of Monica Heller, Kari Dehli, Sue Ruddick, Gary Genosko, Etienne Turpin, Irmgard Emmelhainz, D. T. Chochrane, Nasrin Himada, A. K. Thompson, and Christine Shaw guided me when this book was still an early draft. My fieldwork gave me energy and purpose, thanks to the *compagni* from insu^tv: Alessandro Verna, Alfonso De Vito, Luca Manunza, Michela Porcelli, Pie(t)ro Di Iorio, Raffaele Aspide, Raffaele Romano, Sara Cotugno, Aurelia Luongo, Simone Veneroso, Pasquale Scognamiglio, Federica D'Andrea, Gigi Mete, Marco Della Monica, Alessandro Ventura, the lovely folks of Telestreet, Annalisa Pelizza, Ciro D'Aniello, Franco "Bifo" Berardi, Giancarlo Vitali, Franco Civelli, Angese Trocchi, Alan Toner, Enea Discepoli, Otello Urso, Chiara, Carlo, and many others. My friends and family made life in Naples sane and joyful; thank you especially to my parents, my sister, my *nonna*, and Gennaro Navarra.

Hacked Transmissions would not have its current shape were it not for the invaluable input of Richard Grusin, Jack Bratich, Craig Robertson, the Bit Bots and Bites crew, Gabriella Coleman, Fenwick McKelvey, Sophie Toupin, Elena Razlogova, Marco Deseriis, Sandra Braman, Greg Elmer, and Ganaele Langlois. Some of the ideas in this book were presented at the Craft of Scholarship Lecture Series and received the insightful feedback of the members of Media@McGill, which kindly hosted me for a semester in 2015. Thank you to Jonathan Sterne, Jenny Burman, and Tamar Tembeck. Last but not least, I am endlessly grateful to my partner, Lucas Freeman, sanity buoy, book midwife, brilliant *accomplice extraordinaire*.

Appendix

List of Interviews

The recorded interviews in this book were carried out with members of Telestreet channels insu^tv, OrfeoTv, and TeleMonteOrlandoTV between 2008 and 2015. In addition to other countless, more informal conversations that took place over the years, these interviews were crucial to orient my study. In the interviews I cite throughout the book, many interviewees chose to use their nickname handles, which have tied them to the world of Italian activism online and away from the keyboard ever since they can remember. I include their real names here as appropriate, and with permission.

Alfio	Interview with Alfonso De Vito, insu^tv, Naples, March 25, 2008.
Ambrogio	Interview with Giancarlo Vitali, OrfeoTv, Bologna, August 7, 2008.
Asterix	Interview with Raffaele Aspide, insu^tv, Naples, March 26, 2008.
	Interview with Raffaele Aspide, insu^tv, Naples, April 9, 2014.
Aurelia	Interview with Aurelia Luongo, insu^tv, Skype, October 15, 2008.
Bifo	Interview with Franco Berardi, OrfeoTv, Bologna, August 8, 2008.
Ciano	Interview with Antonio Ciano, TeleMonteOrlandoTV, Formia, July 4, 2008.
Ciro	Interview with Ciro D'Aniello, OrfeoTV, Bologna, August 10, 2008.
Fedina	Interview with Federica D'Andrea, insu^tv, Skype, April 28, 2015.

Hadebra	Interview with Michela Porcelli, insu^tv, Skype, February 10, 2010.
Iasus	Interview with Luca Manunza, insu^tv, Naples, March 25, 2008.
	Interview with Luca Manunza, insu^tv, Skype, April 22, 2015.
Nicola	Conversations with various members of insu^tv under the pseudonym Nicola Angrisano took place in Naples, in Toronto, in Berlin, and on Skype, between 2008 and 2017.
Nisa	Interview with Annalisa Pelizza, OrfeoTv, Bologna, August 10, 2008.
Pog	Interview with Pasquale Scognamiglio, insu^tv, Naples, April 5, 2008.
Raro	Interview with Raffaele Romano, insu^tv, Naples, March 30, 2008.
Sandro	Interview with Alessandro Verna, insu^tv, Naples, February 26, 2008.
	Interview with Alessandro Verna, insu^tv, Skype, April 19, 2015.
Sara	Interview with Sara Cotugno, insu^tv, Naples, March 30, 2008.
Simone	Interview with Simone Veneroso, insu^tv, Skype, October 10, 2008.
Wadada	Interview with Pie(t)ro Di Iorio, insu^tv, Naples, April 6, 2008.

Notes

Introduction

1. In many cases, their discussions and actions embraced the widely shared assumption that the power to protest the financial crisis today lies in using the new available communication infrastructure because of its capability to mobilize critical masses (Castells 2012; Jenkins, Ford, and Green 2013).

2. It will become clearer throughout this book that connective activism is about fostering social connection rather than networked mediation for political mobilization. In this sense it is very different from the logic of connective action theorized by W. Lance Bennett (2013) and Alexandra Segerberg (Bennett and Segerberg 2012).

3. The Independent Media Centers (IMC) or Indymedia were the first citizen journalism centers that systematically covered protests from the grassroots perspective of the movements involved in global justice, starting with the 1999 Carnival against Capital in London. Indymedia developed and used the first horizontal online open publishing platforms, which have eventually given rise to so-called Web 2.0 (see chapter 4). It rapidly grew into a worldwide network after covering the 1999 anti-WTO protests in Seattle.

4. All translations from Italian are mine unless otherwise indicated.

5. The diffusion of YouTube and other Web 2.0 spaces outdated Telestreet very soon after its birth: although internet-based media in Italy does not fulfill the same function as traditional television—always on as a background to household activities—platforms like YouTube became more accessible for Italians while Telestreet was attempting to grow. Once broadband internet became more affordable, some nodes moved online, abandoning the airwaves, for which transmission is often rife with technical and logistical problems. Some channels were never able to muster the analog transmission technology and opted for a WebTV version shortly after their start.

6. See chapter 2 for more on *conricerca*.

7. My ties and eventual participation in insu^tv grew organically over the first years of my research on other Telestreet nodes through multiple trips to my hometown of Naples and my friendship with some of its members.

207

208 · NOTES TO INTRODUCTION

8. While I make extensive use of the data gathered during the interviews and conversations with insu^tv, I have chosen to only selectively quote from my transcriptions and study results (a full list of interviews appears in the appendix). This is because I am wary of singling out others' ideas in a context where ideas cannot be attributed to specific individuals. Moreover, from an ethical research perspective, it is often hard to make choices about what piece of information to include when the time spent with our so-called informants is not only data collection time but also our time of work and friendship. This time spent together was based on trust and not on self-censorship, and although I did my best to anonymize information while still providing a multilayered tale, I fully claim responsibility for my statements and interpretations.

1. Making Sense of Telestreet

1. See, for example, the law Decreto Legge 27.07.2005 no. 144, *Gazzetta Ufficiale* 27.07.2005, on urgent measures to fight international terrorism.

2. Karen Barad has used the notion of diffraction as a guiding practice, as "a method of diffractively reading insights through one another, building new insights, and attentively and carefully reading for differences that matter in their fine details, together with the recognition that, there, intrinsic to this analysis is an ethics that is not predicated on externality but rather entanglement" (2012, 77). As a guiding practice in my writing, diffraction is brought about by new *compositions* of ideas, methods, and media (including this book). The process of producing compositions with and through research on Telestreet is also a way of focusing on the importance of where knowledge comes from when reading insights through one another—experimenting with ethical patterns of relationality (Barad interviewed in Dolphijn and Tuin 2012, 50).

3. From this perspective, it can be argued that change *is* an immanent relationship in itself. Brian Massumi's insights are worth quoting at length: "The idea is that there is an ontogenesis or becoming of culture and the social . . . of which determinate forms of culture and sociability are the result. The challenge is to think that process of *formation,* and for that you need the notion of a taking-form, an inform on the way to being determinately this or that. The field of emergence is not presocial. It is *open-endedly social.* . . . That interaction is precisely what takes form. That is what is socially determined—and renegotiated by each and every cultural act. Assume it, and you beg the whole question. . . . Not assuming it, however, entails finding a concept for interaction-in-the-making. The term adopted here is *relation*" (2002, 9). By separating the ontological status of the relation from that of its terms, the notion of change shifts from merely negating, subverting, or deviating from the preconstituted terms and codes of a relation within a structuring grid to the simultaneous emergence of both individuals *and* society. Individuation is

very much about relations and compositions as modes of being themselves, that is, as simultaneous with the terms engendered (Simondon 2006, 38).

4. The concept of transduction captures the process of gradual physical, biological, mental, or social becoming—individuation—that puts into communication and structures different zones where it takes place: "Each region of the structure that is constituted in this way then serves to constitute the next one to such an extent that at the very time this structuration is effected there is a progressive modification taking place in tandem with it" (Simondon [1964] 1992, 313). This description of transduction reflects Simondon's attempt to account for the nonlinearity of processes of emergence while still finding a common denominator for different processes of individuation (for instance, the formation of crystals of snow, the transition from the perception of the cold snow to the emotions felt touching it, to the effects on the individuality of a person, to their relation with their surroundings).

5. Simondon's theorization of individuation offers a comprehensive framework to discuss not only the subjectivation of humans at these multiple scales but also the development of technology and its role in processes of subjectivation. This will become clear in the following chapters.

6. Chapters 4 and 5 delve deeper into the role of information within processes of emergence, engaging information theory, cybernetics, and Simondon's understanding of information.

2. Intimacy and Media Making

1. Bifo is quoting André Breton's "Manifesto of Surrealism" (1924).

2. *De-lirium*: mid-sixteenth century, Latin, from *delirare*, "deviate, be deranged" (literally "deviate from the furrow"); from de- ("away") + lira ("ridge between furrows"). *Oxford English Dictionary*, s.v. "delire," accessed April 1, 2009, https://www.oed.com. The latter is a ploughing metaphor.

3. The antipsychiatry movement was particularly strong in the sixties and seventies, denouncing institutional asylums as abusive and violent structures for control and decrying the unequal power relationship between doctors and patients that often led to questionable diagnoses. In Italy, the psychiatrist Franco Basaglia led the democratic psychiatry movement and, with the support of trade unions and the student movement, was able to make asylums and compulsory hospitalization illegal (Nasrallah 2011).

4. Drawing on Charles Pierce and Louis Hjelmslev, Deleuze and Guattari describe the sign (and language) as entirely immanent and socially determined by stratification ([1972] 1983, 240–62; 1987, 39–74).

5. These kinds of pamphlets (e.g., OASK, Senso, la congiura de' pazzi) were called *fogli trasversali* (transversal sheets) and were all produced and circulated in a similar context.

210 · NOTES TO CHAPTER 2

6. This notion of desire refutes the transcendent, idealist, or psychoanalytic approach to "desire as lack"—that is, the drive to fill a lacuna and procure pleasure, discussed in the canonical work of Plato, Georg Wilhelm Friedrich Hegel, and Jacques Lacan. Deleuze and Guattari talk about a kind of "desiring-machine" that connects and disconnects the flow among larger interconnected machines while producing flows itself. The second volume of *Capitalism and Schizophrenia, A Thousand Plateaus,* replaces the concept of a desiring-machine with that of the assemblage.

7. The Vietnam War contributed to shattering the Italian myth of the United States as a country of dreams come true and shed light on its imperialist tendencies. Rather than the United States as a general abstraction, Italian activists identified with their rebelling universities, the Wobblies, the hippie communes, and the Black Panther Party (Ginsborg 1989, 406–9).

8. The theories questioned the labor theory of value and distinguished between labor power (the object of Marxism as a science) and the working class (the subject of Marxism as revolution) (Del Re 2013).

9. It is often accompanied by a theorization of the universal guaranteed minimum wage or basic income (Virno and Hardt 1996).

10. This critique of identity is taken up in Deleuze's book *The Logic of Sense* (1969), through the example of Lewis Carroll's *Alice in Wonderland* and *Through the Looking Glass* (Berardi, Jaquemet, and Vitali 2009, 78).

11. During this period there were two sides to Italian feminism: one that focused on the development of self-awareness (often based in the work of psychoanalysis) and one that was decidedly *operaista* (workerist) (Dalla Costa 2002). The latter produced important breakthroughs in Marxist analysis of gender.

12. The demands for money were primarily a response to the fact that women were financially dependent on men but they were also coupled with demands for the reduction of the working week to twenty hours, freeing time for social reproduction and making visible the labor of producing the laborer. Other women in the institutional left and from other strands of feminism critiqued this position and sought work outside the home. Even within autonomist feminism, some working-women found themselves marginalized by the demands for paid housework (Cuninghame 2008). Alisa Del Re's (2013) analysis of the relation between work and personal time led her to advocate for social services and welfare programs like subsidized childcare to be relieved of work, waged or not, both outside and inside the house. Rather than being completely opposing positions, these could be described as "parallel streams of struggle, progress in both arenas constituting a necessary condition for women's autonomy" (Culbertson 2012).

13. Lotta Femminsta was a splinter group of Potere Operaio. Groups like the International Feminist Collective coordinated actions across countries and held international conferences. Unlike many feminist movements of the time, the

International Feminist Collective also considered race a further layer of oppression, for example in Selma James's *Sex, Race, and Class* (2012). Worth mentioning is also a lesser-known tradition of exchanges between autonomists and black Marxists like C. L. R. James and Raya Dunayevskaya but also race and labor activists like Grace Lee Boggs. Finally, lines of solidarity ran at the intersection of patriarchy, class, and cultural marginalization. Mariarosa Dalla Costa (2002) recounts that "Afro-American women were part of this circuit. They used to say that the strong Italian presence in the circuit had made it conceivable for them to take part in it, because Italian women had little power (a kind of Third World women in their eyes)."

14. Here it is worth mentioning the work of Lea Melandri, a pathbreaking feminist from Milan, who was closer to the self-awareness than the *operaista* movement (the former had a strong footing in the city). Melandri brought together women from different classes through the groups on sexuality and writing *(gruppi di scrittura e sessualità)* and through what she defines as "experience writing" *(scrittura d'esperienza),* where one interrogates the connection between thinking and body memory that shape subjectivity (Melandri 2002, 125).

15. For more information on the terror attacks, see, e.g., De Lutiis (1984) 1994; Willan 1991.

16. The reasons and dynamics behind this coup attempt are not yet clear. The trials linked fascist groups to the government, its secret services, the Free Masons, and the mafia. After a series of harsh sentences, the appeals to the trial ended with an acquittal of all the individuals involved, with the exception of some jail sentences for illegal weapon possession. For more information, see Flamini 2007.

17. In the first fifteen years under the Reale Law (nr. 152 on 22/5/1975), the Italian security forces shot 625 people (254 dead and 371 wounded), of which 208 had not committed and were not about to commit any crimes (Balducci 1990).

18. In his analysis of the relationship between Italian politics and violence, the "Anatomy of Autonomy" (Berardi 2007), Berardi makes a distinction between forms of violent struggle that are necessary for direct action (picketing, occupations, taking to the streets) and forms such as the militarization of the movement through autonomous armed cells, that is, terrorism. This distinction clarifies the contradictory stance of Radio Alice developing as a project that repudiates violence and the radio's support of the riots in March 1977.

19. Shortly after the riots, in September 1977, a convention against repression brought together seventy thousand members of *autonomia* groups and sympathetic international intellectuals to rescue the movement from its crisis. The event merely resulted in the reemergence of an old fracture on the forms of political organization and left the groups ill-equipped to produce any alternatives to the "armed struggle" and to their own looming demise (Berardi 2007, 160). The debate between those who refused any kind of structures that shaped the movement from the inside and those who advocated for a clear political direction of the movement

212 · NOTES TO CHAPTER 2

to reach political mediation with the dominant powers had been an underground force that shaped and reshaped the various groups ever since its beginning. This hard-to-reconcile tension between class subjectivity and political subjectivity is still a major part of the debates that shape Italian autonomist movements (and many others) in the present.

20. Again, here I am careful to stress that the "madness" of a person refers to their behaving outside the norm rather than their being abnormal.

3. Delirium at Work in Berlusconi's Mediascape

1. In 1978 there were 434 private television channels (Barbacetto 2004, 38).

2. Assemblages are a more conceptual and philosophical framing of what the mathematics of topology conceives as manifolds. Like manifolds, assemblages can be made visible by mapping the potential relations among various terms without assigning a specific value to each term (Deleuze and Guattari 1987, 12). In other words, the relation among these terms is differential (Deleuze 1994, 179).

3. For this economic analysis, I draw on Jonathan Nitzan and Shimshon Bichler's theory of differential accumulation. *Differential* accumulation refers to the processes through which economic actors compete to accumulate *in relation to each other* and identifies the kinds of practices that obtain and consolidate power; in our time the practices are characteristic of neoliberalism. With the lens of differential accumulation, I show production from the perspective of power rather than the worker. For Nitzan and Bichler, productivity bears directly on power, while capital accumulation, state formation, and criminal activities are all key elements of a single process to accumulate capital as power (2009, 280). On the whole, struggles for differential accumulation among powerful actors continuously order and reorder society, and their analysis can outline a topology of qualitatively changing power arrangements and the discursive and nondiscursive formations that sustain them (Cochrane 2011).

4. Capital is also redistributed when profits rise faster than it takes for wages to catch up.

5. When looking at assets as capitalized power, government is incorporated into capital and its influence is discounted into corporate stocks and bond prices. In a context in which this process can be made predictable and manipulated through corruption and other practices, accumulation increases more easily, affecting the market/social makeup through more concentration of power into the hands of fewer capitalist groups. These groups, in turn, can condition institutions and shape the logic of capital, often making powerful corporations into de facto regulators (Nitzan and Bichler 2009, 297–99).

6. In his collection of documents and transcripts of all the trials and investigations, Gianni Barbacetto also mentions Berlusconi's membership in the secret

NOTES TO CHAPTER 4 · 213

Masonic Lodge P2, involved, among other things, in an attempted coup d'état. In 1981 fellow members, P2 head Licio Gelli, Communication Minister Michele Di Giesi, and other high-ranking government officials procured Berlusconi the exclusive rights to broadcast live and nationwide a world soccer championship, despite legal restrictions. On many other occasions, Berlusconi's channels were rescued and RAI sabotaged by the prompt intervention of other friends (Barbacetto 2004, 40–41). The secretary to Communication Minister Oscar Mammì left his job right after the law was passed and received from Fininvest a gift of 460 million lire (61).

7. Virtual money transactions enable the economy to thrive even in the absence of "real" capital in the hands of consumers who are subject to job and financial insecurity. Debt itself takes over the function fulfilled by state assistance that guarantees access to basic rights such as housing and education. For a discussion of subjectivation through debt, see Maurizio Lazzarato's *The Making of the Indebted Man: An Essay on the Neoliberal Condition* (2012).

8. Membership in Forza Italia was limited to an initial four thousand members for many years before it was opened again. It still has a screening process.

9. The personalization of politics in Italy was significantly aided by the change to the electoral system from a proportional voting system to a majority one in 1993. Like in the United States, a majority voting system favors the showcasing of top candidates in political debates in the media.

10. Affects were implicated in the reactions of the viewer to the mediality of the medium transmitting the images (Grusin 2010, 81). I believe that Berlusconi's control of the media helped him win, not because he could monopolize the information flows but because he could use marketing and knowledge of affective manipulation developed over the years to reshape the language of politics.

11. Papì is the nickname used by many of Berlusconi's employees (especially young women on his television channels) to address him (Anonymous 2009). While it literally means "daddy" and points to his touted father role for the country, it also has a very strong sexual connotation.

4. Activist Energetics in the Information Milieu

1. Amid the dominant demonization or infantilization of the students, coverage of the 1990 movement also made history in Italian journalism because some mainstream media outlets directly provided a platform for the students to speak for themselves. In this sense, news outlets were partly responsible for the spread of the occupations across the Italian peninsula. Already in December 1989, the left-leaning daily *L'Ora* in Palermo had allowed one of its new journalists, Titti De Simone, who was involved in the occupations, to chronicle the events from within the occupied university. In early January 1990, with a reportage by the

214 · NOTES TO CHAPTER 4

national weekly *L'Espresso* and RAI talk show *Samarcanda*—which had live interventions by the students in the universities—a different representation of the occupations spread across Italy and garnered support (Denaro 2006).

2. As someone who witnessed some of the discussions, I recall that not everyone agreed with associating a political movement with a logo because they felt it was necessary to keep capitalist aesthetics and communication tactics outside politics.

3. One of the social centers squatted that year in Naples was named Tienament (1989–97)—as homage to Chinese students and as a pun on a Neapolitan dialect expression meaning "remember, or keep in mind."

4. Okkupanet reminds us that, while occupation and "Occupy" became a meme in the second decade of the new millennium, many of its tactics and discourses have been part of social movements for a long time, not just in Italy. See, for example, Feigenbaum, Frenzel, and McCurdy 2013.

5. The chat communication features of networks like DECnet and BITnet had already led Jarkko Oikarinen to develop Internet Relay Chat (IRC) in 1988 (Oikarinen 1997). IRC became very popular and is still a common communication tool to chat among hackers.

6. These discourses on heterogeneity within collective subjectivity can be found again in theorizations of the multitude as the vanguard subject of struggle in neoliberal societies (Hardt and Negri 2000, 2004, 2009; Virno 2004).

7. Telecommunications engineer Claude Elwood Shannon (1948) conceived of information as a ratio of signal to noise. His research was concerned with efficient communication of messages and with how signals can overcome noise as they travel through channels. Shannon's theories are helpful to understand the kind of guerrilla communication I have described so far. In Simondon's theories of individuation (2006), information is a structuring force that constantly gives shape to—literally *informs*—structures and systems. His understanding of information is key in framing movements like La Pantera and Telestreet as formations that are subject to constant inputs to change within a milieu where seeds for transformation abound. For a more in-depth discussion of the difference between Simondon's and Shannon's theorization of information, see the work of Thomas Lamarre (2012), Muriel Combes (2013, 51–55), and David Scott (2014, 39–42).

8. Individual perception supports processes of subjectivation (see chapters 3 and 5) while social dynamics connects individuals to groups and broader social formations (see chapters 6 and 7).

9. For a history and characterization of social centers in Italy, see the work of Pierpaolo Mudu (2014).

10. For Maxigas, a scene points to the idea of bodies and machines located in specific sites and performing concrete functions that are part of hacker cultures (Autistici/Inventati 2017, 13). Decoder was founded in Milan in 1986 as a group

interested in social uses of new technologies like the bulletin board system BBS FidoNet (Di Corinto and Tozzi 2002, 220). The Italian FidoNet created the local node of the Association for Progressive Comunication (APC): the Associazione PeaceLink—telematica per la pace (Peacelink Association—telecommunications for peace) (1992) (Di Corinto and Tozzi 2002, 294).

11. Buttressing the work of these tech collectives was free and open-source software (F/OSS) like Dynebolic, which, from 2002 onward, provided media activists with a toolkit for F/OSS multimedia production and audio streaming (eventually video too). Dynebolic runs Linux from a CD-ROM on recycled computers, without having to install the operating system, making media production portable and affordable (Dyne.org 2002). The development of free software for activism fulfilled the multiple aims of bypassing corporate monopoly on hardware and software, guaranteeing more anonymity for users and creating programs and interfaces for information production and circulation. At the same time, discussions about intellectual property became part of a sustained effort to create a knowledge commons. The discussions on cyber rights and on intellectual property eventually engendered projects like Creative Commons (Italy), the Italian version of a transnational "copyleft" set of licenses that guarantees the preservation of some rights for authors while leaving out corporate control.

12. "La Neta" means "the real story" in Mexican slang. Martinez-Torres also discusses prior collaborations to set up BBS-based networks like PaxMex in the 1980s (Martinez-Torres 2001). For an in-depth history of the use of emerging technologies for social struggle in the Americas, see the work of Dorothy Kidd (2004) and Brian Murphy (2002, 2005).

13. The EZLN's use of informational guerrilla tactics became proof of the possibility to tamper with the relationship between government and investors that is key to the flow of capital, by affecting the dominant power's potential to use information for economic gain. Even before the hackers of Anonymous developed more powerful tools for distributed denial-of-service (DDoS) attacks, RAND Corporation research was already defining activist informational guerrilla as *netwar* (Arquilla and Ronfeldt 1997, 369–95; 2001, 171–99; Ronfeldt et al. 1998, xi–xii), pointing to the damaging effects these forms of digital direct information-based action could have on governments and economic actors.

14. The police brutality of Genoa is relived to various degrees still today at protests where governments have standardized their methods of dissent preemption through the protocols of the Miami model (Renzi and Elmer 2013). These include but are not limited to surveillance of online communication, preemptive arrests of organizers, surveillance and infiltration of groups, large police presence, and the use of military less-than-lethal weapons. See, for example, *Preempting Dissent: Policing the Crisis* (Elmer and Opel 2014) and *The Miami Model* (Indymedia 2003).

216 · NOTES TO CHAPTER 4

15. Jeffrey Juris (2008) has discussed in detail the process and debates leading up to the summit and the role of discussions about violence in fragmenting the movement, drawing attention to the lack of internal coordination among organizing groups from Genoa onward.

16. It is possible to observe the continuity between the first debates on consent-based online discussions with Okkupanet and Indymedia's Principles of Unity (http://perthindymedia.net/principles-of-unity), meant to structure interaction among network nodes. Similar strategies and discourses resurface in the moderation criteria of NGVision, the video platform of Telestreet.

17. For instance, the organization of the Florence Social Forum widened the political cracks that had opened after Genoa and strained a movement that was already ailing from repression: "But in Florence it was like a bomb went off. In Florence everything vanished. Everyone huddled around what little was left standing. And for the little that remained, the evictions began, the charges rained down, it was a massacre. A political and human massacre, because people stopped talking to each other, even people within A/I" (Caparossa, qtd. in Autistici/Inventati 2017, 79).

18. A/I provides encryption and anonymity services and does not keep logs of the communication it supports. Nevertheless, on some occasions, police have been able to copy all the data on its servers with the pretext of looking for specific email accounts (Autistici/Inventati 2017, 89).

19. The effect of this growth will impact social movement communication not only because tech collectives will have to compete with more established platforms that are expressly designed with for-profit aims in mind but also because the growth of Web 2.0 will significantly impact discourses on surveillance and privacy: "For example cryptography spread, but in a completely different way from the cypherpunk ideas that had fueled *Kriptonite* or the early A/I collective. E-commerce firms sanctioned and imposed it, whilst users mostly found the complications involved in cryptographic tools to be tiresome, and were happy to trade their privacy for free services" (Autistici/Inventati 2017, 73).

20. The movement was also staffed with an army of militant co-researchers producing knowledge on the new forms of labor—service, migrant, care, and informational—that were becoming more common in the country's service economy (Mattoni 2008). This kind of work created a renaissance of autonomist research on class composition in the new labor force of cognitive capitalism (Tsianos and Papadopoulos 2006; Mattoni 2008; Neilson and Rossiter 2008; Berardi 2009). For a general analysis of the economy, see the work of Andrea Fumagalli (2007) and Nick Dyer-Witheford (1999); for work on labor, race, and immigration, see Sandro Mezzadra and Brett Neilson (2013) and Miguel Mellino and Anna Curcio (2002); for work on gender and precarity, see Alice Mattoni (2008); for precarious work at call centers and in journalism, see Enda Brophy (2017) and Nicole Cohen (2016). Much of the research on precarity has been published on sites like Quaderni di San

Precario (http://quaderni.sanprecario.info/) and has formed the basis for a rethinking of the relationship between communication and the economy in the field of media studies (McKercher and Mosco 2007; Roggero 2011; Brophy 2017). See also *Communication and Critical/Cultural Studies* 11, no. 1 (2014) (e.g., Bratich 2014; Thorburn 2014).

5. Squatted Airwaves, Hacked Transmission

1. The final chapter asks what it would mean to inquire into these recompositions as a form of *conricerca* and as a way of learning from the past to strengthen the future. What can an energetics of movements tell us about media and change and about strategies to strengthen movements and media use?

2. Perception is the act of increasing the information in a system and is at the basis of psychic individuation. The processing of information is what allows the viewer system to reorient every time the system's equilibrium is upset. Muriel Combes explains that a "physical system is said to be in metastable equilibrium (or false equilibrium) when the least modification to the parameters of the system (pressure, temperature, etc.) is sufficient to break the equilibrium of the system. . . . Before every individuation, being can be understood as a system that contains potential energy" (2013, 11). Every metastable system contains potential and its energy is potential because in order to structure itself it requires a transformation of the system.

3. Isole nella Rete is part of the European Counter Network (ECN), a virtual network created in 1989 as a bulletin board system (BBS), which then acquired an internet server in 1996. The network was created after a series of European meetings that started in 1984 (Di Corinto and Tozzi 2002). The ECN is a platform connecting different elements of the extraparliamentary left in Italy and Europe, similar to North American initiatives like Riseup.

4. P2P has a horizontal architecture without suppliers and consumers: everyone partakes in both functions. For these reasons, it can produce use value among freely cooperating nodes rather than exchange value for the market (Bauwens 2005). P2P content-delivery systems have paved the way for the development of all kinds of applications, ranging from music exchange to streaming media and serverless portal systems for anonymous and autonomous web portals.

5. NGVision closed down in 2012, mostly because it had been superseded by commercial video platforms.

6. See Creative Commons, "About," accessed January 2, 2019, https://creative commons.org/.

7. Since all of Telestreet's nodes are strictly noncommercial, there is no advertising. It is worth mentioning that Disco Volante TV was the only channel officially shut down under the pressure of local commercial broadcasters who were afraid of losing viewership and therefore advertising revenues.

218 · NOTES TO CHAPTER 5

8. Procura della Repubblica presso il Tribunale di Ancona, Richiesta di Archiviazione 562/04, in *Art. 408/411 c.p.p., 125 e 126 D.L.v. 271/89* (Ancona, March 1, 2005).

9. Chapter 8 discusses how regulations on digital broadcasting rendered Telestreet's transmission system obsolete and how its ensemble had to be reconfigured again through social media and other available components.

10. To many Telestreettari's dismay, the proposed regulation came to nothing after the collapse of the center-left government and the return of Berlusconi's center-right coalition. Other Telestreet members did not consider this a major defeat since not all nodes were interested in legalizing the network because of the hurdles that come with working within institutional settings. For these people, the molecularity of the Telestreet assemblage allows for creative recomposition in a way that molar, institutionalized media assemblages like public and open channels cannot. Although "Bill Gentiloni," the draft legislation that Telestreet proposed, was never approved, the meetings and discussions for its preparation mark an important moment because of the conflict and of the self-examination that ensued in the network. The discussions about the bill were also the last moment of intense collaboration among many different Telestreet nodes before their general dispersal.

11. The concept of modulation foregrounds the continuity of the process within a metastable system and, as such, always entails the potential for further transformations.

12. While the term *community television* is rather ambiguous and can refer to a variety of grassroots media (Rodríguez 2001; Carpentier 2007), my use of the term is closer to its definition as open-access television, one that has been promoted by activists like George Stoney and projects like Paper Tiger TV (Boyle 1999; Halleck 2002) and that is supported by legislation in many countries.

13. Telestreet has also featured video by Otello Urso, a blind camera operator for SNK TV in Catania.

14. During this interaction, the ceremony host blatantly directed the awards into the hands of the person pushing Civelli's wheelchair, who, in turn, gestured toward Civelli. The exchange is a good reminder that the impact of viewing certain content on television does not always last long enough to replace social habits.

15. Unfortunately, Disco Volante was never able to recover from the blow of the long legal battle and slowly phased out of existence as some of the key people driving the group burned out or had to take leave because of health problems.

6. Subjectivity, Therapy, Compositionality in the Porous Spaces of Naples

1. As part of the interiority that keeps individuals constantly in tension with their environment, the preindividuality of the Neapolitan is only different from that of others insofar as its relation to the outside may be shaped by a more sustained

engagement and intimacy with impermanence. In this sense, many other informal environments are conducive to similar processes of individuation that could be considered an aspect of resilience.

2. Here I am building on Simondon (2006), for whom society is not the result of the reciprocal presence of several individuals; nor is it a substantive reality to superimpose on individual beings, as if it were not dependent on them.

3. The funds to upgrade, outfit, and maintain these spaces come from money raised through large parties that are organized at the university. The university only covers the water and electricity costs (TerzoPiano n.d.).

4. In reality, the protests against the forum were "an invention" of Neapolitan activists. Insu^tv member Wadada explains that the forum itself was not high on the protest agenda of the global justice movement but activists mobilized against it mostly as an occasion for coalition building and to call attention to the impact of neoliberal policies on the city (Stein n.d.).

5. Ten years later, the Coordinating Committee against the Ship Sails lobbied for the demolition of the housing projects because of their inhabitability. In 1998 some of these notorious buildings were finally demolished and new "human-friendly" housing was created in the same area (Festa 2003, 392). Three more buildings will be demolished in 2019. Among the causes of the degradation of the area is the fact that many of the public spaces and community centers that had been planned were never built (Pagliardini 2011).

6. Disobbedienti is an autonomist network active in the global justice movement since 2001 and close to the Italian social centers. Its antecedents were called Tute Bianche (White Overalls). See Azzellini 2009.

7. In general, a critical revision of the history of the unification of Italy in 1861 likens the process to one of colonization of the south by the Savoy monarchy and managerial class from the north. Even Gramsci makes reference to this (Gramsci and Togliatti 1972, 490–91).

8. I prefer to use the term *near colonialism* to discuss the framing of the Southern Question through Fanon's work in recognition that real colonial relations are built on genocidal histories and not on metaphors, no matter how useful (see Tuck and Yang 2012).

9. Southern Italians are often called by northern Italians *terroni,* a derogatory term that means a person of the dirt.

10. Since 2000, Adunata Sediziosa is the yearly festival of the Campania Region's radical grassroots that showcases autonomous cultural production and political debates while fundraising for projects.

11. The choice of a media representative also posed a problem later on when the mainstream media developed the tendency to look for a voice of the movements to talk about actions (Hydrarchist 2005). Having one appointed speaker has often led to the pigeonholing of specific actions and groups. It usually detracts

from the weight that many of the issues contested have on people's everyday lives and prevents broader social identification with the practices.

12. There are general splits in the *area antagonista* of the social centers, which mostly run along the lines of anarchist, Marxist-Leninist, and Disobbedienti (Ceri 2003). While these divisions are political, divisions within divisions sometimes go back to individual exchanges or episodes that cause friction, especially in the handling of direct action.

13. After Genoa, media activists were accused of circulating images that could be used by the authorities as evidence in court. While the media center in Genoa became the site of unprecedented (and unpunished) police violence and human rights violations, the more than forty documentaries produced on the protests and the information on the computers confiscated by the Italian police have been used to prosecute activists. Moreover, with Berlusconi's newly elected government, the movement was not able to open up a debate on the events in the mainstream media in the same way it did in Naples. By demonizing any kind of violent clash as a deliberate attempt to silence the voice of other protesters, the media contributed to deepening the split between more and less radical groups, hampering future collaboration and dialogue.

14. Some of the founders of Radio Alice were part of OrfeoTv.

15. Pirate Radio Sarracino and its other temporary incarnations circulated information and covered events like Adunata Sediziosa.

16. The theorization of media production as a form of social therapy had already started earlier in the seventies, when the psychotherapist and activist followed closely the free radio movement in Italy—especially the work of Radio Alice, with his friend Bifo.

17. Fanon never fully rejected traditional psychoanalysis: the colonial subject is still led by her unconscious—a false self overdetermined by the experience of colonization (Luce 2016). Guattari rejects the notion of the unconscious and pushes for the affirmation of a process of subjectification that is driven by desire; it is self-producing but also collective.

18. The etymology of the word *individual* is from Latin *individuus* from *in-* "not" + *dividuus* "divisible" (from *dividere* "to divide") and is the same root in the word *con-dividere,* which means to share. *Oxford English Dictionary,* s.v. "individual," accessed April 1, 2012, https://www.oed.com.

19. Cobas are Italian local unions that are an alternative to traditional, verticalist unions. These organizations started in schools as Co.Ba.S. (Comitati di Base della Scuola, School Base Committees) that hark back to the coordination organs of autonomist and student movements in the 1970s. They are now organs for workers in different sectors.

20. While retaining the conceptualization of the activist group as the continuation of the activist, one can focus on this empathic mode of coexisting among in-groups without having to focus on the group boundary.

7. Insu^tv, Media Connective

1. Their numbers are rising rapidly. The Italian Ministry of Interior claims that in the first two months of February 2017 alone, 136,215 migrants reached the Italian shores and were hosted in refugee centers (Piccolo 2017).

2. Due to its history, Naples has a very well-developed field of informality that folds in the gray and black economic sector (illegal activities, semihidden factories that often produce counterfeit goods, contraband, etc.) and a cultural sector supported by a local music production industry. The so-called neomelodic music industry produces a huge amount of songs in the Neapolitan language and is distributed by local commercial broadcasters often connected to or owned by the Camorra. The TV channels exist in the gray areas of supposed prelegalization and sometimes close down and open elsewhere. In this sense, piracy in Naples has more support than in other places in Italy. Insu^tv is the only noncommercial station in this local mediascape.

3. A focused analysis of the role of gender in Telestreet is beyond the scope of this book because it would require a long digression into the development of Italian feminism and the opposition to it, as well as a discussion of the construction of gender roles through religion, the media, and popular culture. From what I have seen, different nodes in the network have different discourses and practices around gender. In the case of insu^tv, I find it to be one of the rare spaces in Naples in which gender roles do not shape or polarize interaction. This is particularly worthy of notice because, often, the work connected with technology and media is male-dominated, whereas this is not the case with the insulini. There is also a clear interest among many members of the group in exploring the issues of gender and sexuality from alternative perspectives. This is visible in the collaboration with queer collectives like the *transgeneri,* the support of queer cultural events, and the inquiries into alternative relationships to the body and into sex work.

4. Published by Marotta & Cafiero editori, this award-winning book provides alternative stories about the youth of Scampia to counter mainstream media narrations that paint all young people as members of the Camorra. The word *snow* in the title refers to the abundance of cocaine that is trafficked in the area.

5. Beyond the studios, through the airwaves, and online where the episode is archived, GRIDAS's creative social critique and Vo.di.Sca's books, videos, and theater also reached a wider audience with their nuanced self-representation. This is a residual effect of *Domenica Aut.*

6. Revealing the conflicts and groups involved in direct or indirect local struggles, insu^tv develops concrete analytical maps with the help of communication tools. The video material for the more recent *Domenica Aut* episodes are reassembled into downloadable documentaries that circulate the knowledge produced collaboratively.

222 · NOTES TO CHAPTER 7

7. Members of the movement against the high-speed rail (No TAV) and representatives of the new populist party Cinque Stelle were often at the media center.

8. In a genealogy of the discursive construction of the southern Italian as a race through centuries of ethnographic, medical, and literary studies that underlie political decision-making about the region, Antonello Petrillo (2009) offers an uncanny thread that intersects with Fanon's (2004) discussion of the Algerian racialized subject.

9. NIMBY has also been the strategy to undermine the work of other Italian environmental movements opposing other disastrous plans like the construction of the TAV speed train, military bases, and the bridge connecting the Italian mainland to Sicily. On this topic, see Wu Ming's (2016) gripping and detailed account of twenty-five years of resistance to the speed train in northern Italy.

10. Mogulus was one of the first livestreaming platforms. It launched in 2007 to be rebranded as the popular platform Livestream in 2009.

11. Since its inauguration in 2009, the incineration plant has already been closed down and reopened many times due to corruption scandals, malfunctioning, and toxic particle emission (insu^tv 2009b). Italy has been supporting what Naomi Klein (2008) calls disaster capitalism, a mode of investment that uses crisis to develop projects and policies that would otherwise receive more public scrutiny and would be halted.

12. European Commission, "New Forms of Innovation," Theme: Societal Challenges (H2020-INSO-2014, Sub call of H2020-INSO-2014-2015), posted December 11, 2013, Topic: Understanding and Supporting Business Model Innovation, INSO-2-2014 (funding application in author's possession).

13. This bio was submitted to the Toronto Free Broadcasting event at the Free Gallery in Toronto in October 2009, curated by Tejpal S. Ajji, Chris Lee, and Maiko Tanaka. Insu^tv organized an episode of *Domenica Aut* in the west end of Toronto, where I was living at the time. The episode "Everybody Wants Something" (insu^tv 2009a) focused on issues of gentrification and pollution in the area. We also held a public screening of *Wasting Naples* in collaboration with local organizers dealing with waste management problems in the city.

8. De/Re/Compositions, in Process

1. Scampia's dystopian social housing shaped like the sails of a flotilla will become an international icon through the opening shot of the blockbuster Camorra film *Gomorrah*.

2. Burnout and PTSD, for instance, have to do with extended exposure to stimuli that trigger the release of hypothalamic, pituitary, and adrenal hormones as well as other substances released by the adrenal glands to keep one's attention

focused and ready to flee. The ongoing response to stressful situations affects a body's ability to participate in collective activities and be connected to others.

3. Since 2018 insu^tv has been working on a series of events and videos on migration issues and housing justice, and on archiving its videos and unedited footage, using an open-source, distributed, and autonomous digital archiving platform, currently under construction.

4. Discussions, however, have always been unstructured and unfacilitated and at the moment in which it became harder to communicate, some facilitative principles would have been useful to make the meetings more efficient and perhaps productive.

5. Insu^tv's crew are constantly trying to think of new ways to stabilize the migrant contribution to media activism, but so far, they have not been entirely successful because this would require financial resources that are not available. At the same time, through the contacts and previous collaborations with migrant rights organizations, insu^tv is among the few groups that follow and report on the dramatic events affecting migrant communities in southern Italy, something so rare that mainstream media outlets sometimes contact insu^tv asking for footage.

6. A similar format seems to be emerging through reporting work in new journalistic organizations such as Field of Vision, and in some cases *Vice Magazine*.

7. Open DDB is a sister project to Distribuzioni dal Basso, the crowdsourcing platform for activist and grassroots documentary.

8. Open DDB, "Come Funziona?" [How does it work?], accessed October 11, 2017, http://www.openddb.it/come-funziona.

9. In Canada, the Cinema Politica network has been supporting and distributing political documentaries for more than fifteen years and is deeply connected to Canadian social movements in a variety of ways (Turnin and Winton 2014).

10. For more information on the wave of occupation in the cultural sector in Italy, see the interview with MACAO's Cultural Workers Organize (2013).

11. I believe that some of the political discourses of culture workers running projects like *Stalking Asilo* are less conducive to radical experimentation than those circulating in other social-justice-oriented spaces. Although occupied cultural centers are still important endeavors in the landscape of movements for autonomy and against austerity, the individualistic character of much of the work carried out in these professionalized art spaces and the spaces' relation to mainstream art scenes and to local administrations present a less fertile ground for in-depth, systemic critique of the function of culture for social change. Political differences were not the main reason for the end of *Stalking Asilo* but they certainly challenged its development and caused some friction.

12. Ulises Mejias (2010) has written extensively about how the structure of commercial social media practices affects sociality. Among its effects he discusses

224 · NOTES TO CHAPTER 8

that the reliance on nodal connections (nodocentrism) of social networks excludes as much as it connects.

13. From a perspective of connective activism, it is worth asking whether the underlying homophilic structure of social media platforms can be repurposed to foster porosity among groups. As Wendy Hui Kyong Chun (2016) explained in her insightful lecture on the engineering principles of the internet, "the assumption is that birds of a feather flock together."

14. A similar reconfiguration took place in the early twenty-first century with the explosion of the blogosphere. As NGOs, activists, and community groups were able to self-publish and manage their content online without needing to know HTML (Hypertext Markup Language)—the standard markup language for websites—Indymedia became less relevant for social movements' communication.

15. I am not advocating for abandoning social media but for a more critical attitude toward its affordances. Social media can be useful for organizing (Gerbaudo 2012; Costanza-Chock 2014). Similarly, there are some very inspiring instances of radical livestreaming assemblages (Thorburn 2014, 2015).

16. FairCoop is a global cooperative network developing resources and infrastructure that aims to build an alternative global economic system based on cooperation, ethic, solidarity, and north-south redistribution and justice in economic relations (https://fair.coop/). It uses the crypto-currency Faircoin.

Epilogue

1. It is also worth noting that insu^tv had a strong footing in the Neapolitan social movements and therefore had a larger basis of support than other less political nodes from the Telestreet network.

2. There are new projects like the Liquid Democracy Association that develop open-source software tools that support civic and political participation (Brues and Deseriis 2017). Perhaps these will become technical objects that foster new sociotechnical assemblages for connection. Other kinds of media tools that are not proprietary are being developed to support organizing, including new apps to document police brutality and state violence; affordable software and DIY sensors to crunch data and facilitate citizen science inquiries; secure leaking platforms to foster transparency; and open data platforms for civic media projects.

3. Barad often discusses how, as a principle of physics, diffraction allows us to study both the nature of light and also the nature of the apparatus itself (2007, 73).

Bibliography

((i)). 2008. "Indymedia Italia torna online." Indymedia.ch, June 29. http://ch.indy media.org.

((i)) Italia. 2008. "4 luglio—IndYpendence Day—(Ri)apre ((i)) Italia." Indymedia .ch, June 29. http://ch.indymedia.org.

Albanese, Carmelo. 2010. *C'era un'onda chiamata Pantera*. Rome: Manifestolibri.

Alquati, Romano. 1975. *Sulla Fiat e altri scritti*. Milan: Feltrinelli.

Alquati, Romano. 2002. "Intervista a Romano Alquati—Dicembre 2000." In *Futuro anteriore: Dai "Quaderni rossi" ai movimenti globali; Ricchezze e limiti dell'operaismo italiano*, edited by Guido Borio, Francesca Pozzi, and Gigi Roggero. Rome: DeriveApprodi. CD-ROM.

ami. 2010. "Rifiuti, quando l'Europa scopre la Campania: Poco dialogo con i cittadini e ciclo basato su discariche e termovalorizzatori." Agenza multimediale italiana, May 7. http://www.agenziami.it.

Andrei, Massimo, dir. 2004. *Mater Natura*. Rome: Kubla Khan. DVD.

Andretta, Massimiliano. 2005. "Movimenti e democrazia tra globale e locale: Il caso di Napoli." In *La democrazia locale tra rappresentanza e partecipazione*, edited by Francesca Gelli, 281–318. Milan: FrancoAngeli.

Angrisano, Nicola, dir. 2009. *Una montagna di balle* [Wasting Naples]. Naples: insu^tv. Documentary. http://www.insutv.org.

Angrisano, Nicola, dir. 2010a. *Il tempo delle arance* [Gone with the oranges]. Naples: insu^tv. Documentary. http://www.insutv.org.

Angrisano, Nicola, dir. 2010b. *Via Padova è meglio di Milano* [Via Padova is better than Milan]. Naples: insu^tv. Documentary. http://www.insutv.org.

Angrisano, Nicola, dir. 2011a. *Genuino Clandestino—Movimento di resistenze contadine* [The genuine clandestine—farmer resistance movement]. Naples: insu^tv. Documentary. http://www.insutv.org.

Angrisano, Nicola, dir. 2011b. *Lampedusa Next Stop*. Naples: insu^tv and Radioazioni. Documentary. http://www.insutv.org.

Anonimo. 2003. "Telestreet Rome—Give Sky the 'Boot.'" Accessed February 26, 2010. http://slash.interactivist.net.

Anonymous. 2009. "Papí and the Patriarchal State." IDC mailing list, October 1. https://lists.thing.net.

BIBLIOGRAPHY

Anonymous Digital Coalition. 1998. "Call for Virtual Sit-Ins at Five Mexico Financial Web Sites." *The Thing,* January 19. http://www.thing.net.

ANSA (Agenzia Nazionale Stampa Associata). 2005. "Sicurezza: Bulgarelli (verdi), sconcerta viminale su tv strada interrogazione dopo analisi fenomeno in relazione al Parlamento." Rome 19/01/05-16:26. Press release, January 19.

AntTV, Guerrigliamarketing, OrfeoTV, SpegnilaTV, and Teleaut. 2003. "Dalla tv di strada al decoder di quartiere: Su canale Uhf 26 Juventus/Roma domenica 21.09.03 in chiaro a Roma nel quartiere di San Lorenzo." Press release, September 21.

Ardizzoni, Michela. 2008. "Urban Media Practices as Interventions: An Italian Case Study." *Flow,* November 13. http://flowtv.org.

Armano, Emiliana, Devi Sacchetto, and Steve Wright. 2013. "Coresearch and Counter-Research: Romano Alquati's Itinerary within and beyond Italian Radical Political Thought." *Viewpoint Magazine,* no. 3 (September 27). http://viewpointmag.com.

Armstrong, Amanda. 2012. "Debt and the Student Strike: Antagonisms in the Sphere of Social Reproduction." *Reclamations* 6 (June).

Arquilla, John, and David Ronfeldt. 1997. *In Athena's Camp: Preparing for Conflict in the Information Age.* Santa Monica, Calif.: RAND.

Arquilla, John, and David Ronfeldt. 2001. *Networks and Netwars: The Future of Terror, Crime, and Militancy.* Santa Monica, Calif.: RAND.

Atton, Chris. 2002. *Alternative Media.* London: SAGE.

Autistici/Inventati. 2017. *+Kaos: Ten Years of Hacking and Media Activism.* Edited by Laura Beritelli. Amsterdam: Institute of Network Cultures.

Azzellini, Dario. 2009. "Disobbedienti / Tute Bianche." In *The International Encyclopedia of Revolution and Protest: 1500 to the Present,* 8:1006–10. Hoboken, N.J.: Wiley-Blackwell.

Babylonian. 2003. "Google News Reportedly Has Removed IndyMedia.org Due to Pressure." *MetaFilter* (blog), May 19. http://www.metafilter.com.

Balducci, Ernesto. 1990. *625: Libro bianco sulla Legge Reale; Ricerca sui casi di uccisione e ferimento "da legge Reale."* Milan: Centro di iniziativa Luca Rossi.

Barad, Karen. 2007. *Meeting the Universe Halfway: Quantum Physics and the Entanglement of Matter and Meaning.* Durham, N.C.: Duke University Press.

Barad, Karen. 2011. "Nature's Queer Performativity." *Qui parle* 19 (2): 121–58.

Barad, Karen. 2012. "Intra-actions." Interview by Adam Kleinman. *Mousse* 34 (Summer): 76–81.

Barad, Karen. 2014. "Diffracting Diffraction: Cutting Together-Apart." *Parallax* 20 (3): 168–87.

Barbacetto, Gianni. 2004. *B. Tutte le carte del Presidente.* Milan: M. Tropea.

Barthélémy, Jean-Hugues. 2012. "Fifty Key Terms in the Works of Gilbert Simondon." In *Gilbert Simondon: Being and Technology,* edited by Arne De Boever,

Alex Murray, Jon Roffe, and Ashley Woodward, 203–31. Edinburgh: Edinburgh University Press.

Bauwens, Michel. 2005. "The Political Economy of Peer Production." *Post-Autistic Economics Review* 37 (January 1).

Benjamin, Walter. (1924) 1978. "Naples." In *Reflections: Essays, Aphorisms, Autobiographical Writings*, edited by Asja Lacis, 163–73. New York: Harcourt Brace Jovanovich.

Bennett, W. Lance. 2013. *The Logic of Connective Action: Digital Media and the Personalization of Contentious Politics.* Cambridge: Cambridge University Press.

Bennett, W. Lance, and Alexandra Segerberg. 2012. "The Logic of Connective Action." *Information, Communication & Society* 15 (5): 739–68.

Berardi, Franco [Bifo]. 2007a. "Anatomy of Autonomy." In *Autonomia: Post-political Politics,* edited by Hedi El Kholti, Sylvere Lotringer, and Christian Marazzi, 148–70. Los Angeles, Calif.: Semiotext(e).

Berardi, Franco [Bifo]. 2007b. "Franco Berardi Lecture, Feb 9th 07." Micropolitics Research Group, February 12. http://micropolitics.wordpress.com.

Berardi, Franco [Bifo]. 2008. *Félix Guattari: Thought, Friendship, and Visionary Cartography.* Translated and edited by Giuseppina Mecchia and Charles J. Stivale. New York: Palgrave Macmillan.

Berardi, Franco [Bifo]. 2009. *Precarious Rhapsody: Semiocapitalism and the Pathologies of the Post-alpha Generation.* London: Minor Compositions.

Berardi, Franco [Bifo]. n.d. "What Is the Meaning of Autonomy Today? Subjectivation, Social Composition, Refusal of Work." *Multitudes: Revue politique, artistique, philosophique* (blog), accessed March 1, 2010. http://multitudes.net.

Berardi, Franco [Bifo], Marco Jaquemet, and Gianfranco Vitali. 2009. *Ethereal Shadows: Communications and Power in Contemporary Italy.* New York: Autonomedia.

Berlusconi, Silvio. 1990. "Prefazione." In *Elogio Della Follia*, by Erasmo da Rotterdam. Milan: Silvio Berlusconi Editore.

Berlusconi, Silvio. 1994a. "Il nostro Paese ha bisogno di fiducia e di speranza: Il primo discorso del Presidente Berlusconi, Roma, Palafiera—6 febbraio 1994." Speech. http://www.ilpopolodellaliberta.it.

Berlusconi, Silvio. 1994b. "Per il mio paese." *Il discorso della discesa in campo,* January 26. http://www.cini92.altervista.org.

Berlusconi, Silvio. 2001. *Una storia italiana.* Milan: Mondadori.

Beschi, Carlo. 2005. "Indymedia Italia: Quando gli hacker fanno politica." Master's thesis, Università degli studi di Bologna.

Bianchi, Sergio, Manolo Luppichini, and Nanni Balestrini, dirs. 1994. *Batti il tuo tempo.* Rome: Onda Rossa Posse. Documentary.

Blisset, Luther. 2004. "Make Media, Make Trouble: Hacking the Infocalypse in the Italian Telestreet." *Arena Magazine* 7 (April–May). http://www.arena.org.au.

228 · BIBLIOGRAPHY

Borio, Guido, Francesca Pozzi, and Gigi Roggero, eds. 2002. *Futuro anteriore: Dai "Quaderni rossi" ai movimenti globali; Ricchezze e limiti dell'operaismo italiano.* Rome: DeriveApprodi.

Botti, Simone. 1990. "Okkupanet: Un mass media introspettivo e disposto all'autocritica." *Il Manifesto,* March 28, sec. Cultura e Comunicazione, 12.

Boyle, Deirdre. 1999. "O Lucky Man! George Stoney's Lasting Legacy." *Wide Angle* 21 (2): 10–18.

Braman, Sandra. 2011. "Anti-terrorism Laws and the Harmonization of Media and Communication Policy." In *Handbook of Global Media and Communication Policy,* edited by Robin Mansell and Marc Raboy, 486–504. Oxford: Wiley-Blackwell.

Bratich, Jack. 2014. "Occupy All the Dispositifs: Memes, Media Ecologies, and Emergent Bodies Politic." *Communication and Critical/Cultural Studies* 11 (1): 64–73.

Breton, André. 1924. "First Manifesto of Surrealism—1924." Reprinted in *Oeuvres complètes,* edited by Marguerite Bonnet (Paris: Éditions Gallimard, 1988), 1:328.

Bronson, John. 2004. "Silvio Berlusconi Controls the National Airwaves in Italy." *Adbusters* 12 (51): 22.

Brophy, Enda. 2017. *Language Put to Work: The Making of the Global Call Centre Workforce.* London: Palgrave Macmillan.

Brues, Rouven, and Marco Deseriis. 2017. "Adhocracy Helps Create a Future of Political Engagement." Open Democracy, February 17. https:// www.opendemoc racy.net/.

Bruns, Axel. 2008. *Blogs, Wikipedia, Second Life, and Beyond: From Production to Produsage.* New York: Peter Lang.

"Campania: Una montagna di balle spopola sul web; Scandalo rifiuti mai finito." 2009. *Costiera on-line,* November 19. https://ecostiera.it.

Carpentier, Nico. 2007. "The On-line Community Media Database RadioSwap as a Translocal Tool to Broaden the Communicative Rhizome." *Observatorio Journal* 1 (1): 1–26.

Casagrande, Orsola. 2009. "Altra Italia—Braccio di ferro con il sindaco. Aska Torino rischia." *Il Manifesto,* November 18.

Castells, Manuel. 1996. *The Rise of the Network Society.* Malden, Mass.: Blackwell.

Castells, Manuel. (1997) 2004. *The Power of Identity.* London: Blackwell.

Castells, Manuel. 2012. *Networks of Outrage and Hope: Social Movements in the Internet Age.* Cambridge, UK: Polity.

Ceri, Paolo. 2003. *La democrazia dei movimenti come decidono i noglobal.* Soveria Mannelli (Catanzaro): Rubbettino.

Chainworkers.org CreW. 2004. "Kit San Precario." Downloadable propaganda. Accessed March 21, 2017. http://kit.sanprecario.info/.

Chetta, Alessandro. 2009. "Il pm De Chiara: Nel film sulle ecoballe diversi spunti di indagine." *Il corriere della sera,* July 16.

BIBLIOGRAPHY · 229

Chiesa, Guido, dir. 2004. *Lavorare con lentezza: Radio Alice, 100.6 MHz.* Bologna: Fandango and Le Films Des Tournelles-Roissy. Drama film.

Chiurchiù, Luca. 2017. *La rivoluzione è finita abbiamo vinto: Storia della rivista "A/ traverso."* Rome: Derive Approdi.

Chun, Wendy Hui Kyong. 2016. "Queerying Homophily: Re-imagining Network Analytics, Re-imagining Difference." HTC Forum Public Lecture Series, Cambridge, Mass., November 1.

Civelli, Franco, dir. 2003. *Barriere* [Barriers]. Senigallia: Disco Volante TV. TV show.

Cleaver, Harry. 1999. "Computer-Linked Social Movements and the Global Threat to Capitalism." Global Solidarity Network, July. https://la.utexas.edu.

Coates, Kenneth. 2015. *#IdleNoMore and the Remaking of Canada.* Regina, Saskatchewan: University of Regina Press.

Cochrane, David Troy. 2011. "Castoriadis, Veblen, and the 'Power Theory of Capital.'" In *Depoliticization: The Political Imaginary of Global Capitalism,* edited by Ingrid Straume and J. F. Humphrey, 89–123. Malmo, Sweden: NSU Press.

Cohen, Nicole S. 2016. *Writers' Rights: Freelance Journalism in a Digital Age.* Montreal: McGill-Queen's University Press.

Colectivo Situaciones. 2005. "Something More on Research Militancy." *Ephemera: Theory & Politics in Organization* 5 (4): 602–14.

Coleman, E. Gabriella. 2013. *Coding Freedom: The Ethics and Aesthetics of Hacking.* Princeton, N.J.: Princeton University Press.

Coleman, E. Gabriella. 2016. "Hacker." In *Digital Keywords: A Vocabulary of Information Society and Culture,* edited by Benjamin Peters, 158–72. Princeton, N.J.: Princeton University Press.

Collettivo A/traverso. 2007. *Alice è il diavolo: Storia di una radio sovversiva.* Edited by Bifo and Gomma. Milan: ShaKe.

Combes, Muriel. 2013. *Gilbert Simondon and the Philosophy of the Transindividual.* Cambridge, Mass.: MIT Press.

Comitato per il Salario al Lavoro Domestico di Padova. 1976. "Sul movimento maschile." *Le operaie della casa,* June/July.

Conti, Antonio. 2001a. "Inchiesta come metodo politico." *Posse,* nos. 2–3: 23–30.

Conti, Antonio. 2001b. "L'inchiesta oggi." *Posse,* nos. 2–3: 12–21.

Conti, Antonio, Anna Curcio, Alberto De Nicola, Paolo Do, Serena Fredda, Margherita Emiletti, Serena Orazi, Gigi Roggero, Davide Sacco, and Giuliana Visco. 2007. "The Anamorphosis of Living Labour." *Ephemera: Theory & Politics in Organization* 7 (1): 78–87.

Costanza-Chock, Sasha. 2014. *Out of the Shadows, into the Streets! Transmedia Organizing and the Immigrant Rights Movement.* Cambridge, Mass.: MIT Press.

Coté, Mark, and Jennifer Pybus. 2011. "Learning to Immaterial Labour 2.0: Facebook and Social Network." In *Cognitive Capitalism, Education, and Digital Labor,* edited by Michael A. Peters and Ergin Bulut, 169–94. New York: Peter Lang.

230 · BIBLIOGRAPHY

Couldry, Nick, and James Curran. 2003. *Contesting Media Power: Alternative Media in a Networked World.* Lanham, Md.: Rowman & Littlefield.

Cowen, Deborah. 2017. "Infrastructures of Empire and Resistance." Verso blog, January 25. https://www.versobooks.com.

Crary, Jonathan. 1984. "Eclipse of the Spectacle." In *Art after Modernism: Rethinking Representation,* edited by Brian Wallis and Marcia Tucker, 283–94. New York: New Museum of Contemporary Art.

Culbertson, Anna. 2012. "The Terrain of Reproduction: Alisa Del Re's 'The Sexualization of Social Relations.'" *Viewpoint Magazine,* no. 2 (September 12). http://viewpointmag.com.

Cultural Workers Organize. 2013. "'Messages of Rupture': An Interview with Emanuele Braga on the MACAO Occupation in Milan." *Scapegoat: Landscape, Architecture, Political Economy* 4:179–87.

Cuninghame, Patrick. 2008. "Italian Feminism, Workerism and Autonomy in the 1970s." *Amnis* 8. doi:10.4000/amnis.575.

Dalla Costa, Mariarosa. 2002. "The Door to the Garden: Feminism and Operaismo." Paper presented at the Seminario sull'Operaismo, Rome, June 1–2.

Dalla Costa, Mariarosa, and Selma James. 1975. *The Power of Women and the Subversion of the Community: Women and the Subversion of the Community.* Brooklyn, N.Y.: Pétroleuse Press.

Davidkhanian, Caren. 2004. "Italy Tuning in to Local 'Street TV.'" *Hollywood Reporter,* May 11.

Debord, Guy. 1983. *Society of the Spectacle.* Translated by Ken Knabb. Wellington, N.Z.: Rebel Press.

Deleuze, Gilles. 1969. *The Logic of Sense.* London: London Bloomsbury Academic.

Deleuze, Gilles. 1986. *Cinema 1: The Movement Image.* Minneapolis: University of Minnesota Press.

Deleuze, Gilles. 1988. *Spinoza: Practical Philosophy.* Translated by Robert Hurley. San Francisco: City Lights Books.

Deleuze, Gilles. 1994. *Difference and Repetition.* Translated by Paul Patton. New York: Columbia University Press.

Deleuze, Gilles. 1995. "Postscript on Control Societies." In *Negotiations: 1972–1990,* 177–82. New York: Columbia University Press.

Deleuze, Gilles. 2004. *Desert Islands and Other Texts: 1953–1974.* New York: Semiotext(e).

Deleuze, Gilles. 2006. *Two Regimes of Madness: Texts and Interviews 1975–1995.* New York: Semiotext(e).

Deleuze, Gilles, and Félix Guattari. (1972) 1983. *Anti-Oedipus: Capitalism and Schizophrenia.* Translated by Robert Hurley, Mark Seem, and Helen R. Lane. Minneapolis: University of Minnesota Press.

BIBLIOGRAPHY · 231

Deleuze, Gilles, and Félix Guattari. 1986. *Kafka: Toward a Minor Literature.* Translated by Dana Polan. Minneapolis: University of Minnesota Press.

Deleuze, Gilles, and Félix Guattari. 1987. *A Thousand Plateaus: Capitalism and Schizophrenia.* Translated by Brian Massumi. Minneapolis: University of Minnesota Press.

Delisa, Antonio. 2012. "Storia dei movimenti studenteschi—'La Pantera siamo noi' (1989–1990)." *Nuova Storia Culturale / New Cultural History* 6 (December 2). https://storiografia.me.

Del Re, Alisa. 2013. "Workers' Inquiry and Reproductive Labor." *Viewpoint Magazine,* no. 3 (September 25). http://www.viewpointmag.com.

De Lutiis, Giuseppe. (1984) 1994. *Storia dei servizi segreti in Italia.* Rome: Editori Riuniti.

Demers, Jason. 2008. "For a Political Gilles Deleuze." *Theory and Event* 11 (1).

Denaro, Massimiliano. 2006. "1990: Il Movimento studentesco della 'Pantera.'" Master's thesis, Facoltà di Scienze Politiche, Università di Pisa.

Deseriis, Marco. 2015. *Improper Names: Collective Pseudonyms from the Luddites to Anonymous.* Minneapolis: University of Minnesota Press.

Deseriis, Marco, and Alessandra Renzi. 2014. "Nonhuman Solidarities: The Impact of Crowdsourcing on Media Activism and Hacktivism." Paper presented at Digital Labor: Sweatshops, Picket Lines, and Barricades, New School, New York, November 14–16.

Di Corinto, Arturo, and Tommaso Tozzi. 2002. *Hacktivism: La libertà nelle maglie della rete.* Rome: Manifestolibri.

Direzione Generale dell'Immigrazione e delle Politiche di Integrazione del Ministero del Lavoro e delle Politiche Sociali. n.d. "La Regione Campania." Accessed February 2, 2017. http://www.integrazionemigranti.gov.it.

Disco Volante TV. 2003. "Conferenza Stampa Guido Calvi." August 1. http://www.viveresenigallia.it.

Disco Volante TV. 2004. "Premio Ilaria Alpi." June 7. Video interview. Accessed February 2, 2010. https://www.viveresenigallia.it.

Dolphijn, Rick, and Iris van der Tuin. 2012. *New Materialism: Interviews & Cartographies.* Utrecht: Open Humanities Press.

Downing, John D. H., Tamara Villareal Ford, Geneve Gil, and Laura Stein. 2001. *Radical Media: Rebellious Communication and Social Movements.* Thousand Oaks, Calif.: SAGE.

Dyer-Witheford, Nick. 1999. *Cyber-Marx: Cycles and Circuits of Struggle in High-Technology Capitalism.* Urbana: University of Illinois Press.

Dyne.org. 2002. "Dynebolic: Free & Live Creative Multimedia." Accessed February 26, 2010. https:// www.dyne.org.

Elmer, Greg, and Andy Opel, dirs. 2014. *Preempting Dissent: Policing the Crisis.* Documentary produced by Boaz Beeri, Steven James May, Greg Elmer, Andy Opel, and Alessandra Renzi. Toronto.

232 · BIBLIOGRAPHY

Escobar, Arturo, and Sonia E. Alvarez. 1992. *The Making of Social Movements in Latin America: Identity, Strategy, and Democracy.* Boulder, Colo.: Westview.

Esposito La Rossa, Rosario. 2007. *Al di là della neve: Storie di Scampia.* Napoli: Marotta e Cafiero.

EZLN. 1996. "Camino andando comunicados y actividades anteriores del EZLN." Accessed February 26, 2010. http://palabra.ezln.org.mx/.

Fals-Borda, Orlando, and Muhammad Anisur Rahman, eds. 1991. *Action and Knowledge: Breaking the Monopoly with Participatory Action Research.* New York: Apex Press.

Fanon, Frantz. 2004. *The Wretched of the Earth.* Translated by Richard Philcox. New York: Grove.

Federici, Silvia. 2012. *Revolution at Point Zero: Housework, Reproduction, and Feminist Struggle.* Brooklyn, N.Y.: Autonomedia.

Federici, Silvia. 2014. *Caliban and the Witch: Women, the Body and Primitive Accumulation.* Brooklyn, N.Y.: Autonomedia.

Feigenbaum, Anna, Fabian Frenzel, and Patrick McCurdy. 2013. *Protest Camps.* London: Zed Books.

Fenton, Natalie, and Veronica Barassi. 2011. "Alternative Media and Social Networking Sites: The Politics of Individuation and Political Participation." *Communication Review,* no. 14: 179–96.

Ferri, Fabio. n.d. "La Pantera siamo noi." *Il megafono quotidiano.* Accessed October 1, 2017. http://ilmegafonoquotidiano.it.

Festa, Francesco Antonio. 2003. "L'alchimia ribelle napoletana: Materiali per una storia della città antagonista." In *Potere e società a Napoli a cavallo del secolo: Omaggio a Percy Allum,* edited by O. Cappelli, 381–423. Naples: Edizioni scientifiche italiane.

Festa, Francesco Antonio. 2008. "Oltre la rappresentanza politica." Unpublished manuscript in author's possession.

Fiori, Dario. 2011. *La rivoluzione della creatività.* Vol. 2, *Riscoprire.* Milan: LibriSenzaData.

Flamini, Gianni. 2007. *L'Italia dei colpi di stato.* Rome: Newton Compton Editori.

Fontanarosa, Aldo. 2006. "Decoder tv, Berlusconi assolto 'Nessun conflitto d'interessi.'" *La Repubblica,* May 12.

Fortunati, Leopoldina. (1981) 1995. *The Arcane of Reproduction: Housework, Prostitution, Labor and Capital.* Brooklyn, N.Y.: Autonomedia.

Foucault, Michel. 1979. *Discipline and Punish: The Birth of the Prison.* Translated by Alan Sheridan. Harmondsworth: Penguin.

Foucault, Michel. 2008. *The Birth of Biopolitics: Lectures at the Collège de France, 1978–79.* Edited by Michel Senellart. New York: Palgrave Macmillan.

Frassanito Network. 2004. "Movements of Migration." European Social Forum, London, October 15–17. Pamphlet.

Freeman, Jo. 1970. *The Tyranny of Structurelessness*. Leeds: Leeds Women's Organization of Revolutionary Anarchists.

Freire, Paulo. 2007. *Pedagogy of the Oppressed*. New York: Continuum.

Fumagalli, Andrea. 2007. *Bioeconomia e capitalismo cognitivo: Verso un nuovo paradigma di accumulazione*. Rome: Carocci.

Gambino, Michele. 2001. *Il cavaliere B.: Chi è e che cosa vuole l'uomo che sogna di cambiare l'Italia*. Lecce: Manni.

Garcia, David. 2006. "Learning the Right Lessons." *Mute*, January 25. http://www.metamute.org.

Garcia, David, and Geert Lovink. 1997. "The ABC of Tactical Media." Nettime mailing list, May 16. https://thing.desk.nl/.

Garrone, Matteo, dir. 2008. *Gomorrah*. n.p.: Fandango. Drama film.

Gerbaudo, Paolo. 2012. *Tweets and the Streets: Social Media and Contemporary Activism*. London: Pluto Press.

Gervasio, Simone. 2018. "La resistenza napoletana alla gentrification." *magzine* (blog), January 22. http://www.magzine.it.

Gherardi, Silvia, and Annalisa Murgia. 2015. "Staging Precariousness: The Serpica Naro Catwalk during the Milan Fashion Week." *Culture and Organization* 21 (2): 174–96.

Ginsborg, Paul. 1989. *Storia d'italia dal dopoguerra a oggi: Società e politica, 1943–1988*. Turin: Einaudi.

Giraud, Eva. 2014. "Has Radical Participatory Online Media Really 'Failed'? Indymedia and Its Legacies." *Convergence* 20 (4): 419–37.

Giurdanella, Antonino. 2014. "La Pantera Siamo Noi." *Mangiatori di Cervello* (blog), November 23. https://mangiatoridicervelli.wordpress.com.

Goddard, Michael. 2018. *Guerrilla Networks: An Anarchaeology of 1970s Radical Media Ecologies*. Amsterdam: Amsterdam University Press.

Gramsci, Antonio. 1995. *La questione meridionale*. Rome: Riuniti.

Gramsci, Antonio, and Palmiro Togliatti. 1972. "Tesi." In *La costruzione del Partito Comunista, 1923–1926*, 488–513. Turin: Einaudi.

Grasso, Gianna. 2003. "13 maggio 2001: Le immagini di Berlusconi e Rutelli e l'influenza sulle scelte degli elettori." In *Le campagne elettorali: VIII Convegno S.I.S.E.* Conference proceedings, Società Italiana Studi Elettorali Venice, December 18–20. http://www.studielettorali.it.

Greedharry, Mrinalini. 2008. *Postcolonial Theory and Psychoanalysis: From Uneasy Engagements to Effective Critique*. New York: Palgrave Macmillan.

Greenwood, Davydd J., William Foote Whyte, and Ira Harkavy. 1993. "Participatory Action Research as a Process and as a Goal." *Human Relations* 46 (2): 175–92.

GRIDAS. n.d. "Storia, vita e miracoli del Gridas." Accessed June 24, 2015. http://www.felicepignataro.org.

234 · BIBLIOGRAPHY

Grusin, Richard A. 2010. *Premediation: Affect and Mediality after 9/11*. New York: Palgrave Macmillan.

Guattari, Félix. 1974. *Una tomba per Edipo*. Edited by Luisa Muraro. Verona: Bertani.

Guattari, Félix. 1995. *Chaosmosis: An Ethico-aesthetic Paradigm*. Translated by Paul Bains and Julian Pefanis. Sydney: Power Publications.

Guattari, Félix. 1996. *Soft Subversions*. New York: Semoiotext(e).

Guattari, Félix. 2012. "Towards a Post-media Era." *Mute,* February 1. http://www.metamute.org.

Guattari, Félix, and Antonio Negri. 1990. *Communists like Us: New Spaces of Liberty, New Lines of Alliance*. New York: Semiotext(e).

Gubitosa, Carlo, and Peacelink. 1999. *Italian Crackdown: BBS amatoriali, volontari telematici, censure e sequestri nell'Italia degli anni '90*. Milan: Apogeo.

Haiven, Max. 2011. "Feminism, Finance and the Future of #Occupy—An Interview with Silvia Federici." *ZNet,* November 25. https://is.muni.cz.

Haiven, Max, and Alex Khasnabish. 2013. "Between Success and Failure: Dwelling with Social Movements in the Hiatus." *Interface: A Journal for and about Social Movements* 5 (2): 472–98.

Hale, Charles R. 2008. *Engaging Contradictions: Theory, Politics, and Methods of Activist Scholarship*. Berkeley: University of California Press.

Halleck, DeeDee. 2002. *Hand-Held Visions: The Impossible Possibilities of Community Media*. New York: Fordham University Press.

Haraway, Donna J. 2016. *Staying with the Trouble: Making Kin in the Chthulucene*. Durham, N.C.: Duke University Press.

Hardt, Michael, and Antonio Negri. 2000. *Empire*. Cambridge, Mass.: Harvard University Press.

Hardt, Michael, and Antonio Negri. 2004. *Multitude: War and Democracy in the Age of Empire*. New York: Penguin.

Hardt, Michael, and Antonio Negri. 2009. *Commonwealth*. Cambridge, Mass.: Belknap Press of Harvard University Press.

Harney, Stefano, and Fred Moten. 2013. *The Undercommons: Fugitive Planning & Black Study*. Brooklyn, N.Y.: Autonomedia.

Hartwig, Robert. 1995. *Basic TV Technology: A Media Manual*. Boston: Focal Press.

Harvey, David. 2005. *A Brief History of Neoliberalism*. New York: Oxford University Press.

Heller, Monica. 2001. "Critique and Sociolinguistic Analysis of Discourse." *Critique of Anthropology* 21 (2): 117–41.

Howley, Kevin. 2010. *Understanding Community Media*. Los Angeles: SAGE.

Hugill, David, and Elise Danielle Thorburn. 2012. "Reactivating the Social Body in Insurrectionary Times: A Dialogue with Franco 'Bifo' Berardi." *Berkeley Planning Journal* 25 (1): 210–20. http://escholarship.org.

Hydrarchist. 2005. "Disobbedienti, Ciao." *Mute*, February 8. http://www.meta mute.org.

Indybay. 2001. "Genoa: Many Eyewitness Reports for Police Raid of Italy Indymedia Center—GSF." July 21. https:// www.indybay.org.

Indybay. 2003. "Google News Bans SF Bay Area Indymedia over Israel/Palestine Controversy." September 3. https://www.indybay.org.

Indymedia, dir. 2003. *The Miami Model*. Documentary produced by Indymedia.

Indymedia Italia. 2002. "Press Release—Indymedia Italy under Attack." https:// stallman.org.

Indymedia Montreal 2016 Convergence Working Group. 2017. "Holding Out for Un-alienated Communication." *Briarpatch*, January/February. https://briarpatch magazine.com.

Indymedia Piemonte. 2012. "Coeclerici vs Indymedia: I provider si ribellano." Accessed June 24, 2015. http://piemonte.indymedia.org.

insu^tv. 2006. "Citta' e Periferia" [City and suburbia]. Naples: insu^tv. Episode of *Domenica Aut*. http://www.insutv.it.

insu^tv. 2008. *Castelvolturno 20 novembre: La polizia devasta l'American Palace e deporta 57 immigrati!* [Castelvolturno, November 20th: Police destroy the American Palace and deport 57 migrants]. Naples: insu^tv. Video. www.insutv.org.

insu^tv. 2009a. "Everybody Wants Something." Toronto: insu^tv. Episode of *Domenica Aut*. MiniDV tape.

insu^tv. 2009b. "Onda su onda—Videonarrazione del movimento studentesco" [Wave upon wave—Video narration of the student movement]. Naples: insu^tv. Episode of *Domenica Aut*. www.insutv.org.

insu^tv. 2009c. *Sgombero dei braccianti marocchini di San Nicola Varco (Sa)* [Eviction of Moroccan laborers in San Nicola Varco (Sa)]. Naples: insu^tv. Video. www.insutv.org.

insu^tv. 2010a. "Assalto al cielo continua . . . prossimo appuntamento ven 19 marzo ore 18." Naples. Poster.

insu^tv. 2014. *Stalking Asilo: Talkshow indipendente* [Stalking Asilo: Independent talk show]. Naples: insu^tv and Collettivo la Balena. TV show. www.insutv.org.

insu^tv. n.d. *Domenica Aut*. Website for TV show. Accessed June 24, 2015. http:// www.insutv.it/domenicaut.

Jackson, Sarah J., and Brooke Foucault Welles. 2016. "#Ferguson Is Everywhere: Initiators in Emerging Counterpublic Networks." *Information, Communication & Society* 19 (3): 397–418.

James, Selma. 2012. *Sex, Race, and Class: The Perspective of Winning: A Selection of Writings, 1952–2011*. Oakland, Calif.: PM Press.

Janković, Radmila Iva. 2004. "Barging into the Collective Body of Images." *ART-e-FACT Strategies of Resistance*, no. 3. http://artefact.mi2.hr.

236 · BIBLIOGRAPHY

Jenkins, Henry, Sam Ford, and Joshua Green. 2013. *Spreadable Media: Creating Value and Meaning in a Networked Culture*. New York: New York University Press.

Juris, Jeffrey S. 2008. *Networking Futures: The Movements against Corporate Globalization*. Durham, N.C.: Duke University Press.

Katsarova, Rada. 2015. "Repression and Resistance on the Terrain of Social Reproduction: Historical Trajectories, Contemporary Openings." *Viewpoint Magazine*, no. 5 (October 31). http://viewpointmag.com.

Kaufman, Eleanor. 2001. *The Delirium of Praise: Bataille, Blanchot, Deleuze, Foucault, Klossowski*. Baltimore: Johns Hopkins University Press.

Kidd, Dorothy. 2004. "Carnival to Commons." In *Confronting Capitalism: Dispatches from a Global Movement*, edited by Eddie Yuen, Daniel Burton-Rose, and George N. Katsiaficas, 328–38. Brooklyn, N.Y.: Soft Skull Press.

Klang, Mathias, and Nora Madison. 2016. "The Domestication of Online Activism." *First Monday* 21 (6).

Klein, Naomi. 2000. *No Logo: Taking Aim at the Brand Bullies*. Toronto: Knopf Canada.

Klein, Naomi. 2008. *The Shock Doctrine: The Rise of Disaster Capitalism*. Toronto: Vintage Canada.

Knight, Ben. 2017. "Interior Ministry Shuts Down, Raids Left-Wing German Indymedia Site." *Deutsche Welle*, August 25.

Kogawa, Tetsuo. 1999. "Minima Memoranda: A Note on Streaming Media." March 12–14. http://anarchy.translocal.jp.

Kogawa, Tetsuo. 2000. "Two or Three Things That I Know about the Streaming Media." http://anarchy.translocal.jp.

Kohl, Christiane. 2003. "Der schwarze Kanal." *Süddeutsche Zeitung*, April 12. https://www.sueddeutsche.de.

Laboratorio Occupato SKA and C. S. Leoncavallo. 1995. *El Sup: Racconti per una notte di asfissia*. Milan and Naples: Spray Edizioni.

Lamarre, Thomas. 2012. "Humans and Machines." *Inflexions*, no. 5 (March): 29–67.

Langlois, Ganaele. 2014. *Meaning in the Age of Social Media*. New York: Palgrave Macmillan.

La Pantera. 1990. *Videogiornale Pantera*. Video newsreel.

Lazzarato, Maurizio. 1993. "General Intellect: Verso l'inchiesta sul lavoro immateriale." *Riff Raff*, no. 1: 65–71.

Lazzarato, Maurizio. 1996. "Immaterial Labor." In *Radical Thought in Italy*, edited by Paolo Virno and Michael Hardt, 132–46. Minneapolis: University of Minnesota Press.

Lazzarato, Maurizio. 2001. "Nomi e utensili." *Posse*, nos. 2–3: 32–41.

Lazzarato, Maurizio. 2007. "Strategies of the Political Entrepreneur." *SubStance* 36 (1): 86–97.

Lazzarato, Maurizio. 2012. *The Making of the Indebted Man: An Essay on the Neoliberal Condition.* Translated by Joshua David Jordan. New York: Semiotext(e).

Lazzarato, Maurizio. 2014. *Signs and Machines: Capitalism and the Production of Subjectivity.* Translated by Joshua David Jordan. New York: Semiotext(e).

Lazzarato, Maurizio, Erin Manning, and Brian Massumi. 2009. "Grasping the Political in the Event." Interview with Maurizio Lazzarato. *Inflexions,* no. 3 (October): 1–9. http://www.senselab.ca.

Letta, Gianni. 2008. "Silvio viaggia con due marcie in più." *Il Giornale,* April 21.

Lewin, K. 1946. "Action Research and Minority Problems." *Journal of Social Issues* 2 (4): 34–46.

Luce, Sandro. 2016. "From Fanon to the Postcolonials: For a Strategic and Political Use of Identities." *Política Común* 9. https://quod.lib.umich.edu/p/pc/.

Ludovico, Alessandro. 2003. "The Revolution WILL Be Broadcast—At Least Locally." *Springerin* 2 (03).

Luppichini, Manolo, and Claudio Metallo, dirs. 2008. *Fratelli di TAV.* Italy. Documentary produced by Effetti collaterali del Treno ad Alta Velocità, Teleimmagini, and CandidaTV.

MacDonald, Cathy. 2012. "Understanding Participatory Action Research." *Canadian Journal of Action Research* 13 (2): 34–50.

Mackenzie, Adrian. 2008. "Codecs." In *Software Studies: A Lexicon,* edited by Matthew Fuller, 48–54. Cambridge, Mass.: MIT Press.

Mancini, Roberto. 2009. "The Day Italy Says No to Berlusconi." *The Guardian,* December 4, 2009.

Martinez-Torres, Maria Elena. 1997. "Internet: Lucha 'posmoderna' de los desposeidos de la modernidad." Paper presented at Annual Meeting of the Latin American Studies Association, Guadalajara, April 17–19.

Martinez-Torres, Maria Elena. 2001. "Civil Society, the Internet, and the Zapatistas." *Peace Review* 13 (3): 347–55.

Marx, Karl. (1857–58) 1973. *Grundrisse.* Harmondsworth: Penguin.

Marx, Karl. 1961. *Das Kapital: Kritik der politischen Ökonomie.* Vol. 1, *Der Produktionsprozess des Kapitals.* Berlin: Dietz Verlag.

Massumi, Brian. 2002. *Parables for the Virtual: Movement, Affect, Sensation.* Durham, N.C.: Duke University Press.

Massumi, Brian. 2015. *The Power at the End of the Economy.* Durham, N.C.: Duke University Press.

Mattoni, Alice. 2008. "La questione femminile nelle lotte contro la precarietà in Italia." *Inchiesta* 160 (July–September): 102–15.

Mattoni, Alice. 2012. *Media Practices and Protest Politics: How Precarious Workers Mobilise.* Aldershot: Ashgate.

Mazzucchi, Andrea. 2009. "Okkupanet, quelle notizie così puntuali sulla Cina." *La Repubblica,* June 9, sec. Scene Digitali.

238 · BIBLIOGRAPHY

McAdam, Douglas, Sidney Tarrow, and Charles Tilly. 2001. *Dynamics of Contention*. New York: Cambridge University Press.

McChesney, Robert Waterman. 2015. *Rich Media, Poor Democracy: Communication Politics in Dubious Times*. New York: New Press.

McDonough, Tom. 2004. *Guy Debord and the Situationist International: Texts and Documents*. New York: October Books.

McKercher, Catherine, and Vincent Mosco. 2007. *Knowledge Workers in the Information Society*. Lanham, Md.: Lexington Books.

Mediablitz. 2004. "'Eterea': Convegno delle TV di strada a bologna." http://www.inventati.org.

Meikle, Graham. 2002. *Future Active: Media Activism and the Internet*. London: Routledge.

Mejias, Ulises A. 2010. "The Limits of Networks as Models for Organizing the Social." *New Media & Society* 12 (4): 603–17.

Melandri, Lea. 2002. *Una visceralità indicibile: La pratica dell'inconscio nel movimento delle donne degli anni settanta*. Milan: Franco Angeli.

Mellino, Miguel, and Anna Curcio. 2012. *La razza al lavoro*. Rome: Manifestolibri.

Merani, Stefania. 2004. "Una tv che fa strada." *Tra Terra e Cielo: Il giornale delle scelte consapevoli*, no. 188 (February), sec. Attualità.

Mezzadra, Sandro. 2012. "How Many Histories of Labor? Towards a Theory of Postcolonial Capitalism." *Transversal*, January. http://eipcp.net.

Mezzadra, Sandro, and Brett Neilson. 2013. *Border as Method, or, the Multiplication of Labor*. Durham, N.C.: Duke University Press.

Ministero dell'Interno. 2004. "Relazione al Parlamento sull'attività delle Forze di Polizia, sullo stato dell'ordine e della sicurezza pubblica e sulla criminalità organizzata, anno 2003." Dipartimento della pubblica sicurezza, Rome.

Miyazaki, Shintaro. 2015. "Going Beyond the Visible: New Aesthetic as an Aesthetic of Blindness?" In *Postdigital Aesthetics: Art, Computation and Design*, edited by David M. Berry and Michael Dieter, 219–31. New York: Palgrave Macmillan.

Monaghan, Jeffrey, and Kevin Walby. 2011. "Making up 'Terror Identities': Security Intelligence, Canada's Integrated Threat Assessment Centre and Social Movement Suppression." *Policing and Society: An International Journal of Research and Policy* 22 (2): 1–19.

Monico, Francesco. 2002. "Tune In: The Television Monopoly Will Implode." *International Herald Tribune*, July 3.

Morandi, Sabina. 2005. "Censura in rete: Per questo fotomontaggio Indymedia è sotto sequestro." *Liberazione*, May 5.

Moroni, Primo, and Nanni Balestrini. 1988. *L'orda d'oro*. Milan: Sugarco Edizioni.

Mudu, Pierpaolo. 2014. "Where Is Culture in Rome? Self-Managed Social Centers and the Right to Urban Space." In *Global Rome: Changing Faces of the Eternal*

City, edited by Isabella Clough Marinaro and Bjørn Thomassen, 246–64. Bloomington: Indiana University Press.

Munster, Anna. 2014. "Transmateriality: Toward an Energetics of Signal in Contemporary Mediatic Assemblages." *Cultural Studies Review* 20 (1): 150–67.

Murphy, Brian M. 2002. "A Critical History of the Internet." In *Critical Perspectives on the Internet*, edited by Greg Elmer, 27–45. Lanham, Md.: Rowman & Littlefield.

Murphy, Brian. 2005. "Interdoc: The First International Non-governmental Computer Network." *First Monday* 10 (5). https:// www.firstmonday.org.

Nasrallah, Henry A. 2011. "The Antipsychiatry Movement: Who and Why." *Current Psychiatry* 10 (12): 4–53.

Negri, Antonio. (1979) 1999. *Marx beyond Marx*. New York: Autonomedia.

Negri, Antonio. (1997) 2003. *Time for Revolution*. New York: Continuum.

Negri, Antonio. 1998. *Spinoza: L'anomalia selvaggia; Spinoza sovversivo; Democrazia ed eternità in Spinoza*. Rome: DeriveApprodi.

Neilson, Brett, and Ned Rossiter. 2008. "Precarity as a Political Concept, or, Fordism as Exception." *Theory, Culture & Society* 25 (7–8): 51–72.

Nitzan, Jonathan. 1998. "Differential Accumulation: Towards a New Political Economy of Capital." *Review of International Political Economy* 5 (2): 169–216.

Nitzan, Jonathan, and Shimshon Bichler. 2009. *Capital as Power: A Study of Order and Creorder*. New York: Routledge.

Noborder. 2003. "Azione NoBorder al CPT Bari Palese." August 3. Video. http:// www.ngvision.org.

Obino, Stefano, dir. 2005. *Il Vangelo secondo precario*. Italy. Drama.

Oikarinen, Jarkko. 1997. "Founding IRC." https:// www.mirc.com.

Open Space. 2016. "Explore Open Space." http://openspaceworld.org.

Orrico, Mauro. 2006. *Radio libere ma libere veramente*. Rome: Malatempora Editrice.

Pacos and Rio. 1997. "Aguascalientes: Spazi liberi." *Blue Line: Periodico di Informazione Internazionale*, no. 1.

Pagliardini, Pietro. 2011. "Diversi pareri sulle vele di Scampia." *De Architectura* (blog), April 11. http://regola.blogspot.ca.

Palano, Damiano. 1999. "Cercare un centro di gravità permanente? Fabbrica Società Antagonismo." *Intermarx: Rivista virtuale di analisi e critica materialista*, April.

Palano, Damiano. 2000. "Il bandolo della matassa: Forza lavoro, composizione di classe e capitale sociale; Note sul metodo dell'inchiesta." *Intermarx: Rivista virtuale di analisi e critica materialista*, January.

Parikka, Jussi. 2012. *What Is Media Archaeology?* Cambridge, UK: Polity.

Pelizza, Annalisa. 2006. "Orfeo Tv: Comunicare l'Immediatezza: Una televisione di strada a Rotterdam." *Inchiesta* 36 (152): 12–18.

240 · BIBLIOGRAPHY

Peters, John M. 2016. "Foreword." In *The Palgrave International Handbook of Action Research*, edited by Lonnie L. Rowell, Catherine D. Bruce, Joseph M. Shosh, and Margaret M. Riel, vii–x. New York: Palgrave Macmillan.

Petrillo, Antonello. 2009. *Biopolitica di un rifiuto: Le rivolte anti-discarica a Napoli e in Campania*. Verona: Ombre corte.

Philopat, Marco. 2006. *Lumi di Punk: La scena italiana raccontata dai protagonisti*. Milan: Agenzia X.

Piazza, Gianni. 2015. "Not Only Liberated Spaces: Italian Social Centres as Social Movement and Protest Actors." In *Making Room: Cultural Production in Occupied Spaces*, edited by Alan Moore and Alan Smart, 200–205. Chicago: Other Forms.

Piccolo, Francesco. 2017. "Immigrazione in Campania e a Salerno: Gli ultimi dati e le statistiche degli anni scorsi." *L'occhio di Salerno*, February 14.

Pickard, Victor W. 2006. "Assessing the Radical Democracy of Indymedia: Discursive, Technical, and Institutional Constructions." *Critical Studies in Media Communication* 23 (1): 19–38.

Plotnitsky, Arkady. 2003. "Algebras, Geometries, and Topologies of the Fold: Deleuze, Derrida, and Quasi-Mathematical Thinking, with Leibniz and Mallarmé." In *Between Deleuze and Derrida*, edited by Paul Patton and John Protevi, 98–119. New York: Continuum.

Precarias a la Deriva. 2004. "Adrift through the Circuits of Feminized Precarious Work." *Transversal*, July. http://eipcp.net.

Precarias a la Deriva. 2010. "First Stutterings of 'Precarias a la Deriva.'" *Caring Labor: An Archive* (blog), December 14. https://caringlabor.wordpress.com.

Pucciarelli, Matteo. 2010. "La Pantera, venti anni dopo l'eredità di un movimento breve." *La Repubblica*, January 30.

Purdue, Derrick. 2007. *Civil Societies and Social Movements: Potentials and Problems*. ECPR Studies in European Political Science. New York: Routledge.

Raboni, Giovanni. 1994. "Berlusconi, il Principe e lo spot." *Corriere della Sera*, February 20, 22.

Raley, Rita. 2009. *Tactical Media*. Minneapolis: University of Minnesota Press.

Redazione. 2009. "Il discorso di Silvio Berlusconi al congress del Pdl." *Il Giornnale. it*, March 23, sec. Politica. http://www.ilgiornale.it.

Redazione. 2012. "Cosa è successo a Indymedia Piemonte?" *Conoscenze in Rete Magazine*, October 18.

Renzi, Alessandra. 2006. "Televisione di Strada Tattica." *Inchiesta* 36 (152): 75–80.

Renzi, Alessandra. 2015. "Info-capitalism and Resistance: How Information Shapes Social Movements." *Interface: A Journal for and about Social Movements* 7 (2): 98–119.

Renzi, Alessandra, and Greg Elmer. 2013. "Property Must Be Defended: Investing in the Bio- political City-Sacrifice." *Theory, Culture & Society* 30 (5): 45–69.

Renzi, Alessandra, and Ganaele Langlois. 2015. "Data/Activism." In *Compromised Data: New Paradigms in Social Media Theory and Methods,* edited by Greg Elmer, Ganaele Langlois, and Joanna Redden, 202–25. London: Bloomsbury.

Renzi, Alessandra, and Stephen Turpin. 2007. "Nothing Fails like Prayer: Why the Cult of San Precario Is More Dangerous than Religion." *Fuse Magazine: Art, Media, Politics* 30 (1): 25–35.

Rete No Global and Network Campano per i Diritti Globali. 2001. *Zona Rossa: Le "quattro giornate di Napoli" contro il Global Forum.* Rome: DeriveApprodi.

Revel, Judith. 2013. "Foucault and His 'Other': Subjectivation and Displacement." In *The Biopolitics of Development: Reading Michel Foucault in the Postcolonial Present,* edited by Sandro Mezzadra, Julian Reid, and Ranabir Samaddar, 15–24. New Delhi: Springer India.

Rodríguez, Clemencia. 2001. *Fissures in the Mediascape: An International Study of Citizens' Media.* Cresskill, N.J.: Hampton Press.

Roggero, Gigi. 2011. *The Production of Living Knowledge: The Crisis of the University and the Transformation of Labor in Europe and North America.* Translated by Enda Brophy. Philadelphia: Temple University Press.

Ronfeldt, David, John Arquilla, Graham Fuller, and Melissa Fuller. 1998. *The Zapatista "Social Netwar" in Mexico.* Santa Monica, Calif.: RAND.

Runyon, Steve. 2009. "Television Technology." Museum of Broadcast Communications. Accessed May 12, 2016. http://www.museum.tv/eotvsection.php?entry code=televisionte.

Ruzza, Carlo, and Stefano Fella. 2009. *Re-inventing the Italian Right: Territorial Politics, Populism and "Post-fascism."* New York: Routledge.

Saviano, Roberto. 2007. *Gomorrah.* New York: Picador.

Scholz, Trebor. 2014. *Digital Labour: The Internet as Playground and Factory.* London: Routledge.

Schrank, Peter. 2009. "The Berlusconisation of Italy." *The Economist,* April 30.

Scott, David. 2014. *Gilbert Simondon's Psychic and Collective Individuation: A Critical Introduction and Guide.* Edinburgh: Edinburgh University Press.

Seisselberg, Jörg. 1996. "Conditions of Success and Political Problems of a 'Media-Mediated Personality-Party': The Case of Forza Italia." *West European Politics* 19 (4): 715–43.

Senior, Kathryn, and Alfredo Mazza. 2004. "Italian 'Triangle of Death' Linked to Waste Crisis." *Lancet Oncology* 5 (9): 525–27.

Serra, Fulvia. 2015. "Reproducing the Struggle: A New Feminist Perspective on the Concept of Social Reproduction." *Viewpoint Magazine,* no. 5 (October 31). http://viewpointmag.com.

Shannon, Claude Elwood. 1948. "A Mathematical Theory of Communication." *Bell System Technical Journal* 27 (3): 379–423.

Shaviro, Steven. 2010. *Post Cinematic Affect.* Winchester, UK: Zero Books.

242 · BIBLIOGRAPHY

Simondon, Gilbert. 1964. *L'individu et sa genèse physico-biologique: L'individuation à la lumière des notions de forme et d'information.* Paris: Presses universitaires de France.

Simondon, Gilbert. (1964) 1992. "The Genesis of the Individual." In *Incorporations*, edited by Jonathan Crary and Sanford Kwinter, 296–319. New York: Zone.

Simondon, Gilbert. 1989. *Du mode d'existence des objets techniques.* Paris: Aubier.

Simondon, Gilbert. 2006. *L'individuazione psichica e collettiva.* Translated by Paolo Virno. Rome: DeriveApprodi.

Simpson, Leanne. 2016. *Islands of Decolonial Love: Stories & Songs.* Winnipeg, Manitoba: Arbeiter-Ring.

Smargiassi, Michele. 2007. "Chiusi io radio Alice ma ora la rimpiango." *La Repubblica,* February 7.

Societacivile.it. n.d. "Cronologia dell'indignazione: Come nasce un movimento." Accessed May 12, 2016. http://www.societacivile.it.

Spinoza, Benedictus de. 1992. *The Ethics; Treatise on the Emendation of the Intellect; Selected Letters.* Edited by Seymour Feldman. Translated by Samuel Shirley. Indianapolis: Hackett.

Stein, Jasmin Kyoko. n.d. "Interviews with insu^tv." Unpublished interviews in author's possession.

Stengers, Isabelle. 2008. "Experimenting with Refrains: Subjectivity and the Challenge of Escaping Modern Dualism." *Subjectivity* 22 (1): 38–59.

Tarrow, Sydney. 2004. *Power in Movement.* New York: Cambridge University Press.

Telestreet. 2004. Interview with David Garcia at Eterea II, Senigallia, March 28.

Telestreet. n.d. "Telestreet." Accessed June 1, 2006. http://www.radioalice.org/nuovatelestreet/index.php.

Terranova, Tiziana. 2000. "Free Labor: Producing Culture for the Digital Economy." *Social Text* 18 (2): 33–58.

Terranova, Tiziana. 2004. "Communication beyond Meaning: On the Cultural Politics of Information." *Social Text* 22 (3): 51–73.

Terranova, Tiziana. 2014. "Red Stack Attack! Algorithms, Capital and the Automation of the Common." *Quaderni di San Precario,* February 12. http://effimera.org.

TerzoPiano. n.d. "Chi siamo?" Terzopiano Autogestito. Accessed September 25, 2019. https://www.autistici.org.

Thorburn, Elise Danielle. 2014. "Social Media, Subjectivity, and Surveillance: Moving on from Occupy, the Rise of Live Streaming Video." *Communication and Critical/Cultural Studies* 11 (1): 52–63.

Thorburn, Elise Danielle. 2015. "Assemblages: Live Streaming Dissent in the 'Quebec Spring.'" In *Social Media, Politics and the State: Protests, Revolutions, Riots, Crime and Policing in the Age of Facebook, Twitter and YouTube,* edited by Daniel Trottier and Christian Fuchs. New York: Routledge. eBook.

Thorburn, Elise Danielle. 2016. "Networked Social Reproduction: Crises in the Integrated Circuit." *Triple C: Communication, Capitalism & Critique* 14 (2). http://www.triple-c.at.

Tilly, Charles. 2004. *Social Movements, 1768–2004.* Boulder, Colo.: Paradigm.

Toronto Free Broadcasting. 2009. "Pirate TV in Action. NICOL* ANGRISANO for INSU^TV." Pamphlet, Toronto Free Gallery.

Torti, Maria Teresa. 2002. "Intervista a Maria Teresta Torti—17 Giugno 2001." In *Futuro anteriore: Dai "Quaderni rossi" ai movimenti globali; Ricchezze e limiti dell'operaismo italiano,* edited by Guido Borio, Francesca Pozzi, and Gigi Roggero. Rome: DeriveApprodi. CD-ROM.

Toscano, Alberto. 2012. "The Disparate: Ontology and Politics in Simondon." In "Deleuze and Simondon," special issue, *Pli: The Warwick Journal of Philosophy* (2012): 87–96.

Trocchi, Agnese. 2004. "Telestreets." *Mute,* January 12. http://www.metamute.org.

Tronti, Mario. (1966) 2006. *Operai e capitale.* Rome: DeriveApprodi.

Tsianos, Vassilis, and Dimitris Papadopoulos. 2006. "Precarity: A Savage Journey to the Heart of Embodied Capitalism." *Transversal,* November. http://eipcp.net.

Tsing, Anna Lowenhaupt. 2005. *Friction: An Ethnography of Global Connection.* Princeton, N.J.: Princeton University Press.

Tsing, Anna Lowenhaupt. 2015. *The Mushroom at the End of the World: On the Possibility of Life in Capitalist Ruins.* Princeton, N.J.: Princeton University Press.

Tuck, Eve, and K. Wayne Yang. "Decolonization Is Not a Metaphor." *Decolonization: Indigeneity, Education & Society* 1 (1): 1–40.

Tufekci, Zeynep. 2014. "Social Movements and Governments in the Digital Age: Evaluating a Complex Landscape." *Journal of International Affairs* 68 (1): 1–18.

Turnin, Svetla, and Ezra Winton. 2014. *Screening Truth to Power: A Reader on Documentary Activism.* Montreal: Cinema Politica.

Van Dijk, Jan. 2005. *The Network Society: Social Aspects of New Media.* Thousand Oaks, Calif.: SAGE.

Vercellone, Carlo. 2006. *Capitalismo cognitivo: Conoscenza e finanza nell'epoca postfordista.* Rome: Manifestolibri.

Virno, Paolo. 1996. "Do You Remember Counterrevolution?" In *Radical Thought in Italy: A Potential Politics,* edited by Paolo Virno and Michael Hardt, 240–58. Minneapolis: University of Minnesota Press.

Virno, Paolo. 2004. *A Grammar of the Multitude.* Translated by Isabella Bertoletti, James Cascaito, and Andrea Casson. New York: Semiotext(e).

Virno, Paolo, and Michael Hardt. 1996. *Radical Thought in Italy.* Minneapolis: University of Minnesota Press.

Wark, McKenzie. 1995. *Virtual Geography: Living with Global Media Events.* Bloomington: Indiana University Press.

244 · BIBLIOGRAPHY

Whyte, W. F. 1991. *Participatory Action Research.* Thousand Oaks, Calif.: SAGE.

Willan, Philip. 1991. *Puppetmasters: The Political Use of Terrorism in Italy.* London: Constable.

Wolfson, Todd. 2014. *Digital Rebellion: The Birth of the Cyber Left.* Urbana: University of Illinois Press.

Wright, Steve. 2005. "Pondering Information and Communication in Contemporary Anti-Capitalist Movements." July 25. http://libcom.org.

Wright, Steve. 2007. "There and Back Again: Mapping the Pathways within Autonomist Marxism." http://libcom.org.

Wu Ming. 2016. *Un viaggio che non promettiamo breve: Venticinque anni di lotte No Tav.* Turin: Einaudi.

Zanotelli, Alex. 2009. "Grida! Lettera agli amici." July 14. http://www.nigrizia.it.

ZERO! and BITs Against the Empire Labs. 1995. *Digital Guerrilla: Guida all'uso alternativo di computer, modem e reti telematiche.* n.p.: n.p.

Zittrain, Jonathan. 2008. *The Future of the Internet and How to Stop It.* New Haven, Conn.: Yale University Press.

Index

Aaarg, 94
AC Milan, 75
activist field, 16, 59, 94, 134–35, 144, 150, 161, 175, 189, 198
Adbusters, 21
Adunata Sediziosa, 144, 219, 220
affect, 95, 99, 155, 125–34, 138, 141–42, 145, 159–60, 171, 186–91, 212, 213, 223
agency, 4, 24, 37, 43, 106, 142–43, 194, 198
Agnelli, Gianni, 88
Airbnb, 182–83
Albanese, Carmelo, 87, 91
Algeria, 142, 222
Alice in Wonderland (Carroll), 210
Alquati, Romano, 10, 11, 47, 48, 139, 195
Alvarez, Sonia E., 95
Amazon, 108
Ambrogio, 52–53, 55–59, 62–63
Andrei, Massimo, 157; *Mater Natura*, 157
Andretta, Massimiliano, 141, 144
Angrisano, Nicol*, 124, 153, 168–71, 179–80
Anonimo, 27, 28
Anonymous Digital Coalition, 101
anticolonialism, 47, 100
AntTV, 27–28
appropriation, 6, 45, 52, 91, 161, 186, 193

Arab Spring, 63, 181
Ardizzoni, Michela, 35
Armano, Emiliana, 11, 48, 139
Armstrong, Amanda, 190
Arquilla, John, 215
Asilo Filangieri, 183
Assalto al cielo (Assault on the sky), 175–77
assemblages, 14–16, 19, 29–34, 39–45, 66–67, 82–87, 94–95, 110–11, 114–18, 170–72, 177–78, 182, 186–98, 210, 212, 218, 224. *See also* sociotechnical assemblage
Asterix (insu^tv interviewee), 39, 158, 177, 191
Atton, Chris, 35
Aurelia (insu^tv interviewee), 146, 149
austerity, 46, 143, 176, 182, 190, 196, 223
Autistici/Inventati, 20, 96–99, 103–6, 214, 216
autonomia, 43–46, 56–63, 67, 74, 81, 98, 110, 140; Autonomia Operaia, 10, 47; autonomist feminism, 39, 43, 53, 56, 199, 210
AVvisi Ai Naviganti, 97
Azzellini, Dario, 219

Babylonian, 106
Balducci, Ernesto, 211
Balena, La, 183
Balestrini, Nanni, 46, 48, 52, 96

245

246 · INDEX

Barad, Karen, 14, 16, 174, 197, 199, 208, 224
Barassi, Veronica, 104
Barbacetto, Gianni, 69, 71, 212, 213
Barriere (film, Civelli), 129–30
Barthélémy, Jean-Hugues, 20
Bassolino, Antonio, 140
Bauwens, Michel, 217
becomings, 4, 8, 14, 24, 26, 37, 51, 86, 113–14, 122, 138, 149–50, 170–71, 194, 199, 208, 209
Benjamin, Walter, 133–34
Bennett, W. Lance, 3, 207
Berardi, Franco "Bifo," 41–42, 47, 57, 60–63, 69, 71, 87, 145, 192, 211, 216
Berlin, 9
Berlusconi, Silvio, 6, 9, 15, 20–27, 33, 35, 65–84, 86–88, 100–108, 111, 114, 120, 125–28, 138, 165, 175, 193, 212, 213, 218, 220; No Berlusconi Day, 23
Beschi, Carlo, 104–6
Betamax, 47
Bianchi, Sergio, 96
Bichler, Shimshon, 15, 67–69, 82, 212
BITs Against the Empire, 97–98
BitTorrent, 120
Black Panther Party, 88, 210
Black Power, 47
Blisset, Luther, 169
Blue Line, 145, 147
Boggs, Grace Lee, 211
boicoopTV, 121
Bologna, 169, 179
Bomboclat (IMC), 103
Books and Breakfast (Ferguson, MO), 61
Borio, Guido, 195, 200
Bosnia, 9, 122
Botti, Simone, 92–95

Boyle, Deirdre, 218
Braman, Sandra, 20
Bratich, Jack, 217
Breton, André, 42, 209; "Manifesto of Surrealism," 209
Bronson, John, 21
Brophy, Enda, 216
Brues, Rouven, 224
Bulgarelli, Mauro, 20
bulletin board system (BBS), 15, 51, 97–98, 101, 111, 215, 217
burnout, 37, 39, 56, 103, 110, 113, 144, 222
Burroughs, William, 50

Calabria, 179–80
Camorra, 1–2, 138, 148, 158, 163, 173, 176, 181, 221, 222
CandidaTV, 6, 29, 32–34, 121
Caparossa, 216
capitalism, 6, 31–32, 42–44, 48, 53, 56, 62, 77, 81–84, 86, 91, 111, 188–89, 216, 222
Capitalism and Schizophrenia (Deleuze and Guattari), 42, 210
Carlo (Telestreet interviewee), 63–64
Carnival against Capital (1999, London), 207
Carroll, Lewis, 50, 210
Casagrande, Orsola, 100
Castells, Manuel, 27, 98, 100, 207
Castile, Philando, 198
cathexis, 178
Catholic Church, 7, 47, 72, 109
Catsin, Monty, 169
Celestini, Ascanio, 166, 168
Chainworkers.org, 109
Chetta, Alessandro, 167
Chiaiano, 1–2, 163, 165
Chiapas, 101, 105, 110, 193
Chiurchiù, Luca, 52

INDEX · **247**

Christian Democrats (Italy), 42, 57, 60, 139
Chun, Wendy Hui Kyong, 185, 224
Ciano, Antonio (Telestreet interviewee), 125–28
Cinque Stelle, 222
Civelli, Franco, 129–30, 218; *Barriere,* 129–30
Classe Operaia (journal), 46
Cleaver, Harry, 101
closed-circuit television (CCTV), 121
Coates, Kenneth, 198
codecs, 119, 126
Cohen, Nicole, 216
co-individuation, 150, 192, 195, 199. *See also* individuation
Colectivo Situaciones, 17
Coleman, Gabriella, 121
collective individuation, 17, 81, 83, 140–41, 147–49, 160, 171, 178, 191
Collettivo A/traverso, 41, 44, 45, 50–52
Combes, Muriel, 115, 214, 217
Committee for Housing Rights (Scampia), 148, 188–89
communication infrastructure, 6–8, 16, 20, 71, 95, 207
Communist Party (Italy), 46–49, 51, 57–58, 72
community media, 9, 122, 128–29, 176
composition, 4, 10–16, 21, 40, 46–47, 99, 126, 135, 150, 174, 185–86, 192–200. *See also* assemblages; decomposition; recomposition
compositionality, 134, 150–51, 170, 197
compositional thinking, 21–22
connective activism, 1–3, 13–16, 38–40, 42, 53, 62–63, 67, 74, 83, 99, 132, 151, 171–72, 177, 187–88, 192–97, 207, 224

connective research, 200. *See also conricerca*
conricerca (co-research), 10–14, 44, 47–48, 113, 139, 207, 217
Conti, Antonio, 10–11, 47–48
Controradio (Florence), 51
Cooperativa Megaride, 155
co-research. *See conricerca*
Cossiga, Francesco, 59
Costanza-Chock, Sasha, 224
Coté, Mark, 11, 189
Couldry, Nick, 35
counterinformation, 47, 74, 104, 159
Cowen, Deborah, 198
Crary, Jonathan, 30
Craxi, Bettino, 70, 72, 88
Creative Commons, 8, 121, 167, 182, 215, 217
crisis, 95
Culbertson, Anna, 210
culture jamming, 21, 102, 164
Cuninghame, Patrick, 54–56, 210
Curcio, Anna, 12, 216
Curran, James, 35
Current TV, 167
Cybernet, 97
cybernetics, 30, 209

Dada, 8, 51–53, 56, 72, 113
Dalla Costa, Mariarosa, 53–56, 61, 188, 210, 211; *Power of Women and the Subversion of the Community,* 55
Dallas (TV), 71, 73, 83
Davidkhanian, Caren, 22
Davos, 136
DDoS (distributed denial-of-service), 215
Debord, Guy, 28–30
DECnet, 92, 214
Decoder (magazine), 97, 214
decomposition, 39, 134, 188, 196–97

248 · INDEX

Deleuze, Gilles, 14, 29, 30, 42–45, 66, 70, 72, 81, 130, 171, 177, 209, 210; *Anti-Oedipus,* 42, 45; *Capitalism and Schizophrenia,* 42, 210; "desiring-machine," 210; *A Thousand Plateaus,* 210
deliberation-without-attention, 80
delirium, 41–44, 63, 74, 81
Delirium of Praise, The (Kaufman), 62
Delisa, Antonio, 87
Del Re, Alisa, 11, 210
De Lutiis, Giuseppe, 211
Demers, Jason, 81
Denaro, Massimiliano, 214
Deseriis, Marco, 169–70, 186, 188, 203, 224
De Simone, Titti, 213
desiring-machines, 210
détournement, 29, 32–34
Diakron, 76
Di Corinto, Arturo, 97, 215, 217
differential accumulation, 15, 82, 90, 212
digital divide, 118, 147
Digital Guerrilla, 98
Disco Volante TV, 6, 12, 16, 28, 31, 122, 123, 128–31, 217
DIY: media, 8, 29–30, 39, 60, 127; punk, 45, 91; sensors, 224; television, 5, 128, 183–88; transmission systems, 4, 15, 22, 114–17, 122–23, 154, 156
Dolphijn, Rick, 208
Domenica Aut (TV), 156–62, 171, 175–77, 183, 221, 222; "Citta' e Periferia," 158, 161; *Wasting Naples,* 38, 162, 166–70, 175–76, 195, 222
Downing, John D. H., 35
Dunayevskaya, Raya, 211
Dyer-Witheford, Nick, 216
Dynebolic, 215

Edilnord Constructions, 65
Electronic Disturbance Theater, 101–2, 145, 193
Elmer, Greg, 215
EmisioNeokinok.Tv, 33
energetics of movements, 14–16, 26, 94, 126, 191, 196–200, 217
energy, 14–15, 26–27, 45, 63, 87, 99, 103, 107–8, 110, 122, 126, 131, 139–63, 172–87, 195–200
entrepreneurial subject, 186–87
Erasmus, Desiderius, 65, 73; *Praise of Folly,* 65
Escobar, Arturo, 95
Esposito La Rossa, Rosario, 158
Eterea, 6–9, 31, 63, 121, 129
ethics: of care, 2; of connection, 16, 171–72, 191, 197–200, 208; DIY punk, 91; publishing, 5; of research, 9, 199
European Counter Network (ECN), 97–98, 217
European Union, 167, 176

Facebook, 3, 185, 186, 187, 198
failure, 8, 86, 111, 142
FairCoop, 224
Fals-Borda, Orlando, 11
Fanon, Frantz, 144–43, 148, 151, 164, 219, 220, 222; *Wretched of the Earth,* 141
fax machines, 91, 98, 101, 193
Federici, Silvia, 1, 54, 62, 188–90
Federico II University (Naples), 88–89, 135
Fedina (insu^tv interviewee), 178–79, 184
Feigenbaum, Anna, 63, 214
Fella, Stefano, 76
feminism, 39, 43, 47, 53, 56, 63, 192, 199, 210, 221

INDEX · **249**

Fenton, Natalie, 104
Fernandez-Savater, Amador, 196
Ferri, Fabio, 88
Festa, Francesco Antonio, 139–40, 143, 144, 146, 219
Fiat, 5, 10, 68, 88
Field of Vision, 223
financial crisis of 2008, 3, 49, 176, 190, 207
Fininvest, 69–72, 76, 81–82, 118, 213
Fiori, Dario, 44–46
Flamini, Gianni, 211
Flickr, 107
FloodNet, 102
Fontanarosa, Aldo, 175
Ford, Sam, 207
Fordism, 10, 46, 74, 113
formation, 29, 208, 212, 214. *See also* information; transformation
Fortunati, Leopoldina, 188
Forza Italia, 73–80, 213
Foucault, Michel, 15, 70, 72, 83, 114, 164, 177
free and open-source software, 8, 117, 119, 154, 215
Freeman, Jo, 104
Free Masons, 211
free radio movement, 5, 12, 47, 50–51, 83, 85, 89, 97, 102, 104, 111, 120–21, 147, 193, 220
Freire, Paulo, 11
Frenzel, Fabian, 63, 214
frequency modulation (FM), 125
friendship, 40, 42–45, 58–59, 63, 113, 122, 144, 154, 185, 189, 208
Fumagalli, Andrea, 11, 216

Gaeta, 5, 12, 125–28
Gambino, Michele, 65, 69
Garcia, David, 29–32
Garrone, Matteo, 158; *Gomorrah*, 158

Gates, Bill, 117
Gaza, 180
G8 Summit (2001), 85–86, 102, 103, 106, 109, 120, 141, 144
general intellect, 50
Genoa, 39, 85–86, 99, 102–11, 120, 137, 141, 144, 149, 196, 215
Genuino Clandestino (Angrisano), 179
Gerbaudo, Paolo, 224
Gervasio, Simone, 183
Gherardi, Silvia, 109
Gianturco, 164–65
Ginsborg, Paul, 46, 210
Giraud, Eva, 104
Girotondi, 23
Giuliani, Carlo, 85, 103, 120
Giurdanella, Antonino, 89
global justice movement, 5–7, 15, 39, 59, 85, 101–6, 108, 110, 113, 140, 146, 207, 219
Goddard, Michael, 47, 196
Gomorrah (film, Garrone), 158
Google, 3, 106, 108
governmentality, 70, 78–83, 114, 131, 148
Gramsci, Antonio, 141, 219
Grasso, Gianni, 80
grassroots media, 5–9, 15, 36, 86, 98–100, 131, 146, 175–76, 218, 219, 223. *See also* DIY
Greedharry, Mrinalini, 148
Green, Joshua, 207
Greenwood, Davydd J., 10
Grifi, Alberto, 47, 130
Gruppo Risveglio dal Sonno (GRI-DAS), 158
Grusin, Richard, 15, 31, 78–80, 115, 127, 131, 213
Guattari, Félix, 14, 29, 41–45, 145–48, 151, 159, 177, 196, 209, 210, 212, 220; *Anti-Oedipus*, 42; *Capitalism*

250 · INDEX

and *Schizophrenia*, 42; *Una tomba per Edipo*, 41
Gubitosa, Carlo, 98
Guerrilla Marketing, 27

Hacker Art, 97
hackers, 8, 30, 97, 117, 120, 214
hacklabs, 3, 97, 108, 113, 120, 154, 197
Haiven, Max, 1, 8
Hale, Charles R., 9
Halleck, DeeDee, 218
happening, 19, 21, 40. *See also* assemblages
Haraway, Donna, 14, 199
Hardt, Michael, 47, 49, 67, 68, 210, 214; *Empire*, 49
Harkavy, Ira, 10
Harney, Stefano, 199
Hartwig, Robert, 116
Harvey, David, 24
Hegel, Georg Wilhelm, 210
Heller, Monica, 12
Hjelmslev, Louis, 209
Hollywood Reporter, 22
Howley, Kevin, 128
Hub TV, 5
Hugill, David, 63, 192
Hydrarchist, 219

identity, 52–55, 59, 94, 110, 135, 142–44, 159, 169–70, 189, 210. *See also* individuation; subjectivation
#IdleNoMore, 198
imagination, 5, 14, 30, 32, 35, 42, 200
IMC Open Source, 107. *See also* Indymedia
Independent Media Centers (IMCs), 102–7, 147, 207
individuation, 37–39, 67–68, 80–83, 86, 95, 110–11, 116, 122–28, 131–34, 140–50, 160, 168, 170–72,

187–99, 208–9, 214, 217, 219. *See also* collective individuation; transindividuation
Indybay, 103, 106
Indymedia, 4–5, 85–86, 100–109, 113–14, 146–47, 193, 207, 215–16, 224
Infoaut, 145
information, 3, 6, 13, 15, 21–22, 26, 30–33, 37, 38, 76–77, 86–111, 146, 159, 174, 186–89, 198, 208, 209, 213, 214–17, 220. *See also* counterinformation
information capitalism, 77, 189
information economies, 56, 74–77, 87, 108
infrastructure, 3, 6, 8, 11, 16, 20, 36, 39, 44, 69–72, 83–97, 121, 181–87, 190–91, 196–98, 207, 224
Instagram, 184, 187
intellectual property, 8, 28, 119, 121, 215
interconnection, 118, 122, 132, 174
Intercontinental Meeting for Humanity and Against Neoliberalism, 101
International Feminist Collective, 210–11
International Herald Tribune, 21
Internet Relay Chat (IRC), 214
inquiry (*inchiesta*, Italian), 9–11, 14, 17, 158, 161–66, 188, 197–99
Iraq war, 5, 96, 103, 144
Italian Story, An, 75
Italy: Article 21, Italian constitution, 123; "communication machine," 67, 73–74, 83; la questione meridionale, 141; mediascape of, 6, 15, 20, 34, 51, 70–74, 78–81, 168–70; Ministry of the Interior's "Report to Parliament on Police Activity, Public Security and Organized Crime," 19, 106

INDEX · 251

Jackson, Sarah J., 198
Jaquemet, Marco, 47, 69, 71, 210
James, C. L. R., 211
James, Selma, 53–55, 188, 211; *The Power of Women and the Subversion of the Community*, 55; *Sex, Race, and Class*, 211
Janković, Radmila Iva, 29, 32, 34, 123
Jenkins, Henry, 207n1
Juris, Jeffrey, 103, 216

Katsarova, Rada, 190
Kaufman, Eleanor, 62; *Delirium of Praise*, 62
Khasnabish, Alex, 8
Kidd, Dorothy, 102, 215
Klang, Mathias, 3
Klein, Naomi, 24, 90, 222
Knight, Ben, 107
Kogawa, Tetsuo, 173–74
Kohl, Christiane, 24

Laboratorio Occupato SKA, 85, 101, 140
Lacan, Jacques, 148, 210
Lamarre, Thomas, 214
Lampedusa Next Stop (film, Angrisano), 181
Langlois, Ganaele, 165, 186
Lazzarato, Maurizio, 10, 30–31, 67–68, 72–75, 187; *Making of the Indebted Man*, 213
Le Corbusier, 139
Leoncavallo, C. S., 85, 96, 101
Letta, Gianni, 73
Lewin, Kurt, 9, 11
Linux, 33, 117, 146, 215
Liquid Democracy Association, 224
livestreaming, 6, 12, 66, 165, 178, 198, 222, 224
Logic of Sense, the (Deleuze), 210

Lomastro, Ciro, 59
Lorusso, Francesco, 59, 85
Lotta Continua, 47, 53, 55
Lotta Femminsta, 54, 210
Lovink, Geert, 29, 31
Luce, Sandro, 220
Ludovico, Alessandro, 121, 130
Luppichini, Manolo, 96, 124

MacDonald, Cathy, 11
Machiavelli, Niccolò, 73
Madison, Nora, 3
madness, 41–43, 62, 73, 81, 212. *See also* delirium
Mafia, 1, 73, 166–67, 211
Ma.gi.ca TV, 28, 38, 173–74, 191
Magistris, Luigi de, 182
Magnammce o'pesone (Mop), 182
Making of the Indebted Man, The (Lazzarato), 213
Malafemmina, 56
Mammì Law, 70
Mancini, Roberto, 23
"Manifesto of Surrealism" (Breton), 209
Manning, Erin, 72
Mao-Dadaism, 51–53, 56, 72, 113
Marshall Plan, 46
Martinez-Torres, Maria Elena, 101–2, 215
Marxism, 43, 49, 53, 60, 145, 210, 220
Massumi, Brian, 14, 25–26, 72, 80, 115, 126, 174, 208
Mater Natura (film, Andrei), 157
Mattoni, Alice, 216
Maxigas, 99, 214
MayDay, 109
Maygay, 155
Mazza, Alfredo, 163
Mazzucchi, Andrea, 92
McAdam, Douglas, 23–24

McChesney, Robert Waterman, 6
McCurdy, Patrick, 63, 214
McDonough, Tom, 34
McKercher, Catherine, 217
media activism, 2–3, 8, 11–14, 16, 19–20, 32, 37, 39, 57, 68, 83–84, 92, 94, 98, 103–7, 137, 145–47, 170, 176, 182, 190–91, 195, 198, 223
Mediablitz, 5–6
Media Democracy Day, 105
Media Indipendenti Napoletani (MINA), 147, 161
media literacy, 6, 23, 159, 162
mediality, 31, 78–82, 114–15, 123–28, 132, 213
Meikle, Graham, 90
Mejias, Ulises A., 223
Melandri, Lea, 211
Mellino, Miguel, 12, 216
Metallo, Claudio, 124
metastability, 95, 111, 171–72, 175, 177, 191
Mezzadra, Sandro, 216
Miami Model, The (film, Indymedia), 215
"milieu," 193, 198
militant research, 8, 10, 14
Minimal TV, 130
Minitel, 147
Miyazaki, Shintaro, 126
modulation, 116, 125–28, 131, 218
Mogulus, 165, 222
Monaghan, Jeffrey, 20
Monico, Francesco, 21
Moore, Thomas, 73
Morandi, Sabina, 106
Moro, Aldo, 60
Moroni, Primo, 46, 48, 52
Mosaico TV, 6
Mosco, Vincent, 216
Moten, Fred, 199

Movement for Black Lives, 49, 61, 198
Movimento Disoccupati organizzati (MDo), 139
MTV, 6, 123
Mudu, Pierpaolo, 97, 214
Mujer a Mujer, 101
Munster, Anna, 173–74
Murdoch, Rupert, 28
Murgia, Annalisa, 109
Murphy, Brian, 215
MySpace, 108

NAFTA (North American Free Trade Agreement), 100
Naples (Italy), 1, 6, 8, 16, 38–39, 88, 113, 122, 133–58, 162–95, 203, 207; garbage crisis, 1–2, 38, 162–70, 182; "The Ship Sails" (Le Vele) of Scampia and Secondigliano, 139, 148, 219
Napster, 120
Nasrallah, Henry A., 209
Neilson, Brett, 216
Negri, Antonio, 49–50, 66, 82, 145, 196, 214; *Empire,* 49
neoliberalism, 15, 66–69, 74, 101–2, 109–10, 140, 189, 200, 212
Neta, La, 101, 215
Net Strike, 101
NGVision, 216, 217
Nicola (insu^tv interviewee), 36–38. *See also* Angrisano, Nicol*
99 Posse, 154
Nitzan, Jonathan, 15, 67–69, 82, 90, 212
No Borders, 36–39
Noi Testarde (magazine), 56
NoWarTV, 5

Obino, Stefano, 109
Occupy, 1, 49, 214

INDEX · **253**

Occupy Wall Street, 3, 196
Officina 99, 5, 140, 149, 153–58, 161,
    164, 173, 183
Oikarinen, Jarkko, 214
Okkupanet, 15, 91–98, 214, 216
ontogenesis, 26, 208
Opel, Andy, 215
Open Distribuzioni dal Basso (Open
    DDB, Distributions from Below),
    181
Open Space, 166
operaie della casa, Le (magazine), 54,
    56
OrfeoTv, 5–6, 12, 16, 25, 27, 33,
    123–25, 146, 205, 220
Organisation for Economic Co-
    operation and Development
    (OECD), 136
Orrico, Mauro, 51
Oury, Jean, 148
Overdose Fiction Festival, 121

Pagliardini, Pietro, 219
Palano, Damiano, 11–12, 48, 140
Palestine, 9, 105, 122
Pantera, La, 87–92, 95–96, 100, 104,
    139, 145, 214
Paper Tiger TV, 218
Parikka, Jussi, 15
Pasolini, Pier Paolo, 47
patriarchy, 12, 54, 200, 211
Peacelink, 98, 215
Pelizza, Annalisa, 124, 203
People's Mic, 3
personality, 10, 75, 78, 82, 145
Peters, John M., 10
Petrillo, Antonello, 222
Philopat, Marco, 89, 96
Piazza, Gianni, 97
Piccolo, Francesco, 221
Pickard, Victor W., 105

Pierce, Charles, 209
pirate radio, 3, 147, 154–55, 176, 220
pirate television, 1, 34, 83–85, 125,
    169, 173–75
Plato, 210
Plotnitsky, Arkady, 66
Pog (insu^tv interviewee), 117, 121,
    146, 149, 154
police, 20, 22, 36, 53, 57–60, 71, 85,
    96, 103, 106, 120, 136–37, 158,
    161–68, 180, 198, 215, 220, 222,
    224
porosity, 13, 16, 39, 133–50, 161, 170,
    185, 188, 190, 193, 224
potentia/potestas, 82–83
Potere Operaio, 46–47, 53, 57, 210
*Power of Women and the Subversion of
    the Community, The* (Dalla Costa
    and James), 55
Pozzi, Francesca, 46, 50, 195, 200
precariat, 10
precarity, 10, 56, 68, 79, 87, 108–10,
    113, 139–40, 142, 162, 171, 182–84,
    216–17
Preempting Dissent (film, Elmer and
    Opel), 215
premediation, 79–80
Produzioni Dal Basso, 166, 179
proxy-vision, 16, 147, 160, 176,
    182–83, 187, 195
psychoanalysis, 41–45, 148, 210,
    220
PTSD (Post-traumatic Stress
    Disorder), 222
P2P (peer-to-peer), 4, 8, 33, 120, 217
Public Enemy, 89
Publitalia, 65, 70
Pucciarelli, Matteo, 88
Pulcinella (theatrical character), 144
Purdue, Derrick, 23, 23
Pybus, Jennifer, 11, 189

254 · INDEX

Quaderni Rossi (journal), 46

Raboni, Giovanni, 73
racism, 12, 164, 180
Radio Alice, 146–47, 170, 197, 211, 220
Radio Gap, 85, 102, 110
Radiolina, 147, 154–55, 162
Radio OndaRossa, 51, 89
Radio Sherwood, 51
RagnaTele, 6
Rahman, Muhammad Anisur, 11
RAI (Radiotelevisione Italiana), 70
Raley, Rita, 30
RAND Corporation, 215
Raro (insu^tv interviewee), 139
Reale Law (Italy), 211
recomposition, 9, 12, 16, 43, 45, 53, 87, 92–95, 99–108, 113, 126, 132, 145, 150, 172, 182, 187–88, 194, 198–200, 217, 218. *See also* composition; decomposition
Redazione, 77, 107
Red Brigades, 57, 60
regulations, 7, 69–70, 75, 78, 118, 123, 218
relation (concept), 26–34, 37–40
Repubblica, La, 88
repurposing, 13, 37–40, 93, 132, 156, 160–61, 174, 181, 184, 187–88, 191, 193–201
repurposing media, 13, 37–40, 132, 150, 171
research. *See* connective research; conricerca
Rodríguez, Clemencia, 35, 36, 128, 218
Roggero, Gigi, 46, 50, 195, 200, 217
Rojava, 180
Rome, 113, 121, 179
Ronfeldt, David, 215
Rosso (journal), 46

Ruberti, Antonio, 88
Runyon, Steve, 115–16
Rutelli, Francesco, 79
Ruzza, Carlo, 76

Sabotax, 96, 100, 139, 145
Sacchetto, Devi, 11, 48, 139
Saint Precario Network, 109
Sandro (insu^tv interviewee), 146, 149, 176, 183, 185–86, 196
Sapienza University (Rome), 88, 91
Sara (insu^tv interviewee), 39, 140, 147, 177
Saviano, Roberto, 153
Scholz, Trebor, 189
Schrank, Peter, 24
Scott, David, 174, 214
Seattle (WTO protests), 86, 102–3, 110, 113, 136, 146, 193, 207
secularization, 72
securitization, 20
Segerberg, Alexandra, 3, 207
Seisselberg, Jörg, 71, 75–79
self-expression, 6
self-valorization, 43, 44, 49–52, 68, 113, 140, 143
Senior, Kathryn, 163
Serra, Fulvia, 39, 72, 98, 189–90
Servicios Informativos Procesados (SIPRO), 101
Shannon, Claude Elwood, 95, 214
Shaviro, Steven, 130
Simondon, Gilbert, 14, 21, 26, 29, 34, 37–39, 95, 115–16, 126, 150, 171, 186–87, 195, 199, 209, 214, 219
Simpson, Leanne, 199
Situationists, 21, 30, 32, 34
Sky Italia, 167
Smargiassi, Michele, 60
social centers, 47, 83, 86, 89, 96–100, 108, 113, 120, 136, 140, 143, 145,

148, 150, 155, 175, 181, 193, 214, 219, 220. *See also* squats
Social Emergency Resource Centers in Boston, 61
social factory, 44, 49, 54–55
Social Forum (European), 5
Social Forum (Florence), 5, 105, 216
social media, 3–4, 8, 15, 33, 76, 93, 107–8, 182–91, 196–99, 218, 223–24
social movements, 1–3, 6, 10, 14, 20–27, 39, 47, 50, 56, 62, 98, 121, 169, 176, 179, 185, 196, 200, 214, 216, 223, 224
social reproduction, 3, 9, 11, 15–16, 39, 41, 44–45, 54–63, 72, 83, 97–98, 113, 139, 148, 150, 188–96, 200, 210
society of control, 30–32
sociotechnical assemblage, 37–38, 87, 123, 132, 165, 186, 194, 224
Soma (media player), 154
SpegnilaTV, 6, 27
Spinoza, Benedictus de, 171
squats, 3, 6, 19, 33–34, 47, 86, 113, 117, 125, 135, 139, 154–55, 161, 214. *See also* social centers
Stalking Asilo (TV show, insu^tv), 183–84, 223
Stein, Jasmin, 148–49, 169, 177, 185, 219
Stengers, Isabelle, 193, 199, 200
Stoney, George, 218
storytelling, 14, 192
subjectivation, 2, 10, 13, 15–17, 43–44, 50, 55, 59, 61–64, 70–78, 81–83, 96–99, 113–14, 148, 158, 195, 209, 213, 214. *See also* individuation
subvertising, 90

tactical media, 14, 21–34, 90, 102, 109, 113, 121, 136, 170, 193, 197
Tarrow, Sidney, 22–24

technical individuation, 34, 37, 123–24, 194. *See also* individuation
technical populism, 78
TeleAut, 25, 27
Telefabbrica, 5
Teleimmagini, 25, 33
TeleMonteOrlandoTV, 5, 16, 125
Tele Ottolina, 6
TelePonziana, 6
Telerobbinud, 6
television. *See* Berlusconi, Silvio; DIY: television; pirate television
tempo delle arance, Il (film, Angrisano), 180–81
Termini Imerese, 5
Terranova, Tizziana, 11, 86, 90, 189
terroni, 219
terrorism, 19–20, 60–61, 87, 208, 211
TerzoPiano Autogestito, 135–39, 146–47, 219
Third Global Forum, 135–44, 147
Thorburn, Elise Danielle, 39, 56, 62–63, 72, 165, 188, 192, 217, 224
Thousand Plateaus, A (Deleuze), 210
Through the Looking Glass (Carroll), 210
Tien'A'ment, 140
Tilly, Charles, 23–24
Titanus Productions, 65
Torti, Maria Teresa, 61–62
Toscano, Alberto, 175, 191, 194
Tosquelles, François, 148
Tozzi, Tommaso, 97, 215, 217
transduction, 21, 26, 31, 209
transformation, 3–4, 12–14, 25–27, 45–46, 66–69, 86–95, 124–27, 161, 174–75, 197, 214, 217, 218
transindividuation, 34, 81, 87, 115, 143, 170, 188, 194, 198. *See also* individuation
Transmediale (Berlin), 9

256 · INDEX

Transmission.cc, 122
transversality, 45–46, 52, 56, 59, 209
Trocchi, Agnese, 32, 121
Tronti, Mario, 49
Tsing, Anna Lowenhaupt, 19, 196
Tufekci, Zeynep, 3
Tuin, Iris van der, 208
Turpin, Etienne, 109
Twitter, 3, 60, 187, 197

UHF (ultra-high frequency) transmission, 4, 27, 126, 169, 175, 178
Utopia (Moore), 73

Van Dijk, Jan, 98
Vatican, 57
Vercellone, Carlo, 68
VHS, 4, 35, 47, 65, 70, 77, 88, 116–18
Via Padova è meglio di Milano (film, Angrisano), 181
Vice Magazine, 223
Vietnam War, 57, 210
Vimeo, 4, 119
Virno, Paolo, 34, 47, 61, 67–68, 72, 74, 77, 210
Virtual Address eXtension (VAX), 15, 91–93, 193
Virtual Geography (Wark), 113
Vitali, Gianfranco, 47, 69, 71–72, 210

VLC media player, 117
Voci di Scampia, 158

Wadada (insu^tv interviewee), 105, 146–48, 177, 219
Walby, Kevin, 20
Wark, McKenzie, 113; *Virtual Geography,* 113
Wasting Naples (film, Insu^tv), 38, 162, 166–70, 175–79, 195, 222
Welles, Brooke Foucault, 198
Whyte, W. F., 10
Wikipedia, 94
Willan, Philip, 211
Windows Media Player, 117
Wobblies, the, 210
Wolfson, Todd, 101, 105, 107
Wretched of the Earth, The (Fanon), 133, 141–42
Wright, Steve, 11, 48, 104, 139, 145
WTO Summit (1999), 86, 102, 207
Wu Ming, 222

YouTube, 4, 107, 119, 185–87, 207

Zanotelli, Alex, 164
Zapatistas, 15, 100–102
ZERO!, 98
Zittrain, Jonathan, 186

ALESSANDRA RENZI is associate professor of critical media production in the Department of Communication Studies at Concordia University, Montreal. She is coauthor of *Infrastructure Critical: Sacrifice at Toronto's G8/G20 Summit.*

CPSIA information can be obtained
at www.ICGtesting.com
Printed in the USA
BVHW040729060320
574250BV00009B/58